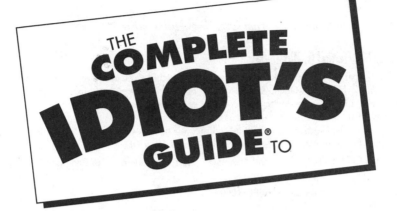

THE **COMPLETE IDIOT'S GUIDE** TO

Past Life Regression

by Michael R. Hathaway, D.C.H.

ALPHA

A member of Penguin Group (USA) Inc.

To Penny, my eternal love, through the mists of time.

Copyright © 2003 by Michael R. Hathaway

International Standard Book Number: 1-59257-065-8
Library of Congress Catalog Card Number: 2003106905

05   04   03   8   7   6   5   4   3   2

Interpretation of the printing code: The rightmost number of the first series of numbers is the year of the book's printing; the rightmost number of the second series of numbers is the number of the book's printing. For example, a printing code of 03-1 shows that the first printing occurred in 2003.

Printed in the United States of America

Most Alpha books are available at special quantity discounts for bulk purchases for sales promotions, premiums, fund-raising, or educational use. Special books, or book excerpts, can also be created to fit specific needs.

For details, write: Special Markets, Alpha Books, 375 Hudson Street, New York, NY 10014.

Publisher: *Marie Butler-Knight*
Product Manager: *Phil Kitchel*
Senior Managing Editor: *Jennifer Chisholm*
Senior Acquisitions Editor: *Randy Ladenheim-Gil*
Development Editor: *Lynn Northrup*
Copy Editor: *Cari Luna*
Illustrator: *Chris Eliopoulos*
Cover/Book Designer: *Trina Wurst*
Indexer: *Angie Bess*
Layout/Proofreading: *Becky Harmon, Mary Hunt, Donna Martin*

Contents at a Glance

Appendixes

Contents

Foreword

Although the history of hypnosis reaches back centuries, it was only toward the end of the nineteenth century that the medical community began to recognize its potential for therapeutic use. Much to the surprise of the experimenting doctors, people under hypnosis sometimes spontaneously described events in what they said had been their previous lives. Naturally, this phenomenon was met with universal skepticism on the part of the doctors, who considered these past life stories as revealing nothing more than the fertile imaginations of their patients.

Then, in the mid-1970s, a few psychotherapists discovered that whether these were true past life memories or imaginary, exploring a past life through hypnosis often resulted in rapid improvements in a client's problems. These therapists worked mostly in isolation, but in the early 1980s, about 50 of them got together under the guidance of Dr. Hazel Denning and formed the Association for Past Life Research and Therapy (now the International Association for Research and Regression Therapies, or IARRT). The Association grew rapidly, attracting therapists from all over the world, and it is still thriving. IARRT publishes a quarterly newsletter and has supported a juried journal since 1986. It also sponsors occasional conferences at which past life therapists attend workshops, meet their peers, and share ideas.

Public interest in past life regression has grown over the years, partially due to considerable media publicity. Most people today know that past life narratives occur. Some people come to past life therapists for help with problems; others are merely curious and attend experiential workshops to see what past life they might access. But the idea of safely accessing a past life yourself is fairly new. It is often thought to be impossible, but in this book, Mike Hathaway presents a graduated series of easy exercises to reach this goal—to explore your past lives yourself, safely and comfortably at home.

This book is a veritable "user's manual" for accessing your own past lives. Mike stresses that you do not need a professional therapist to explore your past lives. Still, the book is not for therapy, and those with serious problems might consider a few visits with a past life therapist to get those problems settled before attempting the exercises in this book.

Interspersed with these exercises is a wealth of factual information, painlessly presented in Mike's refreshingly clear, no-nonsense style. Along the way, we learn something of the history of reincarnation as a belief, the history of hypnosis, the Akashic Records, the stories that children often tell about their past lives, the workings of karma and what to do about it, and finding and using talents and skills that we have developed in our past lives.

Mike presents the process as a journey of self-discovery, a journey that anyone can take. He points out that because we are all unique and have a unique past life history, only we can best understand and use the lessons from our own past lives. Mike's self-hypnosis exercises lead us gradually into finding those past lives and the lessons we learned in them.

You will want to read this book straight through at first, then go back to the beginning and start using the exercises Mike presents. Enjoy your journey!

Thelma B. Freedman, Ph.D.

Thelma Beach Freedman, Ph.D., has a B.S. degree in education and an M.A. and Ph.D. in clinical psychology. She has studied clinical hypnotherapy at the Hypnosis Consulting Center, the Association for the Advancement of Ethical Hypnosis, and the Association for Past Life Research and Therapies. She has practiced hypnotherapy and past life therapy for nearly 30 years. The former director of Hypnosis Associates in Dewitt, New York, she offers a training course in past life therapy for professionals. Her M.A. thesis and Ph.D. dissertation were in the fields of hypnotherapy and past life therapy, and she has conducted research and published articles in those areas. She served four years on the Board of Directors of the Association for Past Life Research and Therapies, and she is a former research chairperson for that organization and a former editor of the *Journal of Regression Therapy*. Presently, she is the president of the International Board for Regression Therapy, the accrediting organization for past life therapists and training programs. She conducts a private practice in hypnotherapy and past life therapy and presents group workshops in past life regression. Her book, *Soul Echoes: The Healing Power of Past Life Therapy*, was published in 2002 by Citadel Press/Kensington Publishing Corporation.

Introduction

If people had told me 30 years ago that I would write a book on how to regress into your past lives, I would have told them they were crazy. It would have been one subject that I didn't really believe in. After all, I grew up a terrorized Baptist. You know what I mean; the evangelical service where the preacher proclaimed that if you even so much as went to a movie on a Sunday afternoon you would truly go to hell. Even though I wasn't comfortable with this strict view of religion, it still was my only basis for belief.

Then a series of events in my life pushed me to open my mind to investigate a world beyond what I had previously known. I was hired as a piano player to accompany a hypnosis stage show, and I was hooked. I had to learn this magic power! A psychologist friend, Dr. Donald Orsillo, loaned me a couple books on the subject, and I was on my way. I became very interested in ghost hunting and started using hypnosis as a tool to contact the unseen. The idea of past lives began to creep into the picture, but I was still unsure how it fit with my belief.

Then a car hit me the summer of 1989 while I was crossing the street (in a crosswalk). Even though I didn't recall going through a tunnel to the other side, I was a different person afterward. I was still alive, and I knew that there must be an assignment left for me on Earth. I began to receive insights and became aware that I had a very special team to guide me. After all, I was obsessed with walking a year before I was hurt, doing up to 10 miles a day. I believe now that I was training for the accident and my life change.

In the process of my studies of hypnosis, I learned about Edgar Cayce, and on a chance visit to the Association of Research and Enlightenment (A.R.E.) in Virginia Beach, Virginia, I had an encounter with an old man who brought me face-to-face with reincarnation. He was in the library, and it seemed that he was waiting for me. Besides telling me about the workings of the library and Cayce, he insisted that I take a small booklet by a Jesuit priest written in the early 1900s that contained reincarnation information that had been removed from the Bible by the early Catholic Church. All of a sudden I knew that there was much more to life than I had thought. The hologram in my unconscious mind had been opened. My belief in a universal power became stronger than ever.

Since that time, my life has been filled with the insights that many gifted and talented psychic people bring me. I really believe that in one of my ancient lifetimes I was a strong and powerful ruler who misused his abilities for self-gain. Perhaps we knew each other then. I really believe that this book holds something special for you within its covers that will help you if you so choose to become in tune again with a part of your soul that is waiting to be rediscovered.

How to Use This Book

The Complete Idiot's Guide to Past Life Regression is divided into five parts:

Part 1, "Echos from the Past," starts your journey through this book by helping you to become aware of the echos from your past that may already have been calling to you through your unconscious mind. As you begin to prepare for your journey back in time, you will get an overview of what different cultures believe about reincarnation, learn about Edgar Cayce, and how to hypnotize yourself.

Part 2, "Peeking Through the Veil," prepares you to look through the thin shroud that has thus far hidden your view into your past lives. You will learn how you naturally experience a trance, how your mind works, how to find your comfort zone, and what it is like to visit a past life regression specialist. You will also find out how children easily remember past life experiences.

Part 3, "Preparing for the Adventure," helps you learn what to expect during regression and how to identify karma. You will practice keeping yourself grounded using your belief, and your inner and outer guidance systems. You will begin to create your past life travel plan and learn how to use your mental DNA to get the best images while you are there.

Part 4, "Going Through the Window," shows you several different techniques to help you have the best past life experience possible. Then you will travel back in time and learn how to get the most out of the information you collected. You will be shown how to resolve the karma that may have accompanied you when you entered this lifetime.

Part 5, "Updating Your Past," shows you how to identify and update the abilities and talents you developed during a past lifetime. You may even want to visit a future lifetime or see what it is like between lifetimes. You may decide you want to have a past life regression party. Finally, you will see how your past can be a very important part of your present and your future.

You'll also find two helpful appendixes: a glossary and a list of resources.

Extras

In addition to the chapters and appendixes, I've included several kinds of boxes sprinkled throughout the text that give additional information, define terms, identify potential pitfalls, and share fascinating anecdotes. Here's what you'll find:

Soul Stories

These boxes contain anecdotes from case studies that will help you understand how past lives can influence people in their present lives.

Words to Remember

Check here for definitions of some of the more significant and commonly used words in the book; you'll also find these terms and more in the Glossary.

Ageless Insights

These boxes provide useful information and miscellaneous tidbits that will help you understand the regression process.

Karmic Cautions

Check these boxes for possible pitfalls you may encounter on your journeys into your past lives.

Acknowledgments

This book would not have been possible without the pioneers in past life regression who have opened the doors and minds of countless people. Foremost in that group would be Edgar Cayce and the work that continues through the A.R.E. in Virginia Beach. More recently, the works of Roger Woolger, Brian Weiss, Robert Grant, and Henry Bolduc, among others, have helped the public become aware of the value of understanding the importance of reaching into the memories of the soul.

There needs to be a great big thank you to the organizations and people behind them who are helping to advance the study of hypnosis and past life research. These include Dwight Damon and the National Guild of Hypnotists, The American Institute of Hypnotherapy, and Thelma Freedman and the Internal Board of Regression Therapy.

I would like to thank Jacky Sach of BookEnds for her tireless effort and guidance representing this and other works. To author Morgan Llywelyn, who is a wonderful teacher and a source of inspiration. Also included is the work and encouragement that the editors of Alpha Books provide.

There are many friends who have encouraged the development of this book. I am surrounded by psychics, including Martha Douglass, David Adams, Ramona Garcia, Pat and Don Bleyle (who has passed over), and they all told me about the adventures that I would have, long before they started. The Wednesday Night Metaphysical Group brings me insights that have helped stretch my mind, and Jan Weinraub, who has an incredible library of books, has provided a wealth of information for this and other works.

Then there is the team on the other side. I believe old friend Ellen Turner, someone who knew and was linked to Edgar Cayce through many of his lifetimes, heads the list. Incidentally, her grandmother was a sister to William James, who had a summer estate near where we live. Author Robert Grant had written to tell me of her passing and said she had told him that it was time to go because she had assignments on the other side. Three weeks later my first offer of a book arrived over the Internet.

I would like to thank Pastor Sean Dunker-Bendigo and the good congregation of the Madison Baptist Church for still allowing me to be a member despite my nontraditional views of religion. Finally, to my incredible and talented family, including the Whitmans, Bennetts, Davises, and Hathaways, especially son Brian, daughter Brenda, husband Marc, and the little man Carter Davis Laforce, thanks for your support. The real proof in past lives, however, is the greatest miracle in my life, my soul mate and wife, Penny, whose abilities as an editor are incredible. Without her, this and other works would not have been possible. Thank you.

Trademarks

Part 1

Echos from the Past

Do you enjoy a good mystery? Do you like to imagine what it would be like to interview the witnesses, collect the clues, and solve the case? If you like intrigue, you are about to become a detective on a case with a fascinating scenario.

Your assignment is to put together someone's missing past. Your search may connect you with royalty, wealth, and possibly even murderers. You might find that the pieces of the puzzle come together easily, or you may have to search for the smallest clues.

There is a risk that goes with this case. It may develop into a passion as you find yourself going deeper and deeper into the history of your suspect's past. After all, it is yourself and your soul that you are assigned to investigate.

Chapter 1

What Do You Mean, I've Lived Before?

In This Chapter

- ◆ What is past life regression?
- ◆ Your conscious, unconscious, and universal minds
- ◆ The karmic connection between past and present lives
- ◆ How your past lives influence you in this life
- ◆ Hypnosis and hypnotic trances
- ◆ Why do people experience past life regression?

Do you believe that you lived before? You may have asked yourself that from time to time. Maybe you are particularly interested in a certain period of history. You might imagine how the people actually lived or what it felt like to wear their clothes. Whether you believe in past lives or not, you can benefit from this book.

No one can say absolutely for sure that you really lived in the past. There are many theories and no actual proof. You are the judge for yourself, and it is up to you to decide. As you read this book and participate in the various exercises, you will have an opportunity to investigate the workings of your mind. No one else's mind is the same as yours. If you enjoy a good mystery, then you are about to take part in one—the search for your past lives. If you have an imagination and are willing to follow where it goes, you may be in for a fascinating adventure into the journey of your soul.

You Are What You Were

Are you comfortable living in today's world? Is there a period in history that you find absolutely fascinating? If so, do you read books about it or listen to music of that time? Do you imagine what it would be like to live back then? Do you visit places that have historical sites related to that time period?

You may wear your hair a certain way or dress in a style that was popular in a different time period. It doesn't have to be hundreds of years ago. Your interest need only go back to before you were born this time. In fact, everything you do in some way or other has the potential of relating back to a different lifetime, including the way you dress, the way you walk, the way you eat, and even the way you think. Chances are, when you were a child, you may have been much more open to past lives than you are as an adult. Society has some very narrow beliefs about reincarnation.

Your interest in different time periods can be influenced by the memories that are stored in your unconscious mind. When you are in an open frame of mind, images of your past lives can float up to the surface of your conscious mind. Once they become part of your conscious thinking, you are influenced by your memories from another time without even knowing where they came from.

A *past life regression* is the process of going back into a previous lifetime through your unconscious mind while you are in a relaxed self-hypnotic state. Your soul will reincarnate or experience many different lifetimes before its journey is complete. Each lifetime or incarnation adds to your soul's memories, such as an interest in the things you knew from before. The process of *reincarnation* happens each time a soul enters a new lifetime. When you experience a past life regression, you are actually going back to the memories of one of your previous lives.

Soul Stories _____

Dick needed to lose weight. He weighed more than 300 pounds. His doctor told him that he was gambling with his life. He wondered if a past life might have had something to do with his weight problem. A hypnotherapist helped him regress back to a time after the Civil War when he headed west and made his living as a gambler. He finally died fighting over a card game. Now Dick was able to understand that he had brought his love for gambling into this lifetime where it had surfaced as his reckless love for food. He was able to stop gambling with this life and start eating healthy food and exercising.

Mental DNA: How the Mind Works

The way your mind works is different from anyone else's on earth. Just as you have a physical *DNA* that can be traced backward in your bloodline to your origins, you also have an individual mental DNA that is connected to your soul. Just as physical DNA helps determine your size, weight, coloring, and hair (among other physical characteristics), your mental DNA is shaped by past life experiences as well as your physical makeup.

Mental DNA may sound complicated, but it is really quite simple. You don't have to change a thing about yourself to understand it. In fact, it's a process you have naturally been doing your entire life. When you become aware of the way you think in terms of your sensory images, you will be helped in many aspects of your life, besides that of learning from your past lives. Let's see if we can put this into perspective and understand how your mental DNA images relate to your conscious, unconscious, and universal minds.

Words to Remember

DNA, or deoxyribonucleic acid, is a chemical found at the center of the cells of living things that controls the structure and purpose of each cell. It carries genetic information.

You have three different minds—your *conscious mind*, your *unconscious mind*, and your *universal mind*. The conscious mind is your analytical mind. Some of you have a very active conscious mind, and you have a hard time trying to stop thinking. It is very easy for the conscious mind to become confused. Besides handling all the momentary decision-making, thinking about the past and the future, the conscious mind also is constantly being sent messages from the unconscious mind. The conscious mind makes up only about 10 percent of your total mind.

That means that the unconscious mind makes up the difference, or 90 percent. The unconscious is your memory bank. It does the same thing as a computer. It stores the information that you send to it and brings the data back when it is requested. It keeps on file an image record of everything you have ever experienced. Your experiences also include the memories from your different lifetimes.

Your universal mind is connected through your unconscious mind to a high information source in the universe. It is an intelligence that houses all information. It can communicate in forms of energy, angels, guides, dreams, and other unexplainable ways.

Your mind works in three different tenses—the past, the present, and the future. Every time you recall a memory, you are reaching into your unconscious memory bank. Some of you may be stuck in this tense, and you constantly replay a certain memory over and over. It may be a memory you are familiar with, or it may be something that you have no idea where it came from.

When you imagine something before it actually happens, you are projecting into the future. You consciously imagine the future by using your present and past experiences.

Ageless Insights

You create your memories through five different senses: seeing, hearing, feeling, tasting, and smelling. Everything you experience through your eyes, ears, body, emotions, nose, and mouth are recorded in your unconscious memory and brought back to the surface of your conscious mind when you recall the experience. When you remember, you replay the experience in one or more of your senses.

It is also possible to dream of the future in ways that are connected to neither your conscious nor unconscious minds.

Guess what? Everybody doesn't remember in the same way. Have you and someone else ever compared an event you both witnessed? Did you remember it the same way? Chances are you didn't. Here's why. Our five different senses—seeing, hearing, feeling, smelling, and tasting—are not processed, stored, and recalled equally by everyone's unconscious minds. The way you experience your memories is different from anyone else. It is your mental DNA for the most part that determines the difference. (You'll learn how your mental DNA makeup is determined in Chapter 8.)

You Are a Member of the Karma Club

Did you know that you are participating in a play? At times you may feel like you are. Your play has many different characters and many different themes. In fact, you are in a traveling group of the same actors, and in most every production you have a changing role. Sometimes you are the main character, and sometimes you may have a supporting role. You may be the hero or you may be the victim. You may be royalty or you may be a peasant. You may be the winner and you may be the loser.

You are a member of the Karma Club Players. The script for each production has a lot of flexibility. The play begins with a basic theme, but it can change as the play continues on. Each scene fades into the next without a break.

Sometimes you're offstage a long time, and sometimes you have only a short break. You have the opportunity to make changes as the production progresses. So do all the other players you are acting with. Your actions on stage will help determine the next role you play after you have exited the current segment. You might have a similar role, or it might be very different. It all depends on how you and the other actors played your parts in the last scene.

In the Buddhist religion, *karma* represents the unfinished business that carries over into your current lifetime from one or more of your past lifetimes. Each incarnation has a specific set of lessons for the soul to work on. These lessons can vary widely from control to greed to love to relationships. You revisit the karma in order to help you progress on your soul's journey toward a higher understanding of the workings of the universe.

In Hinduism, it is believed that your mental or physical acts will determine the conditions of your life and rebirth. That is, what you have done in the past can affect your current life, and what you do now can affect your future lives. There is both good and bad karma, meaning that you can advance or be required to improve upon the conditions you have created. This means that your play will be affected by the way you act your role.

Words to Remember

Karma is the force produced by a person's actions in one of their lives that influences what happens to them in their future lives.

So what's your role in the Karma Club? Do you think you have a specific script to follow? If so, how do you know what it is? Do you believe you were born with certain karma? Do you feel life is a challenge that you must overcome in order to succeed, or do you feel you are traveling hand in hand with the universe at a rate that feels comfortable and positive?

You, the actor, have been given one more key element by the universe, that of *free will*. Free will means you may or may not go by the script you were given for this lifetime when you were reincarnated onto the earth plane. You have the potential to advance way beyond this life's lessons, or you could lag way behind. You make the choice whether or not you will follow your lessons, which is the opportunity of understanding your own free will.

Karmic Cautions

If you choose not to work on a karmic lesson, you may have to repeat it in another lifetime. If these are relationship lessons, how you progress as a group will determine how the characters are assigned in the next lifetime. The Karma Club is much more patient with you than you may be with it.

Free will works two ways. If a warning signal pops up relating to someone you think you have negative past life karma with, it's a good idea to pay attention to your intuition. It's also important that both of you have the opportunity to resolve the old behavior patterns. It's very possible that positive gains can be made from the situation in this lifetime.

As you can see, you are not in this alone. Everyone is a member of the club. That is a perspective you often forget. It's easy to feel isolated as you progress through the scenes in this lifetime. Many times the memories from before are so strong that you try to follow the same script as before. That script may be outdated now, and failure to recognize this can create potential problems that can result in more of the same karma in future lifetimes.

Relationships: Past, Present, and Future

Karma based on relationships in past

Much of your karma in this lifetime is based on relationships from the past. Perhaps there is one or more individual in your life who you feel you've known from somewhere before on some different plane. You may have that feeling about someone when you meet him or her for the first time. It's as if your relationship is as comfortable as an old pair of shoes. There seems to be some unexplainable bond—an instant connection— and it's possible that you both feel the same thing. You like and dislike the same things and find yourselves magnetically drawn together.

It's also possible that when you meet someone for the first time you have an unexplainable dislike or mistrust for him or her. You may go to great lengths to avoid that other person even though they are known to have the highest integrity. It is possible there is another person or persons who feel the same way about you, and it seems as if there is nothing you can do to gain their trust.

You may have friends that seem as if they should be part of your family. You may be like siblings or have more of a parent-child bond with them than with your own family. You may feel out of place in your family almost as if you had been adopted, but you know that is impossible. It's as if you got switched in the hospital, and your real parents are out there someplace but not with your blood relatives. All these feelings may be coming from past life karma that is continuing over into this lifetime.

You may have a "fatal attraction" for someone who comes into your life. There may be such a powerful connection that you disregard all caution in the need to tighten the bond. This bond, however, may have been developed during a different lifetime where the roles were different than they are now. Sometimes it's an accumulation of karma from several lifetimes that needs to be addressed. How you address it can have a major impact not only on your life, but on the lives of others connected to you.

Knowledge of your past lives can help you get a fresh perspective on your relationships with other people. They could be anyone in your family, your friends, your business associates, or any new acquaintances you may meet in the future. Once you have become comfortable examining your past lives, what you learn from them can be a great help in dealing with your relationships.

Soul Stories

Jenny was a college student who developed an instant attraction for a young married professor, and he felt the same for her. They were contemplating an affair when Jenny went to a hypnotist specializing in past life regression. It turned out that the two had been very close as stepbrother and sister in a past life during which he was killed in a traffic accident, and Jenny had died of a broken heart. The professor also went to a psychic, who told him he had died in a past life in a traffic accident. That information unfortunately did not stop them from entering into the affair, with disastrous results. Had they kept their relationship to a brother-sister friendship, perhaps the ending would have been different.

Knowing how you worked with someone in the past can give you a good indication of what it would be like to be involved with the person in the future. You may get an indication of potential pitfalls or strengths and talents that someone might have just under the surface of their conscious mind. Your past life knowledge can give you an opportunity to be on the lookout for danger signals as well as an indication of a hidden talent that you might encourage.

For the fun of it, imagine each person you see every day as if they lived during a different time in history. Make notes for yourself on what you imagined. Is there a common time period or theme? Make note of their clothes, their haircut, and the way they walk and talk.

Keep Your Eyes on the Watch: Hypnosis

Did you know that you have been *hypnotized* before? You have. Actually everyone experiences *hypnotic trances* many times a day. For example, have you ever driven down the highway so absorbed in your thoughts that you forgot to turn off where you wanted to? If so, you have experienced "highway hypnosis." You were driving safely and aware of the road, and yet you were absorbed in thought. You were paying attention and not paying attention at the same time. Have you ever been absorbed so deeply in reading or watching television that you failed to hear someone speak to you? If so, you were in a reading or television trance.

Words to Remember

A **hypnotic trance** is an altered state of consciousness in which the unconscious mind is open to suggestion and loses its ability to make critical decisions. **Hypnosis** is an altered state of consciousness where the unconscious mind accepts suggestions without question.

A hypnotic trance is basically a state of mind where you deepen your focus on something to an extent that you are not consciously aware of other things that are taking place at the same time. There will be much more on the subject of hypnosis in Chapter 5.

Mesmerize Me

When Austrian physician Franz Anton Mesmer (1734–1815) first discovered that he could put his patients in a deep trance, he thought he was able to move about an invisible fluid within their body. He would place them in a tank filled with water and iron filings and give them suggestions while he touched them with a magnetic rod. When the patients came out of their trance, they had been healed of their ailments.

Mesmer was hailed as a great physician and was credited with developing animal magnetism until it was proved there was no invisible fluid inside the human body. After he moved to France, he was denounced by the French government and called a fraud. America's Ben Franklin was part of that commission. He was very firm in his belief convincing others who were wavering. What Mesmer didn't realize was that it was the power of suggestion given the patient in trance that brought about the healing. Today the word *mesmerize*—which was coined from Mesmer's name—means the same as *hypnotize*.

James Braid (1795–1860), a Scottish surgeon, changed the name "mesmerism" to "hypnotism." Hypnosis is derived from the Greek word *hypnos*, which means "sleep." Many stage hypnotists still use the word *sleep* while inducing a trance, and to the audience, that's what it looks like. It really isn't sleep but a heightened state of awareness focusing on the relaxation suggestions given by the hypnotist. This is exactly what you are doing to yourself when you focus on a thought, music, reading, or sport. You are actually hypnotizing yourself.

Self-Hypnosis

Actually, all hypnosis is self-hypnosis. You put yourself into a trance; the hypnotist is only the facilitator. You'll learn much more about this in Chapter 5, but for now, consider the question: What does hypnosis have to do with past lives? The answer is simple. You're in a trance when you experience past life recall. The recall comes from your unconscious mind, which creates the memory images that come back up to the surface of your conscious mind. Any time you remember an image you go into a trance, and every time you go into a trance you are experiencing a form of self-hypnosis.

The stage hypnotist carefully tests his subjects to evaluate how deep in trance they are going. He will remove subjects that are only in a light trance because they may not follow the suggestions that he gives as well as a subject in a deeper trance. The stage hypnotist will excuse a light subject and keep the ones in deep trances. When he has done this, he is ready to complete his demonstrations.

A hypnotherapist and other trained professionals use a suggestibility test to measure the trance potential of a subject. The easier the subject accepts the suggestions given, the more likely he or she is to enter a deeper hypnotic trance state. There is a term known as a "fantasy prone personality" that describes someone who easily enters a deep trance. The more someone is open to imagination, the greater the potential that person has for experiencing a hypnotic trance. (You should seek out a professional licensed or certified hypnotist or therapist when you are seeking to experience a past life regression.)

Ageless Insights

Relaxation is the key to experiencing self-hypnosis. There are many depth levels of trance. Some are very light, such as a daydream; others can be so deep that the person experiencing it could have a medical operation and not even feel it. Of course, that is only done under the guidance of a professional.

You don't need to enter a deep trance in order to experience a past life regression. As long as you are willing to work with your imagination and analyze what happened after the experience rather than during it, you may be amazed with the results.

Hypnosis takes relaxation one step further. When you have relaxed, hypnosis adds a goal to work toward. In the case of a past life regression, it might be to go back to a specific time or to find a lifetime with a lesson related to this lifetime.

The goal might be to find a connection to a current relationship or to determine why you may have a reoccurring and unexplained health problem. When a self-hypnosis session is nearing its end, you can give yourself a suggestion to help you after it is over. As you go through this book you will understand and learn how simple and natural it is to put yourself in a hypnotic trance.

Could you get "stuck" in hypnosis? Could you wind up being trapped in a past life and forget the life you're in now? Quite a few years ago there was a television comedy called *Soap*. For a period of weeks one of the characters did get stuck in a past life. The audience watched and laughed at this poor soul as he tried to understand the modern world from the viewpoint of someone who was snatched out of a lifetime several hundred years before. Fortunately, that does not happen to someone experiencing self-hypnosis. It is possible you might relax so much that you fall asleep and wake up normal and rested.

Top Reasons to Go Backward

Why would you want to experience a past life regression anyway? There are many reasons that people choose to visit a past life. Here are some of the most common:

- ◆ You may learn something from a past life that can explain how you feel about yourself in this lifetime.

- ◆ You may learn something from a past life that will help explain a relationship with someone in this lifetime.

- ◆ You may discover a hidden talent or ability in a past lifetime.

- ◆ You may gain insights into a medical condition by visiting a past life.

- ◆ You may discover how to resolve old karma.

- ◆ You may find an answer to why you have a fear or phobia in this lifetime from a past lifetime.

- ◆ You may discover the answer to certain dreams you have had or are currently having.

- ◆ You may use past life information for writing and/or research.

- ◆ You may be able to trace some of the actual lifetimes that your soul has had.

You may go backward just for fun, without any other specific reason except to have an interesting and positive experience.

The Least You Need to Know

- ◆ Whether you believe in past lives or not, past life regression can help give you new insights that may be useful tools for your present life.

- ◆ Like your DNA, your mind is different than anyone else's.

- ◆ Karma can be a good thing if you allow yourself to resolve it positively; unresolved karma can follow you from life to life.

- ◆ Insights from the past may be beneficial to you in the future.

- ◆ Self-hypnosis is a natural phenomenon that you experience many times a day.

- ◆ There are many reasons why one might choose to revisit a past life.

Chapter 2

Who Was I?

In This Chapter

- ◆ Does reincarnation exist?
- ◆ Bringing up the subject of reincarnation
- ◆ Your soul remembers
- ◆ Are your experiences real or imagined?
- ◆ Following what your heart tells you

As a child, you probably thought about what you wanted to be when you grew up. You might have wanted to be a doctor or a lawyer, maybe a cowboy, or an actress. You might have even imagined what it would be like to the point where your playing seemed like reality to you.

Perhaps you were acting out what you *had* been in the past. It could have been the memories of another lifetime that were coming through your conscious mind. You were young enough to blend the realities of a past life with your imagination of what you might be in this life. The images you brought forward were transferred onto your future. Who were you anyway?

Is This All There Is?

Have you ever wondered about who you really are? Why you even exist? It's easy to get lost in these thoughts on a clear starry night when you gaze into the universe and see the countless possibilities for other life. Or perhaps you think that there is nothing more than being born, living, and dying. No before. No after. Is there anything to the idea of reincarnation, or are you just here for the duration of your lifetime?

If that were the case, would life itself have any purpose? For the premise of this book, just imagine that there might be something to this whole thing of life beyond life. Believing that might give you the opportunity to view life in a way that goes beyond your life.

If there is something beyond your current lifetime, then how do you know? At the moment, there is no hard, scientific proof of that. Dr. Ian Stevenson of the University of Virginia has done the largest body of reincarnation research over a 40-year span. He has compiled more than 3,000 case studies that strongly indicate the possibility of past life experiences.

Ageless Insights

If you would like to investigate some of Dr. Stevenson's findings, you may want to read his book, *Where Reincarnation and Biology Intersect* (see Appendix B). Published in 1997, it documents 200 stories supported by photographs and other evidence of children's past lives.

For a moment, let's consider what it might have been like back in the beginning of your soul's existence. The soul is defined as the "principle of life, feeling, thought, and action in man," and is considered to be a separate part of the mental, physical, and spiritual self. It is believed to survive beyond death.

Where did you start? Perhaps if there is such a thing as a Universal Energy Force, in the beginning you were a part of that energy. And like a mist from a cloud, you were spawned into the pure essence of knowing.

In a hypnotic trance, the great seer Edgar Cayce was able to access the Akashic Records and look up the history of a soul (see Chapter 4 for more on Cayce and the Akashic Records). He envisioned one of the soul's early existences in the lost culture of Lemurs. There the soul had no physical form. In another lost ancient land, Atlantis, he saw souls that had evolved into a human form as well as souls that had no form. If this is true, after the soul is created it goes through an evolution to gain its physical form.

Linda has always had a flair for the psychic. When she was little, the rest of her family referred to her as a "gypsy." Like many psychics who have natural intuitive gifts, she has never been completely comfortable with her abilities. She decided to use hypnosis to take her back to a past life where she had developed the talent she has in this lifetime.

In a trance she drifted back to a place she called the "Island of the Sun." There were no physical forms during that incarnation. It was here that souls learned by absorbing the pure thought form of the universal mind. It may have been during this time that she had no physical form, just pure life energy. Linda had regressed to a very early lifetime where she had no physical form.

When you are close to the end of your soul's reincarnations on earth, you are known as an old soul. Old souls are people who just don't seem to fit in with others. They know more than they can tell anyone; if they try, they are looked at as odd or a misfit. An old soul can spend a great deal of energy trying to block the knowledge that their soul contains. Many of them would be much happier living simple lives of self-pleasure as many of their friends and families do.

When you reach the stage of old soul and have completed your lessons, you will again shed your earthly body and return to pure energy. At that time you may assist fellow actors who have not yet completed their play. Your role may be as an angel, a spirit, or just a miracle.

Why Does Everyone Leave When I Bring Up the Past?

Have you ever discussed the subject of past lives with anyone? If you haven't already, you might bring up the subject one of these days. Just ask, "Do you think you lived before?" See what happens. Watch the expressions on the faces around you. Watch their facial expressions and listen to the next sentences. Do they quickly try to change the subject or move to another part of the room, or do they hang on your every word?

Perhaps you are that member of your family who attempts to step outside the bounds of normal communication. You may have already addressed this subject, as well as many others, which are often considered not quite proper for family discussions. Whenever you bring up something in this culture that is not in the norm, those with narrow viewpoints become very uncomfortable. The less open that your friends and family are to different views, the more likely they are to reject the idea of reincarnation. To complicate matters even more, many Western religions do not accept the concept. In fact, just to bring up the subject of past lives in some places of worship is absolutely taboo.

Ageless Insights

If you find a resistance to talking about past lives, don't be surprised. You may have to travel outside of your current circle to find understanding and encouragement. If the concept of past lives is intriguing to you and you decide to investigate further, you can look forward to a great adventure.

On the other hand, you may find that when you approach the subject of past lives, everyone does not leave the room. You may discover that some of your friends and family who you never would have suspected of being interested in the subject may already be doing their own investigations.

Thanks to the popularity of books such as *Many Lives, Many Masters* and *Through Time Into Healing* by Brian Weiss (see Appendix B for details), the topic of past lives has been taken out of back room seances and placed on national television and radio. If you are one of the many who are now seeking to understand the purpose of life, perhaps a major part of that quest will be the knowledge gained from your past lives.

The Soul Knows

The universal energy that forms the makeup of your soul contains your personal code and soul map. It also has a complete record of the history of your journey to this point. This history is available if you allow yourself to be open to it.

The greatest block to accessing this knowledge is your ego mind. That portion of your mind seeks self-satisfaction, and you have the right to accept its wants and needs over your soul's master plan. As you learned in Chapter 1, free will is the term given to your ability to do as you want rather than follow your soul's life plan. If you choose not to follow your purpose you will have the opportunity to do it over in a future lifetime.

The ego's desires and needs sometimes greatly overshadow the soul's purpose. While on Earth, the ego is more often than not the commander of your ship. It does not like to listen to the communications of your soul's purpose. You knowingly or unknowingly are in the middle of the battle for control between your ego and your soul's plan.

Have you ever wanted to do something that a part of you knew was wrong for you? That was your conscience speaking to you. Perhaps you listened, and perhaps you didn't. If you didn't and forged ahead against your own advice, you may have felt very guilty later.

Many times when you give in to your ego, you create new karmas such as those you may be trying to resolve from a previous lifetime. The more you become aware of your ego's drive, the more opportunity you have to allow yourself to quiet your conscious mind and open to the communication of your soul.

There have been many documented stories of near-death experiences where a person's soul left their body. Some of them began to review their *life maps* with kindly beings. When they were brought back to life, they often felt that they had been snapped back into their human body with a sensation described as hitting a brick wall. Hypnosis can help them to go back and revisit what happened when they were suspended between life and death. In fact, it is possible to follow a person's soul from death to the other side and gain insights on how the lessons are reviewed.

Sometimes you are not ready to know or understand the information regarding the other side. What you want to know and what your soul wants you to know may be two different things. When you visit the other side through hypnosis you may not go where you think you want to go. The answers you expect may not be what you actually receive.

The more you reach into your past, the greater the opportunity you will have to reach and surpass the potential of soul development that you have been given in this scene of your play.

You may want to pick a quiet place and have a conversation with your soul. If you are inside, you may want to put on some relaxing music and experience a relaxing smell like lighting a candle. Just let the muscles in your body relax and focus on your breathing. Feel the companionship of your mind, body, and soul all there together with you to help you become in tune with your whole self. As you feel this special connection, ask your soul for permission to begin to examine your past so that you may use this knowledge to help you become and stay in tune with your life map.

Words to Remember

The great universal plan is to let your soul go at its own pace and gain the experiences to match the knowledge it already has. Each time any soul experiences an incarnation, it has the opportunity to advance along its learning plan. That plan while the soul is experiencing the earth's plane is known as a **life map**.

Karmic Cautions

Sometimes in life you are put in situations where you have to deal with your soul's purpose. The great equalizers are the resistances that your ego encounters. You may look at life as a challenge or as an opportunity. The more you clash with your purpose, the less improvement your soul makes in this lifetime.

Is It Real or Your Imagination?

Have you ever imagined that you lived before? If you have, what did you imagine? Perhaps as a child you used to tell other family members about different lifetimes. Perhaps you have dreamed of yourself in faraway lands at different times. Perhaps you like to read stories about a specific time in history. Perhaps you can imagine what it would have been like to live then.

When you read, have you ever gotten so far into the story that it changed your perspective of where you were? When you finished, did the scenes remain so vividly in your imagination that it seemed as if you existed in a time warp? You may have been trapped between the realities of the location where you were at the time and the story that you were living in the book.

You may not need a book or movie to be able to experience another reality with your imagination. It may happen when you visit a place that is steeped in history, and all of a sudden you find yourself engulfed in an unfolding story from a different era. As you remain there soaking in the images, they get stronger and stronger and you find yourself stepping into this parallel reality, until something jerks you back to your conscious world.

These images may have been so real that they still remained with you some time after you returned. Was this your imagination, or had you tapped into a reality that existed on another plane? Was this a resonance of your soul that began to vibrate distant memories of the past when you happened to visit that location? Was this experience one that has been recorded in your soul's memory, or was it something that you imagined? If you have ever had an experience like this, whom could you tell it to? If you shared this story with friends or family, how would they respond to it? Would they advise you against telling the story to anyone else out of loving fear that others would think you were crazy?

Soul Stories

Children often recognize a location from a past life. They may tell you stories about certain locations and the people that inhabited them. When Jan was little, she could tell her parents how to find their way as they drove their car in places they had never been before. Was this a memory of the area from another lifetime or a psychic ability?

Are you able to write stories that come from your mind about a different period in time? Do you imagine them vividly when you write? Can you put yourself in the story and feel the experience with all your senses? Can you write descriptions of situations as if you had been there when they actually happened? Can you imagine what it would feel like to live there and experience the emotions? Can you draw pictures of a past time from the images that you have in your mind?

If you have an active analytical conscious mind, it can get in the way of your imagination. In other words, you are always trying to find a reason for the thoughts that just pop into your head. The more you can wait to think about what you're thinking until you have finished the process, the better your "imagined" images will be.

Here's a case in point. When Rob wanted to experience a past life regression, his active mind prevented him from going into a deep trance. However, he did imagine back to the Second World War and found himself flying combat in a fighter plane. At the same time as he answered the hypnotist's questions, he was also analyzing why he was imaging that particular scene.

"I've always been very interested in the Second World War," he said emphatically in the middle of the session. "I think this is just my imagination from all the reading I've done and movies I've seen on the subject." The hypnotist suggested that Rob just go along with his imagination as he continued to ask more questions that focused on the details.

The hypnotist was able to lead Rob deeper into his imagery and take the pilot through the crash that caused his death after his plane was seriously damaged by enemy fire. Then he brought Rob back out of his trance. "That was odd," Rob stated as he took a moment to get his bearings back. "I know I was just making up that story, and yet when the plane was going down, I really felt dizzy."

Do you think Rob just imagined the whole thing? How do you think he became interested in World War II in the first place? Perhaps he had a soul memory that was powerful enough to lead him to his interest in that time period. Has he been experiencing a second reality originating from World War II that he was trying to resolve in this lifetime?

So what do you do with your imagination? Do you believe the echoes of your mind reminding you of your distant past life experiences in time, or do you dismiss it all as a product of your mental fantasies? You can chalk it up to imagination if you want to. You can listen to those who tell you there is nothing there. Or if you want, you can investigate further. You can become the detective of your own mind and search for clues to the identity of your past.

Follow Your Heart

Now that you've had an opportunity to consider how and where the journey of your soul began, how does it fit with your heart? Is there something inside of you that vibrates with a feeling of recognition when you think about having lived before? Do you, like Rob, miss the clues you are giving yourself because you are not paying attention? Do you credit the whispers from your past to your active imagination?

If you do, you're not alone. Many people never have the opportunity to connect to the rich heritage of their own past lives because they are too focused on the present and the future. Your past can be a wealth of information that can help you as you move forward into the future. No one knows your soul better than you do. You just may not be aware of that yet. As you progress through this book you will be.

You may move at a pace that is comfortable for you, and you do not need anyone else to help you if you want to explore alone. At the same time, having someone support you can be fun, and they may discover something about your past lives that you might miss. Either way, you will have an interesting and educational adventure.

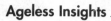

Ageless Insights

You may have such a close connection to your past lives that you are afraid of going back. You need not be. Regardless of who you might have been—a king or a murderer—this is the life you are in now. You can take steps to resolve the karma of your past and build on past strengths as you update them to your current lifetime. You will never be stuck in your past life. You will be able to end your past life session any time you want.

What does your heart say to you? Have you taken the time to communicate with it? If not, let's take a little time right now. Find a comfortable place and let yourself relax. You may feel yourself breathing slowly in and out as you relax more and more. In a moment you may ask your heart and soul the following questions. The answers may not come right away, but they may surface at any time in your dreams, as a thought, or you may be reminded from an outside source.

You may ask your soul for permission to learn of your past lives and to let your heart know the answer. Is it good for me at this time to begin to examine my past lives for the purpose of helping me use the knowledge in this lifetime? May I be aware of the past life influences that have been and are now present in my life?

You may have other questions you want to ask your soul and to feel the answer in your heart. When you have finished communicating with your soul and heart, let yourself drift back to consciousness and allow yourself to be open to the messages.

Is it time for you to give yourself permission to explore your heritage, a heritage deep and rich with the memories of many adventures from your soul's past? A part of you already knows the answers that are inside of you, regardless of what anyone else says. You are the keeper of your soul. The resonance of the vibration that rings true and whispers to your mind can lead you down the path to great adventure as you follow your heart.

The Least You Need to Know

- Although there is no scientific proof, research strongly suggests that reincarnation exists.

- Many people don't believe in reincarnation or are uncomfortable talking about it; you may have to travel outside of your current circle to find understanding and encouragement.

- Your soul knows the history of your past.

- You can decide whether your past life experiences are real or imagined.

- Regardless of what anyone else tells you, you know in your heart the right answers regarding reincarnation.

Religion and Past Lives

In This Chapter

- ◆ Reincarnation beliefs in early cultures
- ◆ The Egyptian belief in an afterlife
- ◆ The controversial views of the Greeks
- ◆ The battle for control among early Christian religions
- ◆ Why there's little room for reincarnation in today's Western religion

If you think the concept of past lives is something new, this chapter will give you a different perspective. In reality, early records show that man has always believed that a part of them would go on beyond their lifetime. From cave drawings and carvings, to the Egyptians, to the Greeks, and all around the globe, reminders of early belief in reincarnation have been uncovered and are still being found today.

You will see how the early Catholic Church determined the view of reincarnation that much of Western religion still maintains today. Discussing your past lives is taboo in most of the Christian religions practiced today. Things are slowly changing, however, and more people are open to the concept of past lives.

Early Beliefs in Reincarnation

The belief that man has a soul has been documented in many cultures around the world since history has been recorded. As you consider the history of the belief in reincarnation, you may compare what you read with how your heart feels about the subject. It's not necessary for you to know exactly what and how you believe to use this book to help you gain new insights.

One of the earliest hints of man's connection with a universal Creator and the beginning of the existence of the soul is found on the island of Crete in the form of a *labyrinth*. Labyrinths have also been documented as a part of Mayan, Celtic, Greek, and even Native American cultures.

> **Words to Remember**
>
> A labyrinth is like a maze except there are no dead ends. Once you enter, you continue inward until you reach the center. If you view the layout of a labyrinth from above, it looks much like the design of a human brain. There is a right sphere and a left sphere. As you progress through it, you are actually balancing your own energy flow.

Early labyrinths may, in fact, have been a type of soul map. It is very possible that early man knew more about our grand design than we do today. The farther you get away from the source, the harder it is to maintain a clear connection. The more lives you have had, the more karmic clutter there is to interrupt your direct line to your beginnings. A meditative labyrinth may help you find the way back to your roots.

Today's labyrinths are used for meditation and healing, although you can walk one without any other reason except for having fun. It is believed that as you walk into it, you are opening to the universe for guidance. On the way out you will have cleared your negative energy and are in balance again.

When you reach the center, you may remain as long as you want to contemplate a question that you may have for the universe. When you are ready, you may retrace your steps back to the opening. The goal of the labyrinth experience is for you to find the connection to your belief and rebalance your connection to the universal energy and your soul.

Actually, you don't even have to walk a labyrinth to receive some of the same benefits. There are hand labyrinths where you can run a finger around inside grooves, and you will feel yourself becoming balanced as you complete the exercise. Some of the hand labyrinths are double so that you can use both hands at once. You can find information on them in a New Age store that specializes in alternative health and self-help subjects.

It is also interesting to note that labyrinths were included in the floor design of early Christian churches and cathedrals. Many of these structures were built over earlier pagan sites. The pagans were very sensitive to the energies of the earth and incorporated them into their worship. A place where the energies converge into a center is called a *vortex*.

Early man may have used the labyrinth as a means of keeping himself connected with his beginnings. The labyrinth itself may have been a soul map showing the way back home to the "Island of the Sun." Each lifetime is a labyrinth, and so is the entire progression of the soul through many lifetimes. When the journey is completed, the soul arrives at the center of the labyrinth in total balance with the universe. Over the history of mankind, this map of the soul seems to have been forgotten.

> **Words to Remember**
>
> A **vortex** is a place where Earth energies converge to create a swirling cylindrical stream that rises upward into the universe. A vortex is a place where souls can be transported to the other side and where the universe can set through reincarnated souls.

Although the true purpose of the ancient labyrinths may be lost, many of the older religions still reflect the belief in the souls it may have stood for. See how this applies to the Jewish mystical teachings and in African tribes, the Australian Aborigines, the Tlingit tribe of Alaska, and the Druids:

- In the Jewish faith, the word for reincarnation is *Gilgul*, which means the passing of a soul when they die into another body. References to Gilgul are found in the Kabala, but are not directly mentioned in the Torah, the Jewish Scriptures. The Kabala is made up of ancient Jewish mystical teachings that first surfaced in the eleventh century and are based on the Torah.

- In Africa, many of the early tribes believed that they would come back for other lifetimes. Those who were unable to have children were looked upon as being cursed by the rest of the tribe. The reason was that they were blocking the re-entrance to human form for the souls that were waiting to be born.

- The ancient Australian Aborigines believed in reincarnation. They were a dark-skinned people who thought that their soul would come back as "Whitefellow."

- The Tlingit tribe of Alaska believed that a pregnant woman or her relatives would dream the name of the soul that was being reincarnated. Past accomplishments would be continued in the new life. Any child who was born without the knowledge of their past was considered to be denied their soul's birthrights.

◆ The Druids believed that their souls would never become extinct. They would continue after death and enter another body. That view may have helped make them the fierce fighters that they were. They knew that, even if they died, a part of them was indestructible.

Ageless Insights

Many of the Eastern religions, including Buddhism, Hinduism, and Islam, developed beliefs in reincarnation before the birth of Christ. The Buddhists believe that reincarnation is caused by unresolved karma. Like the Egyptian belief system, an incarnation that does not reach perfection results in doing the lessons over again. The cycle of death and rebirth is finally ended when the individual is able to overcome their earthly desires and reach the goal of enlightenment. It was also believed that the soul could be reincarnated into lower life forms such as animals, plants, and trees.

The Egyptians

The Egyptians believed that each person had a soul and an afterlife. Reincarnation was only for those that had not learned all their lessons. "The Book of the Coming Forth by Day," often referred to as "The Book of the Dead," prepared one for the afterlife. In order to have access to the afterlife the individual would need to go through a judgment after death. Once the soul was able to successfully pass 42 negative confessions, they would be able to move on to the reunification with Ra, the Egyptian god of the sun.

The only Egyptians who would be able to reach the resurrection were the Pharaohs and their families. They would go on to become gods and sail the heavens with Ra and his boat. The Egyptians embalmed their dead because they believed that their physical bodies needed to be preserved in order to accompany their soul. The royal families were resurrected rather than reincarnated. Elaborate pyramids were built to help them move into the afterlife.

Egyptian kings would teach their sons in line for the throne to strive for their highest selves. The reason for this was that at their death they would review their whole lifetime within a brief moment. It would be at that time that they would be judged on their performance.

Everyone else who failed their judgments was reincarnated back to their earthly state. Here they would begin again to work on perfection. The reward for perfecting the lessons was the resurrection into the spiritual form, and the punishment was the return to Earth.

The Egyptians added to their beliefs over time but did not discard the old. They believed in a divine god and that the universe was created. They believed that man was part of the creation, and they had a set of books called the Canons to help guide them in their beliefs. The Egyptian period began approximately 2500 B.C.E. and continued until it finally died out at the beginning of the Christian era.

Edgar Cayce, who you'll learn about in the next chapter, claimed to have been Ra in one of his ancient lifetimes. While in a hypnotic trance, Cayce was able to relate other people in his current life to his reincarnation as Ra. It's interesting to note that many people today remember a life from the Egyptian period. Perhaps you have an interest in Egyptian pyramids and imagine what it might have been like to live during that time. You may have dreams with Egyptian themes, all possible clues from your past!

Soul Stories

When most people imagine, they see pictures, but John cannot imagine in picture images. When he closes his eyes, everything under his eyelids is blank. He doesn't remember many of his dreams, but one haunts him. He was inside an Egyptian pyramid looking out through a small opening into a room totally filled with gold. Then someone sealed the opening with a stone block and everything went black. John has never liked the idea of visiting the pyramids, especially if he had to go down into a tomb. Although he was nonvisual as a child, he did not have this dream until he was an adult. He wondered if he lost his ability to visualize in his mind in this past life.

The Greeks

Early Greek culture has provided civilization with some of the greatest insights of all time through their beautiful temples, sculpture, and literature. Greek writers, philosophers, and teachers Pythagoras and Plato, among others, believed in reincarnation. Pythagoras (572–479 B.C.E.) was influenced by Orphism, an ancient Greek cult based on the god Orpheus. Orphism was developed in the century before Pythagoras's birth.

Orphism embraced reincarnation and the knowledge that a soul came back to address unfinished karma. Orphism taught that animals should not be killed or eaten, and each human would be judged on their actions on earth and be rewarded or punished as a result of them. Many of these early teachings are incorporated in today's philosophies of occultism and mysticism.

Pythagoras was the first known person to teach soul *transmigration*. He believed that parts of his abilities were carried over from his past lives and that man had "the divine power of reason" given him by the gods. He believed that the soul was the part of the body that survived after death to exist in the underworld where it would be purified, rest, and wait to be born again.

Words to Remember

Transmigration is another word that means essentially the same as reincarnation. It is a term that was incorporated into one of the Christian beliefs until it was finally purged from the church that would be the basis for today's Christian religion.

Ageless Insights

Edgar Cayce seemed to verify what Plato believed when he spoke in a deep hypnotic trance, of early yet unknown cultures where experiments were conducted with the physical bodies that a soul would inhabit. As a result of the experiments, grotesque creatures were produced that eventually had to be destroyed because they were beginning to dominate the earth.

The soul itself had three parts—a rational part, a spirited part, and a desiring part. Pythagoras taught that to achieve balance one needed to live in simplicity, free from desire and ambition. Once these lessons were learned, the soul would attain its goal of rebirth and reach the desired level of purification on earth, ending its transmigrations or reincarnations. The soul would then return to its immortal place with the divine. The belief that the soul would return to be a part of the divine was hotly contested in the early Christian Church. The view that finally won was that human souls were not part of God but something that would always remain separate either in heaven or hell.

Plato (427–347 B.C.E.) believed that the process of reincarnation could take up to 10,000 years to complete. Only philosophers and lovers could reach their destination in less time. He taught that souls were judged after death and were punished in the underground, a place that existed below the earth, before they returned for their next reincarnation. If a soul did not continue to work for purification on Earth, it eventually would be condemned to "Tartarus," a place of "eternal damnation." Plato believed that a soul could go through reincarnations as humans and beasts, and back to human form again over continuing lifetimes.

The Early Christian Church

It was the life of Jesus Christ that eventually created a division in the belief in reincarnation. This division wasn't created by Christ himself, but by the interpretations of his teachings by his followers over the first few centuries that shaped the Christian religion. It was a time of colliding viewpoints that resulted in years of persecution and martyrdom, and many of the prejudices still remain today.

Three different branches of early Christian religion evolved after the death of Jesus. One was from Jesus' disciples who combined their Jewish backgrounds with his teachings, resulting in a form of Jewish Christian religion. The second was through Saint Paul, who is credited with creating the churches that eventually shaped the viewpoint of today's mainstream Christianity. The third form of early Christian religion was based on the Gnostic beliefs. Many of the views of this latter group were eventually banned as the Christian faith was shaped.

For a moment, let's focus on the Gnostics. Very little of their beliefs were known until 1945 when the Dead Sea Scrolls were discovered at Nag Hummadi in Upper Egypt. Many Gnostic writings were found, including copies of known works from the early Christian time period as well as previously undiscovered writings. This form of Christianity seems to have incorporated a belief system that is comprised of many other beliefs. The Gnostics included Greek, Egyptian, pagan, astrology, Judaism, Asian, and other Christian views.

The Gnostic philosophy was developed before the birth of Jesus. Its name is derived from the Greek word *gnosis*, which means "knowledge." Gnostics embraced a mystical view that they knew the secrets of God, the universe, and all of humanity. The scrolls of Nag Hummadi showed that the Gnostics believed in the supreme god and viewed Jesus as someone who helped free the faithful of their earthly views and help them return to their place with the supreme god at the time of their death. He was not considered to have the role as Savior. Salvation was achieved when the soul achieved divine knowledge and was able to escape their physical bodies. The Gnostic leader Carpocrates (c. 140) believed that the soul needed to experience many lifetimes before it returned to the supreme god. The Gnostics believed that they were the true followers in the teaching of Jesus.

With the conflicting viewpoints of just what Jesus was and his role in the concept of a supreme god, each branch of the Christian religion jockeyed for control. Justin Martyr (100–165) wrote that man could not see God, but could only perceive of his existence. He believed that the soul could not transmigrate into other bodies. He did not believe in reincarnation.

Irenaus (130–200) was also against the idea of transmigration, which he stated in his treatise "Against Heresies." Tertullian (145–220) blamed Pythagoras for influencing the Gnostics on the belief of transmigration. The battles over Christian religious beliefs would continue until these differing views came under the control of the ruler of the Roman Empire.

Constantine Makes Changes

When Constantine took control of the Roman Empire in 324, he was already a Christian, the first in its history. As a leader of military forces, he felt that the old ways of honoring many different gods with sacrifices and offerings did not always bring about the results asked for. He felt that one supreme god would provide much better protection for himself and his armies.

Constantine was convinced of a supreme god when he saw an apparition in the sky that he felt had been sent to him from heaven. The vision appeared in the heavens as a cross of light bearing the inscription "Conquer by This." The vision was followed that night with a dream of Christ telling him to make a likeness of the cross and use it for protection from his enemies.

A year after becoming Emperor, Constantine convened the Council of Nicea to rewrite the Christian Creed to fit his purpose. Wording from this edict is still included today in some Protestant church services. Two church bishops, including Arius, refused to sign the document. To Constantine, this act was heresy, and he began a campaign to persecute the followers of other Christian beliefs. This, of course, included the belief in transmigration.

Part of the Creed of Nicea stated that Jesus was the only Son of God. Constantine would not budge from this viewpoint and instructed all his bishops that they must accept the statement. There was no more room for the belief in reincarnation, a pre-existence, and the possibility that a soul could reunite with God. Other believers had to either comply with Constantine's belief or flee.

Many people with pagan beliefs were also in the jurisdiction of the Roman Empire. They resented the change to Christian religion. As a way of encouraging transition from the old religion to the new, the Romans built cathedrals over older pagan sacred sites. Many of these are still known today for their alignment with Earth energy sites called vortexes. Many of the early Christian holidays were established on the same dates as the pagan ones.

Karmic Cautions

The city of Jerusalem remains a hotbed of religious dissention even today. It is a sacred place to Islamic, Jewish, and Christian religions, but until old karma is resolved, it will remain in conflict.

Constantine proclaimed that Christianity would be the religion of the Roman Empire. He also decreed that anyone persecuted for this belief would be compensated. He had the Church of the Holy Sepulcher built in Jerusalem and forbade the Jews to visit the city but only once a year.

Even with all Constantine and his successors' efforts, the old beliefs were adhered to by the devout. It took the Fifth General Council in 553 to finally complete Constantine's objectives. Only a few Christian mystics continued to follow the old beliefs. One group that survives today and has direct ties to their Gnostic roots is the Mandaen Sect located in Iraq and Iran, and consists of approximately 15,000 members.

What About Today's Religion?

Perhaps this quick review has given you an idea of how today's religious beliefs have been formed. The Christian religion split into Catholic and Protestant with neither one accepting reincarnation. There are churches such as the Unity Church that are more open to these beliefs. Edgar Cayce recommended this church as being more supportive of the readings he gave while in a hypnotic trance state. The Spiritualist Church encourages the development of psychic abilities which can be closely tied to past life abilities.

At the end of the nineteenth century there were very few people who embraced the belief of reincarnation. Thanks to the groundwork laid by Madame Helena Blavatsky, who founded the Theosophist belief, and the rise in popularity in the twentieth century of Edgar Cayce, more and more people began to accept the possibility of reincarnation. Many people in the West have turned to Eastern religions to provide more depth to their search for their beliefs.

Basically, there are two types of religion—authoritative and permissive. Authoritative carefully controls all critical reasoning processes. The people who are attracted to this kind of religion prefer to have something concrete to follow. They want to have things presented to them "cut and dried." They are not included in the decisions of what and how to believe. They are just told to follow and don't question.

The permissive form of religion is much more open to a wide variety of views as long as they work to benefit others. This type is much more receptive to the whispers in your mind from your distant past. The common goal is to work for the good. You do not have to believe in any special way to experience a past life regression.

Today you have the world at your fingertips. You can access knowledge that can give you a balanced view of all the world's different religions. Many of you are now blending the views of the East and the West in search of what personally fits them.

In the 1930s, Edgar Cayce gave a series of readings that led to the establishment of a study group called "Search for God." Their theory is that if you live your life in "Christlike consciousness," you will live in balance with your soul's purpose. Remember, your soul already knows the answers to your search for your belief. Perhaps as you continue through this book, you will learn what you already know.

The Least You Need to Know

 ◆ Beliefs in reincarnation have been around since the beginning of man.

 ◆ The Egyptians were the most elaborate in their preparations to enter the afterlife.

 ◆ The Greeks developed transmigration beliefs that carried over into conflict with early Christian religion.

 ◆ Constantine set the tone that led to the purging of all beliefs in reincarnation from the Christian Church.

 ◆ Even today, most Western religions do not accept the view of reincarnation.

Chapter 4

Edgar Cayce and the Psychic Connection

In This Chapter

- From a common man comes an uncommon gift

- Cayce's self-hypnotic trances

- The Akashic Book of Records

- Visiting a psychic

- Were you important in a past life?

Many people consider Edgar Cayce (1877–1945) the greatest psychic diagnostician who ever lived. He spent his whole life trying to understand the gifts he had left over from previous lifetimes. Through a self-hypnotic trance he was able to visit a person's past lives and give health readings. Often he did not follow his own advice and didn't heed the warnings that if he didn't slow down on doing his readings, his health would suffer. His work was and continues to be a rich legacy of intuitive knowledge that when used for the good is still as valid today as it was over half a century ago.

Edgar Cayce was a poor student who couldn't focus in school. However, one day at age 13 he had a visit from an angel who told him he would become a healer. He spent the day in a haze and ended up staying after school to finish his work. That evening he fell asleep on his spelling book, and when he woke up, he knew everything that was in it. After that day he became a good student by sleeping on his textbooks at night. And true to the angel's word, he turned out to be one of the most noted healers in the twentieth century.

A Common Man with an Incredible Gift

Edgar Cayce was born in Hopkinsville, Kentucky. His grandfather, Thomas Jefferson Cayce, was a tobacco farmer who had several psychic abilities, including water dowsing and the ability to move objects by using his mind (what is known as telekinesis today). Edgar's father, Leslie, was never able to make much as a farmer and attempted to operate a store.

At an early age, Edgar had some experiences that had a strong impact on his life. When he was three, he fell on a board with a nail sticking out that pierced his skull and may have entered his brain. His father filled the wound with turpentine and bandaged it up. That near death experience may have had a lot to do with the eventual shaping of his psychic powers.

The second traumatic event occurred a year later at age four when he witnessed his grandfather being kicked by a horse and then drowning in shallow water. After that time, he would visit with his grandfather's spirit in one of the barns. His mother and grandmother encouraged him to tell them about the communications he had from beyond.

At age 15, he was struck on his spine by a ball at school. He came home and started acting crazy, and his father ordered him to bed. He lapsed into delirium, and when he woke up he told his family what to do to cure him. His grandmother prepared the potion and it was placed on the back on his head as directed. He drifted into sleep, and when he awoke he was completely cured.

Encounters with Angels

From his early childhood, Edgar Cayce was able to communicate with the unseen. At age four he and his childhood friend Anna played with fairies or little folk when they were off by themselves. Cayce soon learned that others did not believe the stories he told of these encounters, so he began to keep them mostly to himself, sharing them only with his mother and grandmother.

Cayce began to get visions of angels, which continued into his adulthood. One encounter in 1899 had a major influence on his career choice in later years. He was told that his prayers had been heard, and he would work with the sick and the afflicted.

Earning a Living

Cayce really wanted to become a preacher and help people in a spiritual way, but the closest he would get to that dream was to teach Sunday school. He worked in bookstores, was an excellent photographer, and had his own photography studio at different times in his early adulthood. He was a devout Christian who read the Bible from cover to cover every year of his life.

In 1903 he married Gertrude Evans. They had three children, but one died from whooping cough. The family lived in borderline poverty, struggling to exist on his modest salary. Just as it seemed they would finally get their heads above water, a disaster such as a fire in his studio would pull them back into poverty again. Cayce spent much time apart from his wife and children as he looked for photography work in other cities. Pressure soon began to mount on him to do health readings for others. Even after he became well known, his family always lived on the brink of poverty. He was simply unable to handle money successfully. And there were always those who doubted his gifts and sought to prove him a fraud.

> **Ageless Insights**
>
> It wasn't until age 46 that Edgar Cayce gave his first past life reading. The idea that man had lived before was difficult at first for Cayce, a devout Christian, to accept. It seemed contrary to the teachings of the Bible until he began to see the Scriptures in a brand new way— a way that supported the concept that man lived more than one lifetime.

A Difficult Road

As Cayce became more and more well known, he began to attract people who wanted to use his psychic powers for self-gain. In the 1920s, he spent time in Texas using his intuitive powers to search for oil. He believed that the profits would be used to build a hospital that would treat those people he diagnosed.

There were also those who wanted advice on investing in the stock market. One of these men was Morton Blumenthal, a New York stockbroker. Blumenthal became a backer of Edgar Cayce's dream to have a hospital. In 1925, the Cayces and Cayce's secretary Gladys Davis moved to Virginia Beach to help establish the National Association of Investigators, and began construction on a hospital that would treat patients with the treatments that came from Cayce's readings while in a trance. Gladys had begun to record the readings as a young stenographer in 1923. Despite the irregularity of a paycheck over a good part of her tenure, she managed to stay with the Cayces until the end of Edgar Cayce's life.

The hospital and the association disbanded in 1931 when Blumenthal withdrew his support in the middle of the depression. His loyal supporters formed the Association for Research and Enlightenment (A.R.E.), which is still growing in numbers today. The old hospital building was re-purchased in 1955, 10 years after Cayce's death, and became the headquarters of the A.R.E. Today, Charles Thomas Cayce, grandson of Edgar, helps the work go forward.

As Cayce adjusted to the idea of reincarnation, his "life readings" would give his subjects the opportunity to learn from past life strengths that could help them grow in this lifetime. He could also give a warning to those who needed to resolve old karma during their current lifetime in order for them to progress along their soul's journey.

Although Edgar Cayce had an extraordinary talent, it may not have been as special as yours might be. You may discover as you regress into your past lives that you have an ability that you have not yet identified. You may find yourself to be as great a hypnotic subject as Edgar Cayce.

Hypnotic Trances

When Edgar Cayce entered his self-hypnotic trance, he was so far under that he was not consciously aware of what he was saying or of other things that were happening around him. Early in his reading years, some of his doubters stuck pins into his arms to see if he would feel the pain. He never flinched.

If it hadn't been for local amateur hypnotist Al Layne, Edgar Cayce may never have gone on to become the well-recognized seer who helped thousands of people. Layne had an interest in alternative medicine and particularly osteopathy. Unfortunately for Layne, he took the title of doctor from a mail-order course in osteopathy and later he had to relinquish it because of improper training.

Layne was able to help Cayce speak while he was in a hypnotic trance during the time that he had lost his voice. The problem was that when Cayce came out of the trance, he lost his voice again. Finally, they decided to let Cayce look for his own cure while in his trance. That worked and he was finally able to speak again outside of the trance state.

Layne wondered if Edgar Cayce could help others the way he had helped himself, so he became Cayce's first patient and requested a trance reading on his existing stomach problems. The prescription that came out was stretching exercises and suggestions for medication. He followed Cayce's trance advice, and his condition improved greatly. It was not long before people heard the news of Al Layne's recovery, and others wanted to have Cayce do a reading for them. Over the next year, it is estimated that approximately 80 readings were given as Cayce's reputation began to grow.

It took about 10 years for the "psychic diagnostician" to be thrust into the national limelight. Dr. Wesley Ketchum asked Cayce to do readings on some of his patients. As a result of the cures, Ketchum presented a paper at a meeting of homeopathic physicians that resulted in widespread publicity.

Many times in his life, Edgar Cayce wished that he had never been given the gifts that he had. Besides health readings, he used his ability to search for oil in Texas and forecast the stock market. Some people wanted to take advantage of his abilities and tried to control how his work would be used. However, unless his readings were for the betterment of mankind, the results failed.

Going to the Akashic Book of Records

While he was in a deep, self-hypnotic trance, Edgar Cayce had the ability to visit the *Akashic Book of Records*, a kind of universal memory bank that he called the "Source."

There he could review his subject's history and report on the karma that had carried over from different lifetimes to their present lifetime, comparing the situations. In doing this, Cayce could see how actions in a past life may have resulted in conditions of the current life—physical, mental, or even relationships. His prescription for correcting a subject's conditions would often relate to resolving issues from their past.

Words to Remember

The **Akashic Book of Records,** also known as the "Book of Life," contains a record of every soul that has ever existed. It is believed to hold every deed, word, feeling, thought, and intent of every soul in the universe.

Cayce's life readings would reflect on the history of the soul and relate past conditions and relationships that could have a direct bearing on their current lifetime. He could see the strengths that his subjects had in their past lives and through trance offer potentials for further use of their abilities in their current lifetime. Cayce's readings would also contain warnings for the future if the person did not resolve past life karma. Good karma would be the abilities from a past life that continued to be used for the highest purpose. Bad karma might manifest itself in current physical conditions brought on from improper actions in a past life. An example would be an existing condition brought into this life from ridiculing someone in a past life who had the same condition.

One of the regression scripts in Chapter 16 is designed to let you visit your own Akashic Records. Your records, however, may not be in a big musty volume as you might think. It could be that your past is a video library filled with separate tapes or films containing the history of your individual lives.

When Julie visited the Akashic Records, for example, she was surprised to enter a very sophisticated electronic center, almost like she was visiting the flight deck of the Starship *Enterprise*. Once there she was able to tap into the source of information, and it showed her the images of the past lives that she needed.

Your "electronics" are already programmed inside you ready to connect you up with the great library of the universe. As you grow in your understanding and become more proficient in accessing your internal Akashic Records, you will be able to refer to this vast source of information almost any time that you like.

The Psychic's Gift

Have you ever gone to a *psychic?* Some of you may depend on psychics for guidance to help you in many of your personal decisions. On the other hand, you may never have gone to a psychic before and wouldn't even know what to expect out of the experience if you did go. As you have learned from reading about Edgar Cayce, "ordinary people" like yourself have extraordinary gifts and may be just as psychic as the psychic you visit.

Words to Remember

A **psychic** is a person who is highly sensitive to non-physical or spiritual influences. The word *psychic* pertains to the soul. It is your soul's memories of past life experiences and talents that help you to be sensitive, and the closer your past life memories are to the surface of your mind, the more psychic you are.

The term *psychic* means soul knowledge that is accessible to you through your unconscious mind. Because the soul contains the memories of your past lives, your psychic ability is directly linked to your past life abilities. These gifts that were developed in your distant past are still there waiting to be rediscovered and used by you in a positive way in this lifetime.

Going to a psychic does not always mean that you are going to be told about one of your past lives. Just as every one of you has different talents and gifts, so do professional psychics. Some of them use spirits and guides to connect them to the other side so that they may communicate with your family members and friends who have passed over. Some psychics may have the ability to see into the future and predict events that may happen sometime during your lifetime. Other psychics can look into the past. They can learn what you were like in a past life and report back to you.

If you went to 20 different psychics who specialized in past lives, it's possible that you could get 20 different reports. Each psychic's view would be coming through their varied abilities. Their angle would be different than the next psychic's. As you collect all these views, you begin to get a clearer picture of what your past lives were like.

Soul Stories

When Angela does a past life reading on someone, she centers herself first by touching a part of her client's body. From that touch she absorbs energy from the client that creates visual pictures in her mind relating to one of their past lives. She proceeds to give a reading on what she is watching. Her clients are given an opportunity to identify the images from the past in relationship to their current life situations. As an example, Angela may see the client as an ancient sailor on a small vessel. The client can relate to this image because the client has a great love of the ocean and has always wanted to sail away on a long voyage.

Just as psychics learn to trust that what they are telling a client is true, you are learning to trust your response to what the psychic tells you. Psychics can be helpful catalysts who may assist you as you begin to unlock a mystery from your past. When a psychic helps you discover the possibilities of a past life, you then have the opportunity to continue the investigation yourself. The goal of this book is for you to do just that.

Getting a Psychic Reading

If you're interested in exploring a psychic reading of your past lives, you will want to choose a psychic who has that particular ability. If you know people who visit psychics, ask for their recommendations. You can also attend a psychic or metaphysical fair. Many times a psychic must meet a certain standard and have a good reputation to take part in one. Ask the management for suggestions. Fees can vary greatly depending on the psychic's popularity and reputation. Readings can run from $20 to well over $100.

Here are some questions that you may want to ask a psychic before plunking down your money:

1. How long have you been doing readings?

2. What, if any, is your training?

3. What is your fee?

4. How long is the session?

5. What methods do you use to get your information?

6. What is your area of psychic specialty?

7. Can I record my session with you?

A few words of caution: Some of the psychics listed in phone books or who have 1-900 phone numbers may or may not have the gifts to give you a creditable past life reading. Some of them are just out to get your money and will try to keep you on the line as long as they can (you usually pay by the minute). There are also many professional psychics who are very skilled in feeding back information that you knowingly or unknowingly give to them. It's a good idea to always be a little skeptical—and to be on the watch for out-and-out frauds.

Can You Believe What They Say?

It's important to remember that you are the one with the soul memory. You have permission to believe—or not—anything that anyone else, including a professional psychic (or even the information in this book), tells you. Part of being psychic is the resonance felt when the piece of information you receive rings true.

When you experience a sensation internally or externally, from something you are told or that you read, pay attention. There might be more to it. You may actually get a gut feeling, a heart feeling, or even a vibration in your *third eye* that tells you that you are being reminded of something you know from a past life experience. These reminders can be pleasant or unpleasant. You can feel warm and fuzzy or imagine peaceful music. You could have the sense of something old and pleasant such as baking cookies, or the warmth of a fire. You could also experience a pain, a bad taste, an unpleasant odor, a shiver, a cold or clammy feeling.

Words to Remember

Your **third eye** is located in the center of your forehead at a point that is above and centered between your two seeing eyes. It is the energy center where your "psychic sight" comes into your body from what Edgar Cayce called the "Source."

All of these reactions can be triggered by something you learned long ago. The question to ask yourself is, "Where did I first learn to experience the sensation?" As you learn to trust your own feelings, they will be a great help in determining the validity of your past life connections.

As you begin to collect information on your past lives, the more that you develop a trust in your own intuitive abilities, the more you will be able to sift through the information that somebody else tells you. You will be able to determine how it fits with how you feel. It is possible that a psychic will provide you with information that is right on the money, and in the same session you may receive something else that isn't accurate.

When you begin collecting clues, look for both ones that fit and ones that don't. Set aside the ones that you do not understand at the moment, but keep them handy, as they may be useful in the future. In other words, if you hear something from someone, and that might not be just a psychic, pay attention to how you intuitively respond to that information. If you feel that something feels right, make a mental note of it, and when you have a chance, write it down. Chances are that the true information will be presented to you more than once.

Think of the way you gather information as if there were a whole group of people painting a picture together. The image itself, like a mosaic, brings in each individual's unique gifts and talents, all working on the same general theme to the picture. You are the person in charge of putting together the mosaic of your past lives.

I *Knew* I Was Important!

Edgar Cayce was sometimes reluctant to tell a subject that they had been an important person during one of their lifetimes. He feared that if they knew they had been wealthy or powerful, they would aspire to the same lifestyle over again in this lifetime. Working toward recovering the same experience from the past may not be intended for this life. The soul may need to learn a different lesson relating to the misuse of the wealth of power of a past life. The individual must overcome their free will that wants to recover the past and focus on the lessons of this lifetime. As I've mentioned, when your free will takes over and your lessons are not addressed, you will have to tackle the same lessons in a future life. Following your free will can create all kinds of havoc and chaos, not only for yourself but for others around you. It's never too late to get yourself back in tune with your life map.

One of the best ways to verify that someone may have been important in a past life is to observe their behavior. Do they order others around and expect to be treated like royalty? Do they spend way beyond their means because they fail to see their current financial situation? Perhaps you call someone else "princess" or some other royal name that fits their personality. Here are some other signs that you may have been important in a past life:

- ◆ Do you have feelings that you may have had a high position in the past and resent it that people do not treat you the way you know they should?

- ◆ Does your free will want to control you in ways that are not the best suited for your life situation?

- ◆ Do you feel that you deserve better than you have?

- ◆ Do you resent that others have money and power you feel rightfully should be yours?

- ◆ Do you feel the need to share your vast knowledge with others?

- ◆ Do you have natural leadership abilities that always point you to positions of being in charge?

Being important in a past life can be a good thing if you recognize your past abilities and are willing to put them to use for the good in your current life situation.

CAUTION

Karmic Cautions _____

Whatever you were in a past life, you need to know what your role is in *this* life. It's easy to forget that when your ego takes over. The way you acted in the past may not be appropriate for you now.

It's okay to feel that you may have had a life of great importance in the past. Chances are that you have. It's possible that you have had several lives that others may never have the opportunity to experience. The more you understand these lives, the more you can use the experiences to help you fulfill your purpose in this life. You now may have a good many subjects from a life of royalty that you need to make amends to for your previous actions and bad judgments.

The Least You Need to Know

- From his humble beginnings, Edgar Cayce grew to become one of the world's most renowned psychic diagnosticians.

- Self-hypnosis can be used to develop your intuition.

- Hypnosis can help you visit your Akashic Records.

- A good psychic may help you get past life insights.

- Regardless of whether you were important or not in a past life, what matters is how you use your past experiences in this life.

Chapter 5

How to Hypnotize Yourself

In This Chapter

- ◆ Understanding what hypnosis is all about
- ◆ Hypnosis and your imagination
- ◆ A relaxation exercise that focuses on your breathing
- ◆ Finding your self-hypnosis zone
- ◆ How you can use hypnosis every day

If you've ever been to a stage hypnotist show, you know that there is a certain mystique that the hypnotist presents to his audience. He wants you to succumb to his hypnotic powers. But in reality, he doesn't have any hypnotic powers—*you* do. Hypnosis is magic, and the magic is in your mind waiting for you to let it begin to work its wonders. Then again, you have been using your powers and probably didn't even realize it.

Many people think that to experience hypnosis you need to go to a hypnotist who will put you into a deep sleep. They believe that while you are in this sleep trance the hypnotist has a secret power to change you somehow. When you leave the session you will magically be changed. That's really not the case. The hypnotist doesn't have the magic power, you do. The hypnotist's job is to help you change a habit or even take you into a past life.

In this book, you will become the hypnotist of your self. Self-hypnosis can become a very effective tool for you, not only in examining your past lives, but for many other things as well. As you become experienced in the use of self-hypnosis, you will be able to use this state of relaxation to give yourself suggestions that will help you regress to your past lives.

The Different Kinds of Hypnosis

You already learned in Chapter 1 that hypnosis is an altered state in which your unconscious mind accepts a suggestion without question by your conscious mind. What actually happens in hypnosis is a gradual shifting of your focus from the reality around you to another reality that is created by suggestion. That reality is real to you but may not be noticed by others. On the extreme end of altered states of reality are *phobias*.

reality
↓
↓
phobias

Words to Remember

A **phobia** is a fear that becomes so powerful the one who experiences it temporarily loses touch with their surroundings and enters a second reality that is connected to a traumatic moment in their past. (That past may not be in this lifetime!) When the phobia starts, the memory is experienced again without the person realizing what is happening.

You can experience that dual reality on a lesser scale when you step into your imagination. That imagination may be based on real moments in your life. There may be no known basis for the images you experience—at least not yet.

Basically there are two different types of hypnosis: authoritative and permissive. Authoritative hypnosis is done through direct commands such as "you will" or "you are." This was the predominant method before the last 20 years. Authoritative hypnosis creates the expectation that the subject will be influenced by some special power that the hypnotist uses when he puts his subjects in a deep trance.

"When I start counting from five to zero, your eyes will get heavier and heavier. You will go deeper and deeper into a trance." These are phrases that would be used in an authoritative hypnotic induction. If you were the subject, would you accept someone else's direct command without question, or would you analyze and resist what you were told to do?

Authoritative hypnosis works well for those who are used to taking orders. If you are "highly suggestible," meaning that you accept what someone else tells you without question, then you would be a good subject for this hypnotic technique. The truth is that only one in five people will enter a deep trance through authoritative hypnosis.

This book uses permissive hypnosis. Any suggestions will be phrased with "you may" rather than "you will." The idea behind permissive hypnosis is that you are really in charge of your own hypnosis. You are going to hypnotize yourself. Remember, there is no need for you to enter a deep trance to experience hypnosis for a past life regression. You will always be aware if the phone rings, of traffic going by, or of people talking. Yet at the same time, you may not need to be as aware of these interruptions as you might be at other times.

The type of hypnosis that you will be experiencing is derived from Neuro Linguistic Programming (NLP), which was developed in the 1970s and is widely used today. This concept will help you build image models for collecting past life information. It can help you change your focus from your conscious reality to the reality of your past lives. It will allow you do so without the fear of reliving a negative memory from the past.

> **Ageless Insights**
>
> Your goal in hypnosis will be to keep your analytical mind out of the way so that you will accept suggestions that you give yourself. The more you get used to the hypnosis process, the easier it will be to enter your own trance. It's useful for much more than past life regression. It can help you relieve stress and make positive decisions.

hypnosis — imagination & communication

words produce images in your mind

So to sum it up, hypnosis is really a combination of imagination and communication. Communication creates the imagination. Almost every word produces an image in your mind. At the same time, an image projects a thought or a communication. The two are linked together. In the following chapters you will learn that no one on earth creates images the same way that you do. Therefore, no one else will experience hypnosis exactly like you.

Use Your Imagination

Even though the explanation of what actually happens when you enter a hypnotic trance can sound very complicated, hypnosis is really a lot easier than you might think. It is very natural, and you already do it all the time!

If you can imagine, you can experience hypnosis. As you already know, imagination is part of hypnosis. You will learn more about how you imagine in Chapter 6. For now, just imagine the way you naturally do it, and you will be experiencing natural self-hypnosis.

Let's see how you imagine. Do you have a special place where you like to go and relax? This place could be real, or you may have a place that you think about in your mind. If you don't have one or can't remember such a place, it's all right to make one up. See how many questions you answer with a yes in the following imagination exercise:

1. Make yourself comfortable and think about a place where you like to relax. Close your eyes, if you'd like. Can you put yourself there in your imagination? Can you experience what it feels like to be there? If you can't, that's okay because your imagination experience is the way you naturally do it, not necessarily the way these questions suggest that you do it.

2. Can you imagine a picture of your place? Can you see yourself in the picture as if you were watching a video of yourself? How clear can you picture your relaxing place?

3. Can you hear your favorite relaxing music or another sound such as water flowing? If you can imagine hearing these sounds, does the experience help you to relax?

4. Can you imagine a relaxing smell? If you can remember one, can you experience the feeling of being relaxed when you smell it? Can you picture what you imagined smelling?

5. Can you imagine the taste of a relaxing food? Can you imagine how this food feels in your mouth? Can you smell it? Can you picture it?

All of these questions are designed to show you that you do imagine, and the way you imagine. You may have been able to answer all of the questions with a yes, or you may have only answered some that way. Whatever your total was is the right one for you. You will learn more about how differently each one of you imagines in the chapters to come.

Soul Stories _____

I can tell you that most of my answers to those questions would be no. I discovered when I was studying hypnosis that I cannot imagine pictures, sounds, external feelings, smells, or tastes. I knew I was different, but I didn't know how much. That still didn't discourage me from learning my own way of doing hypnosis. I have lost more than 50 pounds using self-hypnosis, and the amazing thing is that it has stayed off for more than 10 years. I have even undergone eye surgery while using self-hypnosis.

The goal of this little exercise is to prove to you that you could experience hypnosis. It is really as easy as imagining. There is no way to do it wrong. Each time you imagine you will do it differently, even if it's the same subject. Each time you will focus a little differently. Sometimes the focus will be deeper, and sometimes when your conscious mind is cluttered with other thoughts, it may not be easy to let your imagination go.

You have just completed your first exercise in self-hypnosis. It wasn't very hard to do, was it? Next, you will have the opportunity to experience a hypnosis exercise to help you focus even more on relaxing. You may already practice meditation or other forms of relaxation. If you do, you may use any technique that will help you focus and relax.

Karmic Cautions

Imagination can have a positive influence on you. Unfortunately, it can also have a negative influence. If you focus on worries and fears, it's easy to slip into negative self-hypnosis. This can be especially true if you worry about future outcomes or continually go over a negative memory from the past. If you receive a negative image, try to refocus on a positive one.

Take a Breath and Relax

There are a couple of ways that you can try the following relaxation exercise. You can read it first and memorize the wording, or you can record the words and play them back to yourself as you experience the induction. You can also have someone else read them to you as you experience the exercise. You may notice that many words are repeated over and over. There is a purpose to that—it is to help remind you to experience the words.

If you're ready, find a comfortable place to sit or lay down that is away from interruptions. You may want to wear something comfortable and not too tight. You may start by taking a deep breath, if that is comfortable for you, and slowly exhale. Do this several times. Next, focus your mind on the center of your forehead—your third eye—and continue to breathe slowly and deeply. As you do this, let your eyes go out of focus and feel yourself begin to relax. You may be aware of sounds and other things happening around you, and that's okay. You will always be aware, but you need not focus on them.

Sometimes it is really hard to let your body relax. You may have all kinds of thoughts bouncing around in your head. There may be negative thoughts interfering with your relaxation. Slow, deep breathing can help you bring yourself to a calmer state.

You may be aware that you have many muscles in your body, and at all times there are some that are relaxed and some that are stiff. If you feel a muscle stiffen up, relax it and let yourself feel even more relaxed as you continue to breathe in and out comfortably and slowly. With each breath you may feel yourself relaxing more and more. You may let your eyes close and feel yourself relaxing even more. If at any time you want or need to, you may always open your eyes, take a deep breath, exhale, and come back to the surface of your conscious mind, relaxed, refreshed, and ready to continue on with your day or night.

In a moment you are going to count downward from five to zero, and with each number you will feel yourself going ten times deeper into self-hypnosis. It is a good feeling and as you go deeper and deeper you will feel yourself relaxing more and more. As you go deeper and deeper you may feel yourself becoming more and more in tune with your focus on your forehead. If you are ready, you may start with the first number.

- FIVE. You may feel all the muscles from the top of your head down over your forehead to your nose, cheeks, mouth, chin, and neck relaxing. You may suggest to yourself to relax and go deeper and deeper as you slowly count yourself down to zero. In between each number you may allow yourself to breathe deep and focus your mind on your forehead. With each number you tell yourself that you will go ten times deeper.

- FOUR. You may now allow yourself to become more and more comfortable as you relax all your shoulder muscles down to your upper arms, to your elbows, your forearms, your wrists, hands, and all the way to your fingertips. As you relax, you may feel yourself going ten times deeper than before. You may feel yourself relaxing more and more as you go deeper and deeper.

- THREE. You may now feel the muscles in your body relaxing down over your chest and your back, all the way to your waist. You may feel yourself going deeper and deeper. You may feel yourself relaxing and going ten times deeper with each count downward. You may feel very comfortable as you breathe slowly in and out.

- TWO. You may let your muscles relax all the way to your knees as you go 10 times deeper into self-hypnosis. You are getting closer and closer to being very relaxed and in a comfortable self-hypnosis trance as you count yourself down to zero. With each breath you are relaxing more and more.

- ONE. You are almost there. You may feel yourself relax all the way down to your ankles as you breathe slowly in and out, ten times deeper than the last number. You are feeling yourself becoming more and more relaxed. Now, as you slowly count yourself all the way down from five to zero, you may enter a deep relaxing self-hypnosis trance.

- FIVE. FOUR. THREE. TWO. ONE. ZERO. You are now in a very comfortable self-hypnosis trance state as you feel the muscles in your total body relax. You may feel a positive, soothing energy flow through your entire body. Take a few moments to enjoy where you are as you feel positive, relaxed, and very comfortable.

When you are ready, you may begin slowly counting back to the surface of your conscious mind when you reach five. You may go back to this place at the same or different trance level every time you experience self-hypnosis. You will continue to have a positive and relaxed feeling after you end your self-hypnosis trance. If you're ready, you may start counting yourself back up.

- ◆ ONE. You are slowly counting yourself back to the surface of your conscious mind. You may continue to breathe slowly in and out.

- ◆ TWO. You are slowly coming back to the surface of your mind feeling relaxed and comfortable.

- ◆ THREE. You feel so relaxed as you continue to come back upward. Three. You are getting closer and closer to the surface.

- ◆ FOUR. You are almost there.

- ◆ FIVE. You may now take a deep breath, exhale, and open your eyes feeling calm, relaxed, and positive after your self-hypnosis trance. Isn't it great to feel calm, comfortable, and relaxed?

Finding Your Zone

Just as you would go about improving your skills in a hobby, a sport, or an occupation, the same applies to learning to use your imagination. At first you may feel a little awkward at letting your thoughts go where they want to go. You may be used to being in control, and it may be hard to let yourself relax and imagine. Remember, you are in control of yourself and can always change your imagination back to reality. All you have to do is take a deep breath, and open your eyes feeling positive and relaxed.

When you get used to doing self-hypnosis relaxation exercises, you can create shortcuts so that you don't need to spend as much time preparing to become focused. In sports, that focus is called being in the zone. A basketball player may have a certain routine before shooting a free throw. She may bounce the ball a specific number of times, for example, or take a deep breath and exhale. A baseball player may tap the plate or adjust his uniform the same way before stepping up to bat. These rituals are a way to remind athletes to go into the zone. Once they enter it they are in a heightened state of focus. They can slow down a pitch or shorten the distance to the basket in their minds.

An athlete will actually practice their routine or ritual to remind them that they will enter their zone when it is time. Many of them actually do mental training to help them remember what it is like to be in their heightened state of focus. The more comfortable they become with their ritual, the more they will automatically enter their zone. If they forget to go through their routine, they may not be able to focus when they need to.

You are now going to learn how you can get yourself into the "self-hypnosis zone." In other words, you can develop a routine or ritual that will help remind you to go into your heightened state of focus. The goal is to help you to focus faster when you want to zero in on information that you may be giving yourself relating to your past lives.

The word that describes what you are doing in self-hypnosis is called an *anchor*. An anchor can be a special word, or it can be a physical action. It could be a combination of both. You can create anchors to help you go into a heightened state of focus that no one else even notices. You could use an anchor just to bring back a memory of what it is like to be relaxed. You could anchor your imaginary place where you are relaxed and visit it right then and there when you use your anchor.

When you start the action of getting into your self-hypnosis zone, you are triggering your anchor. To trigger an anchor means to bring back your heightened state of focus by your special word or physical action.

> **Words to Remember**
>
> An **anchor** is a special word or physical touch or movement that can help you recreate a state of heightened focus.

Does this sound complicated? It really isn't. An anchor can be as simple and easy as using a word such as *relax*, or placing your thumb and finger together. You can do both at the same time. You can find any word or action that is comfortable and easy for you to use. When and how do you use it? The answer is "any time you want to," and you can develop the trigger for your anchor when you are in a relaxed state of self-hypnosis. You'll learn how to do this in the next section.

When you learn this trigger to put yourself "back in the zone," you will actually be giving yourself a post-hypnotic suggestion. This simply means that when you are in your relaxed state, you will give yourself a suggestion that when you say your special word or experience your physical action, you will return to your relaxed state of heightened focus even if you did not go through the longer relaxation exercise.

Obviously, you may not be as relaxed as if you had completed the whole routine, but you should be able to heighten your state of focus. It is very good for you just to be able to relax when you need to, as well as focus on your past lives.

Creating a Daily Practice Schedule

This self-hypnosis exercise can be beneficial to you in many ways. If you develop a habit of experiencing it at least once a day it can help you stay focused and relaxed. It will also be very helpful to you as you progress through this book.

Some of the potential benefits of using self-hypnosis include the following:

◆ Reduce stress

◆ Lose weight

◆ Stop smoking

◆ Lower blood pressure

◆ Perform better athletically

◆ Communicate more effectively with yourself and others

◆ Be a better student

◆ Overcome a fear

◆ Increase creativity

Remember that no one else will experience self-hypnosis exactly like you. You may not have been able to relax as much as was suggested. That's okay. If you felt any benefit, you experienced something positive. There are many ways to experience self-hypnosis, and the relaxation exercise you completed earlier in this chapter is a great way to begin preparing to use self-hypnosis to journey into a past life. You will be adding to this script and learning how to progress into a trance faster and deeper.

A script is the words a hypnotist uses to help you enter your trance. When you are doing self-hypnosis, it's the words that you say to yourself either by recording them and playing them back during the exercise, or saying and experiencing them at the same time. The script should lead you step by step into a more heightened state of focus or into your zone.

The following exercise shows you how to create an anchor to help you focus:

1. Start by experiencing your self-hypnosis relaxation exercise that appears earlier in this chapter. Count yourself all the way down to zero to your relaxed state. When you have gotten there, imagine your special place, and for a few moments let yourself experience how good it feels to be there.

2. When you are ready, give yourself a special word or place your thumb and finger together or do both. Suggest to yourself that any time you want to experience how good it feels to be in this heightened state of relaxation you will trigger your special anchor(s), and you will be able to experience this state instantly. Suggest that you will be able to have this relaxed feeling, but you will always be aware of where you are at the time you experience it.

3. While you are in your heightened state of relaxation, practice triggering your anchors several times. Suggest to yourself that you will be able to have this experience any time you use your triggers at a focus level that is right for where you are. In other words, if you are in a place where you can experience your anchor stronger, you may do so. However, if you are in a place where it is impossible to go into a deeper state of focus, you may feel less of an effect.

Ageless Insights

It's important for you to practice the longer relaxation exercise at least once a day. At the same time, practice triggering your anchors so that you can return to your relaxed state several times a day. Plan on specific times so that it becomes part of your daily routine.

4. When you are done, suggest that you will remember your anchor after you count yourself back up out of hypnosis. Now count yourself back from one to five, take a deep breath, exhale, and open your eyes.

Now try triggering your anchor and go back into your relaxed state of heightened focus. Take a moment to experience the benefits and take a breath, exhale, and return to your normal conscious state.

Once you get into your self-hypnosis routine, you will be amazed at how it will help you relax. The easier you can relax, the more it will help you as you prepare to experience a past life regression.

The Least You Need to Know

◆ Hypnosis is not the complicated process that you may have been led to believe.

◆ Deep breathing is a good way to help you relax.

◆ No one else experiences hypnosis exactly like you do.

◆ You can create positive hypnotic anchors for yourself that help you find your zone.

◆ The more you use hypnosis on a daily basis, the better at relaxing you will become.

Part 2

Peeking Through the Veil

Now you are ready to start honing your investigative skills. You will learn to understand your own mental DNA and develop a profile of your own thinking. You can look for the clues within yourself that will help put together your own case for your past lives.

Some of your research may go back into your childhood. It was here that you might have showed your strongest connection to your past. Then you will consider the situations in your current life that may have their roots in a past life.

You will read some other case histories and learn not to get thrown off-track by unexpected experiences. You will realize that you have a whole team helping you in your quest. Are you ready to proceed?

Chapter 6

You Live in a Trance

In This Chapter

◆ Learn to create a hypnotic trance

◆ Identifying an interest in things from another era

◆ Living in a different time period

◆ Have you ever experienced déjà vu?

◆ The link between dreams and your past lives

In this chapter, you will discover that you may have been spending a good part of your life in a trance all along. It could have been a pleasant trance or at times a negative trance.

How so, you ask? Can you remember when you were in school, and you had a very boring teacher? No matter how hard you tried to stay focused on the lesson, your mind would keep wandering off to something else. You might even have left the classroom in your mind. All of a sudden the teacher decided to call on you. You didn't have a clue as to what he was talking about, and you got in trouble for not paying attention—in effect, for being hypnotized. That boring teacher had helped put you in a trance.

Have you experienced driving on the highway and losing track of time? All of a sudden you realize that you have gone right by your destination.

You were experiencing something called highway hypnosis. A trance can occur when your conscious mind just spaces out and your unconscious mind takes over. The trance continues until something brings your focus back to your conscious mind.

What Do You Imagine?

In the previous chapter you imagined a special place where you could feel relaxed. In this chapter you will begin to focus on what you naturally experience in your mind. In other words, what do you daydream about?

Some of you may spend a lot of time in your mind, while others may not have the same opportunity to let their mind wander. Bob, for example, developed a great imagination when he worked on an assembly line. He spent eight monotonous hours a day repeating the same task. If he kept track of the time, it moved very slowly. He found that by playing in his mind the time slipped by much quicker. He made it a habit not to look at his watch. His workday consisted of four segments with a mid-morning break, lunch break, and mid-afternoon break. It usually took him a few minutes to slip from his conscious awareness into his imagination. Once he shifted his focus, he was free to wander wherever he wanted.

Bob was able to perform his job and at the same time create a trance for himself that changed the dimensions of time. He would enter a trance and stay in it until it was time for the scheduled breaks. Out of this boring job he naturally developed the ability to use a form of self-hypnosis to enter a heightened state of focus. The focus was on his imagination. This ability has stayed with him.

You may already have a great imagination that was developed because you were bored, or possibly because you were in a situation in your life where it became part of your survival. This is particularly true for those of you who grew up in dysfunctional families where the actual reality was too difficult to endure without going someplace else in your mind. If this is the case, you have developed a wonderful ability out of unfortunate circumstances that can be a great tool for experiencing a past life regression.

Imagination can be separated into several different categories:

- **Functional** imagination is when you use your mind to work on a specific project. It might be something that you want to achieve and bring into a physical reality. To do this you make it real in your mind first and then follow the plan until it is completed. Those of you who work with directions or patterns will build or make it first mentally. Functional imagination is used to make something an actual reality.

◆ Some of you may be able to create wonderful **fantasies** in your mind that have no possibility of becoming reality. A fantasy can be a healthy and relaxing escape from your daily routine. It is a place where you can go with your mind that is not possible in actual reality. It is the land of fairy tales and science fiction.

◆ A **creative fantasy** happens when you use your imagination to develop ideas in your mind. It is a blend of function and fantasy. Much of your creativity actually comes from your unconscious mind. That means you may not and need not know where the ideas come from as long as they come when they are needed. Creative fantasy is an automatic process that just happens. Artists, musicians, and writers often use creative fantasy to let unconscious ideas become a reality.

◆ Maybe you spend a lot of time in your mind communicating with your **belief.** You may meditate, pray, or talk to your angels or guides. You are actually reaching out to sources that will help guide you through your life.

◆ You may spend a lot of time engaged in **worry.** You could worry about something that has happened in the past or something that might happen in the future. Your imagination is the fuel that feeds your worry.

◆ **Random** imagination represents the thoughts and images that pop into your mind for no apparent reason. Some of these thoughts may be contained in a part of your memory that you have not tapped into yet—your past lives.

> **CAUTION**
>
> **Karmic Cautions**
>
> If you're not sure what you believe, you dwell on imagining the worst-case scenarios. You are always looking at the "what ifs" in life rather than believing in positive outcomes. Learning your strengths from past lives can actually help you change this type of imagination to a more positive one.

Do You Like Old Things?

Now it's time to begin to zero in on some of the ways that you have been imagining already that may be keys to unlocking the memory of a past life. Perhaps you like old things, whether the study of history or collecting antiques from a certain time period.

Diane always felt as if she was born in the wrong time period. She loves the past so much that she shuns modern cooking appliances and prefers the warm glowing heat of an old-fashioned wood stove. She even got so interested in local history that she became the president of the historical society in the town where she lived. There was no place she felt more comfortable than being surrounded by the relics of a different age. She could even feel in her imagination what it was like to live in an earlier time.

Perhaps you have a passion as strong as Diane's for old things. Jim does. He is a professional musician who developed a strong interest in the music and instruments of the Civil War period. He studied the subject and joined a performance group called the "Yankee Brass" that gets together for one week a year to recreate the music of that time. The members of the group come from all over the country. They play on authentic Civil War instruments, dress in exact replicas of Civil War band uniforms, and perform music from that era. When they play, they not only take themselves back in time, they take their audiences back as well.

You probably know an old-car buff who isn't old enough to remember the age that consumes their passion. You may be drawn to music, art, and literature, or other subjects that come from a different era. You may be drawn to something old without even realizing it. Perhaps you have thought about your interest in old things and perhaps you haven't. As you get ready to experience a past life regression, now is a good time to become aware of what you already know.

Remember as you consider the following questions regarding your interests in old things that you may not have much interest in them at all. Maybe you had enough of them or did not have a good experience when you actually lived with them in a past life. It's okay to feel that way, too.

What old things do you like? Can you identify the time period that they came from? Do you have more than one time period that you are interested in? Do you like very old things from hundreds of years ago or from a time not long before you were born?

> **Ageless Insights**
>
> Keep notes of the things that you are interested in that may relate to one or more of your past lives. You can keep a small notebook with you or close by at all times so that when you have a thought, you can just write it down. Once you have captured it, you can always add it to a more permanent past life diary later.

Do the things you like have a theme to them, such as old bottles, tools, clothes, books, or other things? Do you collect or research as much as you can find that relates to a certain time period?

Do you like old things that relate to certain countries or geographic locations? Can you imagine what it would be like to live during the time those old things came from? Do you feel a sense of comfort when old things surround you?

Feeling Comfortable in a Different Time

Perhaps you feel so strongly about a different period of time that you actually wished you lived there rather than the time you live in now. Besides collecting old things, you may live in a period house, complete with interior decorations and exterior landscaping.

You may have chosen your neighborhood because it looked like what you had in mind. You may feel out of place and awkward trying to exist in a world where you are uncomfortable. If you feel this way, you're not alone. It's easy to spot someone who consciously or unconsciously longs to live in a different time period. Just look at the way the person dresses. Someone with a passion for the old West may look and act like a cowboy. Someone interested in the Civil War may grow a beard like an enlisted man in the army of the North or South.

The goal in past life regression is to update the strengths that you brought with you from an earlier time into the world where you live now.

Do you wish you lived during a different time period? Even if you like where you are now, what other age would you have liked to live in? Do you try to recreate that age where you live now? Would you if you could?

Do you wear clothes, cut your hair, read books, collect art, or watch movies from a different time period? Can you imagine what it would be like to actually live then?

Is there a time period that sends shivers up your spine just by imagining it? There may be a time period that you positively do not want to visit. Just the thought of living back then brings negative images to your mind. You may be so repelled that you don't even want to watch programs or read books about it. These negative images are just as important in researching your past lives as positive images of different time periods. What is it about that period that you can't stand? Is it the food, the social environment, turmoil such as war, the art, music, or something else? Are there certain locations or countries that you absolutely would not want to live in?

Do you enjoy certain foods and ways of preparing them that were popular way back when? Do you need to make sure you are as self-sufficient as possible? Do you wonder or imagine what it would have been like to walk the land near where you live as a pioneer or early settler?

Is there a specific culture that you are absolutely attracted to? Do you try to learn as much about that culture as possible? You may have an interest in Native America. Mark always had a fantasy about a life as a Native American. He went to a powwow and became hooked. He even went so far as to adopt a Native American name and take part in the ceremonies. He was so obsessed that he existed in a dual reality, one fueled by his imagination.

Is there more than one member of your family who longs to live in the same time period? Do you go to or take part in functions where all of the attendees wished they lived in the same time? Do you take on specific roles of someone who actually lived during a different time period, such as a Civil War enactment group? What other thoughts about living in the past do you have?

You may want to make notes of the responses you had to the questions above. You may not have had a response for all of them. That's okay. Every clue you uncover can help identify a past life that you might have lived.

I've Been Here Before

Have you ever had *déjà vu?* Basically this means being aware that an experience you are having may have occurred before. It's like you already know what's going to be said or happen next as if you were reliving a memory. Sometimes the image itself is so powerful that it puts you in the reality of the previous experience. It can be very confusing as you try to balance what is happening to how you already know that it happened.

Déjà vu can be a wonderful feeling, like connecting with an old friend again. It also can be a warning signal to avoid something unpleasant that may have happened in the past. Perhaps you have had either or both of these experiences.

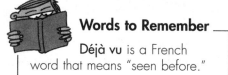

Words to Remember

Déjà vu is a French word that means "seen before."

Déjà vu can happen anytime, anywhere. It could be a conversation with a friend, a chance meeting with a stranger, or a visit to a certain location. Something is triggered in your unconscious memory, and you are suddenly pulled into a memory of the past, only you're acting it out again.

Have you ever gone someplace for the first time and found that you knew where you were going without reading the directions? Perhaps you got lost, and someone else in the car who had never been there before was able to give you accurate directions as if they already knew the way.

Peter had the ability as a child to know exactly where he was when he traveled with his family. He didn't even have to be paying attention when he would announce to the rest of the passengers that the driver had taken a wrong turn. After a while the family learned to trust his instincts even though they didn't understand where he got them.

Have you ever had a déjà vu experience? Have you had more than one? Is there a pattern to any déjà vu experiences that you may have had? Did you have the experiences with the same or different people? Did any of them have a similar déjà vu at the same time as you?

Do you have the feeling that you and someone else have had the same conversation or experience together before? Do you feel that you and a group of people have been together before during different times and are reacquainting with each other? Do you feel that other people who you are with have known you in the past? In other words, do you feel that you might have taught them before and are teaching them now? Or maybe they taught you.

Soul Stories

Have you ever had an experience where you visited a place that you had not been before and felt that you had experienced it in an earlier time period? This happened to author Taylor Caldwell. She and her husband arrived late at night in a hotel in Italy. She gazed out of the window and noted the splendor of the courtyard below. The next morning she was amazed that what she had seen the night before was not what she saw in daylight. She later learned that what she had experienced was the view from the window a few hundred years before. Many of her books reflected knowledge of past cultures that she did not research.

Brenda booked a passage for a day's trip on a boat that was a hundred years old. As she stood on the deck enjoying the warm sun and breeze, she suddenly began to see a different scene. From her relaxed state (light trance), the vessel came alive with people dressed as they would have been on a similar voyage years before she was born. It was such a natural experience for her that the first few moments she didn't even realize what was taking place. When she began to think consciously, she was snapped back to the reality of her current time.

Perhaps you have had similar experiences of déjà vu. Many times it happens when you create a light trance by relaxing your conscious mind and shifting your focus onto your imagination. Or is it really just imagination?

Dreaming About the Past

We all have dreams, but we may not remember them. Can you remember your dreams? Have you ever had a dream that repeats itself either in theme or actual scenes? Dreams are a treasure trove of past life memories. It's very possible that you will actually get more information about your past lives when you are asleep than when you are awake. The reason for this is quite simply the fact that while we are awake our active minds don't give us the opportunity to let the messages come up from the unconscious mind.

While you are asleep, your thinking mind takes a break. While it is taking a break, there are a lot of other things going on. All your experiences of that day and the days before are floating around in your unconscious mind. Just the littlest experience, such as déjà vu or a contact with something old, a conversation, or something else might connect with a memory you have stored. That might trigger an anchor in your unconscious mind that focuses on a memory from the past.

This memory will then work its way up into your sleeping mind as a dream. You can have a dream that goes on for a certain length of time before you even become aware that you are having it. When you wake up, the last moments of your dream may still be very vivid in your mind. A great example of this is a nightmare. You may wake up in a cold sweat from a fear that was created in your dream.

Dreams can come through in many different ways. They might be *realistic*, in which you relive a scene that is very similar to your life now. The cast of characters in the dream play is recognizable to those in your life. However, it is possible that they may be playing different roles. It is possible that someone whom you know remotely, or with whom you have had only a chance meeting, turns out to be one of the stars in your dream.

Dreams can also be *symbolic*. This can be particularly true in dreams that have a certain theme to them. You may see symbols such as animals, bridges, houses, food, or metaphors that play out their story while you sleep. You may see strange fanciful characters. Or you may experience certain feelings or emotions over and over again in different scenarios.

Another type of dream is a *precognitive* dream, usually related to a psychic insight that can also relate to past lives. It is possible to dream of going to a location and experiencing a situation that happened in the past (before you were born). If you visit the place later, you might notice the similarities. You might even be able to locate certain landmarks that you had seen in the dream.

Ageless Insights

Hypnosis is a great tool for revisiting a dream. When you are in a state of heightened focus, it is possible to relive the experience of your dream state and gather many more details. When you wake up from a dream, you could, in fact, put yourself in a trance and examine the dream right away.

You may experience a lucid dream. Unlike other types of dreams, it can continue after you have awakened. It is possible to put yourself back in the dream and control its outcome.

Keeping a dream journal will help you remember dreams that you might otherwise forget. Any notebook will do; keep it and a pen handy so that you can jot down your dream right after you have it. A dream journal will give you an idea of any pattern developing in your dreams and could provide clues to your past lives. Include as many details about the dream as you can, including:

- Where did you have the dream (at home, while traveling, etc.)?

- What was the location in the dream?

- Who was in the dream that you recognized?

- What strangers were in your dream?

- What were you doing before you went to sleep?

- What did you eat before you went to sleep?

Dreams can definitely be a very important window to your past. If you'd like to find out more about dreams, you might start with the books listed in Appendix B.

The Least You Need to Know

♦ Your imagination may include past life memories coming to the surface of your mind.

♦ Your interest in things from a different era may be a continuance of a past life experience.

♦ Wishing you lived in a past time period may indicate that you actually lived there before.

♦ Déjà vu experiences may indicate that you are remembering a past life experience.

♦ Your dreams may be your memory reliving a past life experience.

Chapter 7

Children Still Remember

In This Chapter

- ◆ Children and past lives
- ◆ Acting out a past life
- ◆ Role reversals: were *you* the child?
- ◆ Adjusting to the present lifetime
- ◆ Helping a child keep past life memories alive

As you have learned, many Eastern cultures still believe in past lives. A child brings forward the attributes of their past lives that can be a great benefit to this lifetime. When children are encouraged to tell the stories that are in their minds, they are much more open to sharing the memories that they have brought with them from other lifetimes. Unfortunately, this is not the case in many Western families, and any memory that could have been shared will all too soon be forgotten as the child grows older.

The Tibetans believe that their Dalai Lama is the reincarnation of their God Kings. The current Dalai Lama, born in 1935, is the fourteenth in the known succession of this soul. After the Thirteenth Dalai Lama died, the Tibetan Regent received a vision of a three-story temple near a house that was adorned with carved gables and blue eaves.

In 1937, search parties were dispatched throughout the Chinese territories to locate the child that was the reincarnated Dalai Lama. The landmarks in the vision were found in the village of Takster. The two-year-old boy inside the house with the blue eaves asked for the rosary around the leader's neck. Then he named everyone in the search party correctly and identified items that the group brought with them. The party saw that he had birthmarks that helped confirm that he was the next Dalai Lama.

A Child's Wisdom

When you are born, you bring with your soul memories of the past. You don't have any experiences yet in this life to record in your unconscious mind, so you don't think the same way that adults do in terms of imagination. The older you get, the more information you gather for this lifetime.

Past life skeptics argue that when an adult experiences a past life regression they are tapping into early childhood memories that they have forgotten. Doctor Ian Stevenson, a professor of psychology at the University of Virginia, has spent much of his life studying reincarnation. His work has included field research in countries that embrace the concept of reincarnation. In more than 3,000 case studies, Dr. Stevenson has concluded that children will spontaneously remember past life experiences and report on them as soon as they are able to speak.

Soul Stories

Some children choose not to speak right away. Sarah was so late in communicating verbally that her parents had her examined to make sure she was not physically or mentally impaired. She checked out okay and eventually started to talk. It wasn't until her adult life that she learned through hypnotic past life regression that she had been a monk in a previous life who had taken a vow not to speak out loud. The monk's assignment in that lifetime was to care for animals, and he was able to communicate with them telepathically. Sarah has a special relationship with animals in her present lifetime.

Danny did not speak until he was nearly three years old. He caused great concern for his parents. A younger brother was born and was developing normally. One day the mother took the boys for a walk, pushing the younger one in a stroller. Danny got upset with his brother who would not stay seated and finally blurted out, "Will you sit down!" When he was ready to talk for the first time in this life, he had something to say!

The old saying "out of the mouths of babes" is definitely true in reference to a child's imagination. They can tell fantastic stories that most adults totally overlook if they are not acquainted with past life concepts. When children are old enough to talk, they can be a wealth of information if they are encouraged to let the images of their unconscious mind flow freely.

Children may use words that they did not learn from their family's vocabulary. The words they use can be clues to their past lives. When Brian was young he referred to himself as "The Brian." He would always answer that way if you asked him what his name was. Perhaps he still remembered a title he had earned or inherited during another lifetime.

As soon as she could talk, one little girl started to call her mother "Mommy Anne." It might mean that she knew in her mind that Anne was her current mother, but she had a mother before by a different name.

Perhaps you have heard the following story, which is told in different ways. A young family had a new baby girl. A few weeks after she was born, her four-year-old brother asked to speak to her alone. From the baby monitor they heard him ask, "Can you please remind me about what God looks like? I am beginning to forget." This little story, true or not, hits the nail on the head regarding the complexity of a child's mind.

Karmic Cautions

Pay attention to what a child tells you. If you think of them as "only children," you may miss the ancient wisdoms that are part of their soul. Try thinking of them as old people with memories trapped inside a child's body. You can help them make the transition into this life by giving them the opportunity to tell you about their past lives.

From One Life to the Next

Many children will do more than talk about their past lives—they will try to keep living them. They will bring mannerisms, skills, and habits with them when they come to this life. They may have "natural" creative abilities or excellent rhythm and coordination. They can do things that make you wonder where on earth they could have learned how. Here are three examples:

- ◆ Josh was really good with his hands when he was a small child. He was very interested in carving, and his mother bought him some Ivory soap to practice on. She was amazed to see the results of his work. Josh produced works of art that looked as if they had come from an ancient civilization.

- ◆ David was fascinated with items from the Revolutionary War period. One day he showed his mother a set of plans to build a musket rifle and then proceeded to tell her in great detail how to build and fire it.

◆ Nora used to play an interesting game with her friends when they were small children. She called it "crossing the Himalayas." She would have them line up and walk in single file along a course she had laid out. They had to climb over obstacles as they worked their way over the "vast mountain range." As an adult, Nora discovered that in a past life she had tried to lead a group of children over the Himalayas to escape from invaders of her country. Unfortunately, they were caught by a winter storm and froze to death in the mountains. Unconsciously she was trying to lead her children to safety in this lifetime.

Perhaps you remember (or your parents or other relatives told you) stories of how you acted as a child. Some of these stories may directly link you to an earlier past life that you were trying to continue to live during the first few years of this reincarnation.

Perhaps you had a childhood interest that has stayed with you into your adult life.

Ageless Insights

Sometimes your children will experience past lives through dreams or nightmares. They may try different skills or games they rediscovered in their dreams. Their ability to imagine is the key to the whole process. The more that you allow them to imagine in a positive way, the more clues you will receive.

Let's look at it from a child's perspective. For a moment, imagine what it would be like for you if you suddenly woke up in a different body. This body won't do all the things you want it to do. In fact, it is very small. You know how to move, but it won't move the way you want it to. You know how to walk, but your legs just won't cooperate. Then, when you get big enough to finally do something that you already know how to do, you discover that it isn't the right thing to do in this lifetime.

So there you are with all this knowledge inside of you. How are you going to use it? How are you going to tell anyone about it if they won't believe what you want to tell them? Everyone keeps telling you that you are just imagining things, and it would be better if you just forgot all about them. Everyone wants to treat you as if you were a little child. Perhaps you had an experience like this when you were little.

This example may give an idea of how a child might feel when they are wrestling with memories from the past. Keep this in mind when you have the opportunity to observe and/or communicate with a small child. If you want to ask someone else's child about "before," you may want to get permission from the child's parents. Not everyone is comfortable with the idea of past lives. You can really be a great help to a reincarnated child as they try to adjust to their current earthly assignment. You also may be taught something in exchange for your kindness.

Role Reversals

As children continue to grow and communicate more effectively, they can still retain memories from their past lives. These memories can remain so close to the surface that they will shift their focus from *conscious reality* to the reality of their past. When this happens, they sometimes will blend the two realities together. They can mix up past life assignments and relationships with the present.

Perhaps you as a child decided to take on a different role in your family. You may have tried to take care of your parents. You might have been jealous of one of your parents because you felt they were taking over your rightful place in the family.

Words to Remember

Conscious reality is your awareness of what everyone who is in close proximity to you can experience at the same time.

Perhaps you have or know of a child who isn't comfortable with their current position in their family yet. They may reverse the role of parent and child in their mind. They may want to protect, comfort, love, worry about, or discipline their parents as if they were their children. You might have called a child "little man," or some other term that implies that the child acts much older than his age.

The child may also treat the parent as a sibling. This is a role that can continue into adulthood. You may have a child or a parent who you think of as a brother or sister. You share confidences and other interests and keep in close contact with each other. You may even look much closer in age than you really are. Your physical features may also indicate a close connection.

Just think—you might be your own great-grandmother! When Lisa was a small girl, she visited her great-grandmother's grave-site for the first time. Her great-grandmother had died before she was born. She had an overwhelming feeling of sadness and suddenly envisioned a casket being lowered into the ground. This image stayed with her into adulthood. She also recognized many of the landmarks in the town where her great-grandmother had lived. Through hypnosis, Lisa was able to go back and experience a lifetime when she was her great-grandmother.

Ageless Insights

A child may be the reincarnation of a family member. Past lives can have very short turn-arounds. Sometimes a child will remember people from a past life and greet them by name even though they have never met them before in this lifetime. You may have known someone as a child from a past life or you may know a child who has this ability.

Watching a child play can give you clues to relationships that may have started in the past. Pay attention to the names they give their dolls. Do they have imaginary friends who have names of deceased relatives? If so, how did they know them?

Like Lisa, they may recognize family landmarks when they visit them the first time. They may tell you stories about your relationships with them in a past life. They may comb their hair or want to wear their clothes in a style of a deceased family member. They may even grow to look like a relative who has died. They might have the same birthmark or a scar that relates to an injury of the person they are reincarnating from.

Resisting the Current Lifetime

It may take a child a certain length of time to adjust to life in their current body and time period. Some children just feel out of place with where they are. They may not be happy about it and wish for the life they had before. They may even remind other members of the family that they wish they were in a different place.

It is possible that a child is entering the earth plane this time as an old soul. When this happens the child usually has a highly developed psychic ability accumulated from the lifetimes before. This gift can become their curse if they are not able to understand how they are different from many of their family and friends. They are often misunderstood and even possibly labeled a "misfit" or "odd." They may be labeled as having learning disabilities or other problems that could be the result of a strong psychic ability carried over from the past.

Karmic Cautions

Unresolved issues from a past life or oversensitive psychic ability can be a real problem for teenagers. They are at the most vulnerable point in their lives and are a sponge for information from their past lives. If they don't understand how to deal with these confusing images, they develop fears or phobias from memories that they cannot resolve. It's very important for teens who are having issues of any kind—whether from a past life or in the present—to seek the help of a qualified therapist. Never try to use a book such as this one to take the place of needed therapy.

Edgar Cayce (see Chapter 4) had an experience with a two-and-a-half-year-old boy, Cayce Jones, the son of a good friend. Cayce had given a "life reading" for the child that determined that young Jones was the reincarnation of Edgar Cayce's dead brother Thomas. The reading stated that Cayce Jones would also have the psychic ability that Thomas had when he was alive.

The child acted strangely toward his parents, insisting that he did not belong to them. They asked Edgar Cayce to come to their home and meet the child to see if he could help. Young Cayce Jones recognized Edgar Cayce, whom he had never met before, and demanded that he take him home. He had to wait for the child to fall asleep before he could sneak out of the Jones's home.

Cayce did not dare to visit his friends again for eight years until he was summoned to the house where they had recently moved. Cayce Jones would not enter the house alone because he knew it was haunted. Edgar Cayce determined that he did indeed have his deceased brother's psychic abilities and told him how to deal with the ghost that occupied the house. Even though eight years had passed since their last meeting, Cayce Jones packed his belongings and waited for Edgar Cayce to take him to his "real" home.

If you can help a child become comfortable with his or her past life abilities, the child may more easily be able to overcome any resistance to the current reincarnation. When children understand that it's okay to be different, they will become more secure with their life purpose. You may be a great help to a child whom you know.

Helping Children Keep Their Memories Alive

One of the greatest gifts that a parent can give their children is a sense of their heritage. The more they learn about family genealogy, the more they have the opportunity to appreciate relatives who have gone on before them. At a young age this may start with stories about Grandfather or Grandmother or others who have passed on.

Now that you know children can be a wealth of knowledge from their past lives, you may see in some of their words and actions how they may relate to a past life. Watch how they speak and react to other people—family, friends, and strangers—and you may see past life portraits begin to emerge. If the child talks about people or places or things that seem to be imaginary or that you cannot identify, you may have a good place to start to help them gather information about their heritage.

Many times the past life memories will surface spontaneously. They might be triggered by a place they are in, something they see or experience, music, a taste, a smell, or a feeling that opens up their memory album stored in their unconscious mind. It is always advisable to have a notepad and pencil handy so that you may jot down pieces of information when they surface. If you have time to plan, a tape recorder or a video recorder are great tools for capturing these precious moments. The more variety of ways you have to collect the information, the greater opportunity you will have to piece together the child's past lives.

It's a good idea to keep a journal along with any recorded material. Remember, if you are using a computer, back up your information on an external disk as well as on your hard drive. If you are keeping only written records, make sure that you make copies and never keep them together.

For follow-up sessions, review your material before jumping into new areas. One great advantage in doing this is that you will be "priming the pump" for more information. You can use past knowledge as a cross-reference to see what correlates from session to session. Make sure this is a pleasant experience for the child. If any unpleasantness crops up from the past, steer away from it until the child is ready. If the child is mentally stressed, it is a good idea to seek the guidance and the wisdom of a professional counselor or therapist trained in past life recall and therapy techniques.

Remember that a child's attention span will be short. Gathering the clues should be a positive experience for them. They shouldn't feel bored or deprived of other activities. Try not to interpret what the child is telling you. Just encourage them to provide as much information as they are interested in at the time.

Karmic Cautions

If your child is old enough to realize what you are doing, set aside a quiet time to have a chat. You might call it story time. Rather than you telling them a story, let the child tell you a story. Or you could take turns, but be careful not to lead the child into false memories that might be influenced by your storytelling.

It's also possible that a child may have nothing to say about memories from a past life. The child may not remember them at all. Never press a child into an experience that may be uncomfortable.

It is possible that the length of time might be only a few moments, or it might be several minutes, all depending on your and the child's attention span. It could take a little time to develop a routine that provides consistent information, and as the child grows, the routine and the information may vary. When you have established an initial time period or an order to what you are doing, you can start to collect and organize the child's information.

As you progress, you may find that you are getting clues on more than one past life theme. It is also possible for other elements to be mixed in with past lives. For instance, the child may be seeing an angel, a ghost, or a spirit guide. A spirit guide is a highly evolved being that may come to the child as a voice in his or her mind. Sometimes the child is also able to see the guide. The purpose of the guide is to assist the child through his or her life journey. A deceased relative may visit the child from the other side. At this time in life, the child has not yet learned to become prejudiced about the information that is received, either internally or externally. Everything to a child is natural and real.

They might like or dislike a certain kind of music. These responses can start almost at birth. When Carter was an infant, music was very familiar to him. And yet, every time that he heard Mozart's "Kinder Music" he would get upset and cry. He even woke out of a deep sleep crying in response to that particular song. Perhaps he had an issue with Mozart in a past life.

The Least You Need to Know

- ◆ Children bring past life memories with them when they are born.

- ◆ Children may continue to act out past life situations in their present lifetime.

- ◆ A child may treat you as if you were the child.

- ◆ Some children may have a hard time adjusting to their present life.

- ◆ You can help a child become adjusted to this life and keep memories alive by helping the child understand his or her past lives.

Chapter

Using Your Senses

In This Chapter

- ◆ Understanding the past, future, and present tense experiences of your mind
- ◆ Roles of your conscious, unconscious, and universal minds
- ◆ The mental DNA composition of your mind
- ◆ Determining the strengths and weaknesses of your image recall in each of your five different senses

Imagine living in a house that has three rooms. They are the same size and are constructed side by side with doorways connecting them. You are free to pass back and forth between the rooms, and you can spend more time in any one of them.

The room on the left is filled with memories from the past, and the room on the right is filled with plans for the future. The one in the middle focuses on the present. You can visit these rooms in any of your five different sense images—seeing, hearing, feeling, tasting, and smelling.

Each one of you will live in the house in your mind differently than anyone else, whether you want to or not. That is because you are unique, and you think and remember differently. It's just the way you naturally are and live in the house in your mind.

The Past, Future, and Present

Did you know that your mind focuses in three different tenses—the past, the future, and the present? The past is the total of all your memory experiences up to this moment in your present lifetime. These memories are contained in your unconscious mind and they will continue to be housed there until they come back up to the surface and are noticed by your conscious mind. Have you ever had a memory that you hadn't thought of in years suddenly flood your mind from out of nowhere? If you have, you have experienced *spontaneous memory recall*.

Spontaneous memory recall can be triggered by an experience that taps into your unconscious mind's memory storage area. It might be a similar experience relating to an earlier one that causes a flashback. Sometimes a memory can be so powerful that it actually seems real to you. When this happens, it can be very confusing and even a little scary. This type of experience often takes place when you are already in a light trance such as a daydream and are unwittingly open to spontaneous memory recall.

Words to Remember

Spontaneous memory recall is a memory that is stored in your unconscious mind and suddenly becomes part of your conscious thinking without any effort to remember. This is different than a memory that you may have been trying to remember.

Fears and phobias are usually triggered by a spontaneous memory that brings a disturbing image back to the surface of your conscious mind. You relive it in the same way you experienced it the first time. You are actually in a self-hypnotic trance while you are having an experience like this, and you are unaware of anything but that memory until it has run its course.

Not all spontaneous memories are bad. You can also suddenly remember a very pleasant experience that is almost as enjoyable when you relive it again. Your mind is constantly reaching into your past whether you are awake or asleep.

Besides past memories from your present life, you can recall memories from your past lives. These usually are spontaneously triggered through your unconscious mind. You actually have many more memories than you may realize from past life experiences. Many times these images are overlooked unless you know what to look for. By the end of this book you will.

Besides remembering the past, your mind can focus into the future. You may plan ahead and perhaps even live an event in your imagination before it actually takes place. Perfectionists usually have the ability to experience the future so strongly before it happens that when it does happen, it quite often does not meet the expectations that they had in their imagination. They have pictured every little detail and put the outcome together with perfection. This ability to imagine so vividly can be a real problem for a perfectionist.

You can project a past memory into the future. In this situation you may be so focused on reliving a past memory that you miss what is actually happening in the moment. Again, for the perfectionist, the result is usually a disappointment.

Your mind can also focus on the present. Athletes call it the "zone." When you are in a state of hyper-focus, you are able to mentally change time, distance, and energy. When you are focused in the moment, you may not even be aware of what you are experiencing. It is in this altered state that an artist can paint a picture and not be aware of doing it until after they have finished.

You are constantly moving back and forth between the three tenses of your mind. Every thought or word creates an image that relates to a past memory or a future expectation. You will eventually bring these images back to your present where you have the opportunity to assess them. Under normal circumstances it is very difficult to stay focused for any length of time in any one of the three mind tenses.

Your Conscious, Unconscious, and Universal Minds

You have access to three different minds: your conscious, unconscious, and universal minds. Your conscious mind is your thinking mind. It is constantly processing information it receives from external stimuli as well as the images that surface from the unconscious and universal minds. Sometimes your conscious mind handles so much information that it will overload itself and induce you into a trance or sleep state.

Your conscious mind makes up only about 10 percent of your total mind. It can easily get out of balance with your other minds. This happens when your *unconscious mind* takes over and creates an outcome that your conscious mind is not happy with. When your conscious mind stays on alert too long, it can cause you to experience stress that over time can result in health changes. It is good for you to be able to relax your conscious mind as often as possible so that you stay in balance with your whole self.

Words to Remember

Your **unconscious mind** is the storage area for all your memories up to this point in time. You are constantly adding new information to your database. Your conscious mind is analytical, but your unconscious mind is passive and accepts what is stored there without question.

Your unconscious mind has been compared to a computer that has programs installed in it to do specific tasks. If it does not have the right program, the only way you can change the computer's function is to install a new one. Like your conscious mind, the computer doesn't question the data that it stores.

The unconscious mind may send the conscious mind stored information at any moment, sometimes when the conscious mind is not prepared and expecting to receive it. These images may be so powerful that they can cause you to enter a light trance that shifts your focus from conscious thinking into an unconscious memory experience.

Your universal mind is the part of you that connects to all the knowledge of the universe. You go through your unconscious mind to communicate with your universal mind. Every person is a part of and has the opportunity to access this mind. Many people choose not to, and they miss many opportunities to use their past life strengths and talents in their current lifetime.

Your universal mind is your connection to your soul's memories. These have been collected and stored since the beginning of its journey. Psychic Edgar Cayce referred to the soul's storage area as the Akashic Records, and he would enter a self-hypnotic trance and go there to look up the record of the soul of the person for whom he was doing a reading (see Chapter 4).

How Do You Rate Your Mental DNA?

As you learned in Chapter 1, your mind is different than anyone else's on earth. You will now learn how you process in each of your five senses. It may be that you are strong in all five, or you may be strong in just one of them. For many of us, our visual sense is strongest. We recall our past memory in picture images and visualize what we expect to experience in the future. Everything we observe is recorded in our unconscious mind. Learning how you image can be very beneficial to you in many aspects of your life as well as in a past life regression. (In hypnosis, the word *image* when used as a verb means experiencing a mental impression through your five different senses.)

Consider the following questions to help you determine the type and strength of your visual images.

Seeing with the Mind's Eye

Can you think of a pleasant memory and imagine it in pictures in your mind's eye? If so, can you see these images in color, or are they in black and white? Are your visual images clear or dull? Can you watch your memory as a moving picture? Can you stop the images, rewind them, and play them again?

There are two different ways that you can experience visual images. One way is to be able to watch yourself in the image. It will be like looking at a snapshot or video of yourself as you remember your image from your unconscious mind. This type of visual image does not have emotional feelings attached to it.

The second way is to see the image as if you were experiencing your memory all over again. When you experience a visual memory in your mind, you are also usually connecting one or more of your other sense images to your visual image. Emotional images are often a part of the pictures in your mind.

Some of you may be able to experience both types of visual images. Some of you may only be able to visualize just one or the other, and a few of you will have no visual images in your mind at all. It is not necessary to be able to have visual images in your mind to experience a past life regression.

Can You Hear It?

The second of the five senses is hearing. Technically, it is known as your auditory sense. Can you imagine sounds in your mind? If you can, what do you hear? Can you imagine a song in your head? Can you imagine turning up or down the volume? Can you slow down or speed up the music? Can you listen to music in your mind to calm you down or energize you?

Karmic Cautions

One of the keys to having a successful past life regression is to be able to understand your own mental DNA. Make sure that you understand how your mind works so that you can get the most out of your experience. If you are not visual and you try to have a visual experience, it can be very frustrating to you. Be very aware of this if you are working with someone who only processes in their sense strengths and does not take yours into account.

Can you imagine other sounds, such as nature? Can you remember a conversation with someone and hear it all over again? Do you replay conversations with others in your mind? Can you both picture and hear sounds of the same image in your memory? Can you move around in your visual memory and hear different sounds, or the same sounds from different locations?

Are you sensitive to sound? Do loud noises bother you? Can you listen to something that is mechanical and tell how well it is running by the way it sounds? Do you hear the voices of your guides or your angels? Do you have a positive voice that acts as your guide and comes to you when you need to hear it?

Some of you may not have any sound recall at all. You may not imagine any sound in your mind. You do not need to recall sound to experience a past life regression. The hearing sense is only one of five, so if you have no sound recall at all, you can make up for it with your other senses.

How Do You Feel?

How do you feel about this so far? Actually feeling is one of your five image senses. It is known as your kinesthetic sense and covers two different areas. You can have a *tactile* experience, which simply means touch. If you have a strong tactile memory, then you will be able to recall what something feels like and experience it all over again when you are remembering it.

You will have both comfortable and uncomfortable touch memories. You might imagine how good something felt in the past and then expect that it will feel exactly the same in the future. The same can be true of a memory about something you touched or ate that was very unpleasant. Fears and phobias can be the result of a touch experience that your unconscious mind recalls from the past. That may be why you want no part of touching a spider, a snake, or some other animal or reptile.

> **Soul Stories**
>
> Pat had always had an intense fear of needles. Now that she was pregnant, the thought of all the blood tests that lay ahead of her was overwhelming. She had to find a way to come to grips with her fear. She was regressed into a past life where she had been a prisoner in a Nazi concentration camp during World War II. She had died by a lethal injection. Once she knew the reason for her fear, she was able to face her upcoming blood tests with a positive outlook that helped her through her pregnancy.

Your tactile memories are created from actual physical experiences. These experiences could have happened any time in your life up to this moment and are recorded in your unconscious mind. When you are born, you also bring with you the memories of past life physical tactile experiences. This is why you may be repulsed by the thought of touching something that you have never come in contact with before in this lifetime.

Can you recall the touch of something that is pleasant? If so, how well can you experience this feeling right now? Is it as strong as when you first experienced it, or is it stronger or weaker? Can you change the intensity of your touch image in your mind? Do you also imagine pictures and/or sounds when you recall a touch memory?

Besides tactile images, the kinesthetic sense also includes emotional images. Emotional memories are internal feeling experiences that have been stored in your unconscious mind. You may remember a happy experience that will bring a smile to your face. You may recall a sad experience that brings tears to your eyes when you think of it again.

Can you imagine emotional feelings in your mind? If so, can you increase or decrease the intensity of these feelings? Could you imagine a memory and watch it with little or no emotion and then place yourself in the memory and experience again the feelings that come from your unconscious mind? Can you increase or decrease these feelings?

Do certain sounds or music evoke emotions? If so, are these intense or slight? Can you control them, or do they control you? Some of you may have a very strong emotional image recall, while others of you may have few or no emotional memories. You will experience emotional images in the way that your mind naturally takes in and recalls them. If your emotional sense is not strong, that is okay, as you will make up for it in one or more of your other senses.

Ageless Insights

Do you have emotional experiences that come on you all of a sudden and you have no idea what caused you to have them? These experiences may have their roots in past life recall. An emotional image comes from your unconscious mind and can be triggered by many different things, including a picture, a physical location, a sound, a touch, a taste, or a smell.

Let's Add Taste and Smell

There are two more senses to consider, and they are also very important in your mental DNA makeup. They are your taste and smell senses. The sense of taste is known as the gustatory sense. Everything you have tasted in your life is remembered in your unconscious mind. Some of these are good memories, and some of them are not so good.

Can you remember a taste that is very pleasant to you? Can you imagine a picture of a certain food and experience the taste of it as well as how it feels as you eat it? Can you imagine a food that tastes bad? If so, think of something pleasant instead.

Do you get a bad taste in your mouth when you think of an experience that was unpleasant and not related to food? Do you relate tastes to images in the other senses such as sound, pictures, or feelings? Can you change the intensity of a taste that you are remembering from a past experience?

Your smell sense is known as your olfactory sense. Do you have a favorite smell memory? Can you take a deep breath and experience the feeling right now? If so, how strong is your smell imagery? Can you experience it again the same way as you did before? Do you relate smell images to any one or more of your five different senses—seeing, hearing, feeling, tasting, and smelling? You may or may not have a keen sense of smell. If you don't, that's okay, as your other four senses will pick up the slack.

> **Soul Stories**
>
> Jean has very poor hearing as a result of severe ear infections as a child. However, she does have an extremely sharp sense of smell. She can pick up an old jar that has been empty for more than 50 years and imagine what it had been filled with. She can also pick up old leftover smells from specific locations and then develop an image in her mind of what might have been there a hundred years ago. This is both a good and a bad thing for her. Some of the lingering smells are not pleasant and are a distraction to her.

Making Sense of It All

Have you been able to make any sense of your sense imagery so far? To review a little bit, you have five different senses—seeing, hearing, feeling, tasting, and smelling. Every one of you will process in those five senses differently. No one else on Earth does it exactly like you do. Your mind works backward into your memories from the past, and you recall them through one or more of your five senses. Your mind also projects forward into the future, experiencing events before they happen in those same five senses. In the present, you constantly are processing information through, guess what, those same five senses.

If you are hard of hearing, you will not recall sounds around you very well. If you are visually impaired, it will affect how you remember or project into the future your visual sense. The same thing is also true of feeling, smelling, and tasting.

Let's see how well you remember in each of your five senses. First of all, let yourself relax, using the self-hypnosis exercise you experienced in Chapter 5. Suggest to yourself that you will remember and experience in all your five different senses a very pleasant memory from your past. You can memorize the questions, tape them and play them back to yourself, have someone read them to you, or consider each one by itself, using this book.

Rate each question in terms of a very strong image, a good image, a fair image, or no image. It's possible to be strong in all of them or strong in only one of them. You will score differently than anyone else. There is no pass or fail, just the opportunity to learn your image strengths. When you are ready, answer the following questions:

◆ Once you have focused on your pleasant memory, can you imagine in color? Can you see the image as a moving picture? Can you stop the picture and look at one image? Can you move in and out to get close-up details or see the image from a distance? Can you replay a scene over and over? Can you place yourself in the memory image and move yourself around? Can you go back and forth between experiencing and watching?

♦ Can you hear any sounds or voices related to your memory image? Can you turn up and down the volume of the sounds or voices? Can you slow down or speed up your sound images? Can you move around in the image and hear the sounds and voices from different locations?

♦ Can you experience what the temperature feels like in your memory image? Can you move around and feel different temperatures from different locations? Can you feel textures of different objects in your image? Can you feel what it is like to be someone other than yourself in your image? Can you feel emotions that are in your image? Can you feel someone else's emotions? Can you increase or decrease the intensity of the emotions you feel? Can you step out of the image and not feel any emotions?

♦ Can you experience any taste images in your memory recall? Can you experience different tastes in your image? Can you move around in your image and sample foods if there are any? Can you increase or decrease the intensity of your tastes?

♦ Can you experience smells in your memory recall? Can you move around in the scene and experience different smells? Can you increase or decrease the intensity of your smell imagery? Can you step out of the scene and not have a smell experience related to your memory recall?

What if you have no image recall? Some of you may ask this question after completing the assessment exercise. Mark, for example, found that he did not recall images in pictures, sounds, tastes, smells, and external feelings. He only experienced emotions. He found out that by focusing on the present he was able to receive spontaneous past life memories in feeling images. He learned to trust what his unconscious and universal minds let him know.

Once you have completed this assessment of your mental DNA, you will be able to develop a profile of your image strengths. These will be very valuable for you as you prepare for a past life regression experience.

The Least You Need to Know

♦ Your mind is constantly going back and forth between your past, future, and the present.

♦ Your conscious mind is your analytical mind.

♦ Your unconscious mind contains all your memories from your past.

♦ Your universal mind is the link to your past lives.

♦ Your mental DNA is different than anyone else's in the world.

♦ You may be strong or weak in any one of the five different senses—seeing, hearing, feeling, tasting, and smelling.

Chapter 9

Now Get Comfortable

In This Chapter

◆ Finding a comfortable relaxing place in your mind

◆ Your destination when you experience self-hypnosis

◆ Two trance-deepening self-hypnotic exercises

◆ Enjoying your deep trance experience

◆ Continuing the trance experience after you come back to consciousness

John has always had an active imagination. He was able to tell amazing stories when he was a child. He could also draw pictures that flowed from his unconscious mind. When he experienced a past life regression, he easily slipped into a deep trance.

Eric, on the other hand, had never been able to relax. He felt that he could not let himself enter a hypnotic trance. After he identified the memory of a special place, he started to revisit it using his image senses that were the strongest for him. After a couple weeks of daily self-hypnosis practice, he was ready and open to experiencing his first past life regression.

Your mind may be similar to John's or Eric's, or different from either one. In this chapter you will be able to determine the best way for you to experience hypnosis. Once you have decided what you like the best, practice every day, and you will soon be doing it like a pro.

Where's Your Favorite Relaxing Place?

You are now going to learn how to deepen your self-hypnosis trance. Deepening means to bring yourself into a more intense state of focus using your imagery. When this happens, you are able to step into a holographic image, or in other words, move from the reality around you into the reality of your trance. You may already be naturally escaping in your mind, if you daydream a lot or immerse yourself in a good book, for example. If you do, this will really be easy for you. If you do not, the goal is to let you understand how easy it is to go to your comfort zone.

You will be able to apply your new knowledge of your mental DNA to help you focus even more. As you now know, every one of your minds is different, and the exercises in this chapter are designed to help you use your natural abilities to enter and deepen your self-hypnotic trance. These techniques will be helpful to you as you prepare to experience a past life regression.

Take a few moments and let yourself relax. Now think of a place that is very relaxing and comfortable to you. Don't be surprised if it takes you a little time to come up with one. Some of you are very busy and don't have much time to relax. Still others of you may meditate daily and are easily able to think of a comfortable place.

This place may be one from a pleasant memory where you used to go. It may no longer exist, or it may be hard or impossible for you to go there physically at this time. That's okay. A positive memory that you can revisit in your mind can be a good mental comfort zone. You may have a place in your imagination that you have visited many times and go there when you need to get mentally away. That is also a good place to focus on when you are experiencing self-hypnosis. If you can't think of an actual place, you can make one up if you want to.

Your relaxing and comfortable place in your mind may be an outside or inside image. It could be an experience like floating in water, feeling the warm sun at an ocean beach, or bathing in a warm tub. You could be high on a mountain, relaxing in your bed, cruising on your motorcycle, or reading a book. There are so many places that you can find to relax in your mind that you can choose the same one every time or a different one each time you experience your trance state.

Once you've identified a comfortable place, begin to focus on it through your five different senses: seeing, hearing, feeling, tasting, and smelling. Remember that you may not be strong in all of them even though they are addressed here. You can use the ones that help you focus the best and let you deepen your self-hypnotic trance.

Karmic Cautions

A relaxing self-hypnotic trance can be good for your health. When you fail to allow yourself a chance to escape in a positive way, you can build up stress. This buildup can result in future health problems.

Picture your favorite relaxing place in your mind. If you can, view it both from a distance as if you were looking at it on a television screen, and place yourself in the image where you can move around and see it from several different positions. Let yourself hear the relaxing sounds that are in your relaxing place. Turn the volume up or down and hear different sounds as you move around in the image. Now let yourself feel how good it is to be there. If there are positive and relaxing things to touch, you may allow yourself to do so.

If there are any positive and relaxing tastes in your image, you may experience them. Let yourself experience any relaxing smells that are in your image. You may move around in your mind and enjoy the smells from different locations. Let yourself become aware of what it is like to experience your relaxing and comfortable place in all your senses.

You may also have a favorite relaxing smell that is not a part of your comfortable place. If you do, it's okay to include it in any way that will help you relax. You are also free to add to the imagery with any of your other senses. If you want to try a nonphysical place, you'll be able to after the completion of this exercise.

Take a Deep Breath, and Let Your Eyes Go Out of Focus

Now if you're ready, you may experience how to deepen your self-hypnotic trance by going to your relaxing place in your mind. Find a comfortable place where you will not be disturbed and sit or lie down. Make sure that your clothes feel comfortable and are nonbinding. You may burn a candle with a relaxing smell and use music or other calming sounds if you wish. You may record this *hypnosis script* and play it back, memorize it, or have someone read it to you. You may rewrite the words any way you want to help yourself deepen your trance state.

To begin, take a deep breath of your favorite relaxing smell. If this is a candle or something else that is actually in the room with you, focus on the scent as you exhale and continue to breathe in and out in slow, deep, relaxing breaths. If you are imagining your smell, do the same thing. Suggest to yourself that with each breath you will let yourself feel more and more relaxed.

As you continue to breathe in and out, let yourself focus your mind onto the spot in the center of your forehead known as your third eye. Let your eyes go out of focus as you continue to breathe in and out, relaxing more and more with each breath.

Words to Remember

A **hypnosis script** is the dialogue used by a hypnotist to induce a hypnotic trance in a subject. It can also be the words that individuals practicing self-hypnosis say to themselves to help them go into a trance and may contain suggestions for obtaining their desired goals.

You have many muscles throughout your body, and some of them are stiff and tight, while others are relaxed and loose. All the way through this exercise you may be aware of different muscles that may stiffen up. If they do, allow them to relax, and suggest to yourself that you will go deeper and deeper into your relaxing self-hypnotic trance as you focus on your special comfortable and relaxing place in your mind.

By the way, you'll notice the words "you may" used over and over again in a trance induction. As I've mentioned, there are two kinds of hypnotic language: *authoritative*, which uses "you will"; and *permissive*, which uses "you may." "You may" is considered a much more positive and nonthreatening approach.

In a few moments, when you're ready, you may begin to slowly count yourself downward from five to zero. You may suggest to yourself that when you reach zero, you will be able to experience your relaxing place in your mind in all your five senses. You may totally let yourself experience your image and let yourself have a very relaxing and positive experience.

Count from Five to Zero

As you prepare to count yourself downward, suggest to yourself that with every count you will feel yourself going deeper and deeper. If it is comfortable to you, you may physically feel yourself sinking deeper and deeper as if you were descending down a spiral staircase into the recesses of your unconscious mind. Once you reach the bottom level, suggest that you will step into your special place and experience it in all your senses.

> **Karmic Cautions**
>
> If for any reason you want or need to, you may always take a deep breath, exhale, open your eyes, and come back to the surface of your mind, feeling wide awake, and very positive and relaxed. If you feel uncomfortable during any exercise in this book, you may end it at once.

Are you ready? Take a deep breath of your favorite smell and slowly exhale. At your first number let a positive, relaxing feeling start to flow downward over and through your body from the top of your head, down over your forehead, eyes, nose, mouth, chin, and down to your neck.

- ◆ FIVE. Feel yourself sinking deeper and deeper as you breathe in and out. The relaxing feeling begins to spread through and around your body. You may relax any muscle that is stiff as you continue with each breath to feel yourself sinking deeper and deeper.

- ◆ FOUR. You may let yourself sink deeper and deeper into hypnosis as the relaxing feeling flows down over your shoulders and down your arms, all the way to your fingertips. With each breath you may feel yourself going deeper and deeper into hypnosis as you relax more and more. You are getting closer and closer to your special place in your mind.

◆ THREE. You may experience your favorite smell getting stronger and stronger as you feel yourself relaxing more and more. You may feel a relaxing energy spreading down over the rest of your upper body, all the way down to your waist. With each breath, you may feel yourself relaxing more and more and sinking deeper and deeper into hypnosis.

◆ TWO. The relaxing energy is now spreading downward to your knees. You can feel it flowing over and through you. You feel yourself sinking even deeper and deeper. With each breath you are relaxing more and more and feeling so comfortable.

◆ ONE. As you continue to relax more and more and sink deeper and deeper, you may feel the relaxing energy move down to your ankles. With each breath you continue to relax more and more as you go deeper and deeper into hypnosis. In a moment, you may count slowly from five all the way down to zero when you will be totally filled with a relaxing energy and focused on the special comfortable and relaxing place deep in your unconscious mind.

◆ FIVE. FOUR. THREE. TWO. ONE. ZERO. You are now deep into a very relaxing self-hypnotic trance. With each breath you may relax more and more. You may now prepare to experience the comfortable, relaxing place in your mind.

Enjoy Your Comfort Zone

Now allow yourself to focus on your special relaxing place. You may see it in a very clear picture image. Let yourself step into your image and experience it with all its relaxing beauty. You may move as slowly as you want, and you can stop and rewind your image and replay it again so that you may see it clearer each time.

Soul Stories

Dean loved nature, and it was a comfortable place for him to go in his mind. He would not only experience its positive effects, he began to imagine communicating with the plants and animals. The more he practiced in his mind, the more sensitive he became to the real experience of being in nature. The plants and animals of his mind became real when he wandered among them.

Totally immerse yourself in your special image and experience it through all of your senses at once. Take your time and experience as many different details as you like. Suggest that you will be able to visit this special place in your mind and experience it even more any time you want or need to. You may give yourself a special word or touch anchor to help you come back to your special comfortable place in your mind. Also suggest that you will continue to have your relaxed and comfortable feelings long after you have counted yourself back up to your conscious mind. When you are ready, you may begin to slowly count yourself back up to your conscious mind.

Count Back to Reality

You may now begin to leave your special place in your mind and begin your return to consciousness.

- ◆ ONE. Continue to slowly breathe in and out and experience your favorite relaxing smell. You will feel comfortable and relaxed as you continue your way back to the surface of your mind.

- ◆ TWO. You are continuing upward. With each breath you will feel comfortable and relaxed, enjoying your visit to your special place in your mind.

- ◆ THREE. You are now halfway back. You are beginning to move from your special place experience into the world of your conscious mind. You are feeling very comfortable and relaxed as you breath slowly in and out.

- ◆ FOUR. You are almost all the way back. Let yourself prepare to come back into your conscious mind on the next count, feeling very calm and relaxed from your positive experience in your conscious mind. Continue to breathe in and out slowly as your favorite smell lingers in your mind. Now take a deep breath and hold it for a moment.

- ◆ FIVE. Slowly exhale and let yourself come back to conscious awareness. You may open your eyes and adjust them to the light. You feel very comfortable and relaxed from your visit to your special comfortable place in your unconscious mind.

Ageless Insights _____

Consider this an exercise in imagination. That is really what it is. It's a great way to prepare for a past life regression. If you establish a daily routine of practicing this or the next technique in this chapter, you will form the habit of shifting your focus from your conscious to your unconsciousness. Your goal is to work with your imagination to help the images become sharper and more in focus. This ability to let your mind wander in and experience all your five senses will be very helpful in the chapters to follow.

Take a few moments and allow yourself to reflect on your experience. You may want to make some notes on what you would like to add or change the next time you use self-hypnosis to go to your special place. You are also free to go to other places and have other experiences any time you want.

What If I Don't Have a Special Place?

It's possible that you can't imagine a special place or any place in your unconscious mind. You may be like Jim, who is nonvisual. He could not think of a specific place that he could imagine visiting, so he focused on connecting to his belief. Jim was used to communicating in the form of prayer. As he relaxed and entered his self-hypnotic trance, he asked that a peaceful healing energy flow into his body. He asked his belief to help him with his worries and to guide his words and actions. The more he practiced praying in a self-hypnotic trance, the easier it was for him to bring himself back into the state when he wanted or needed to relax.

In this book, you are not expected to fit into a specific mind mold. You are creating your own self-hypnotic techniques using your own natural image strengths. All you need to do is recognize, develop, and allow yourself to trust what you already are able to do. These exercises will help you focus on your abilities.

Focusing on Your Third Eye

Now let's try a self-hypnotic trance that does not go to a specific real or imaginary physical location in your mind. This place is actually deep in your mind at a place where you can feel the connection to your universal mind. The main focus will come through your third eye.

Imagine for a moment that you are a small, self-contained capsule floating through space. You have within your capsule the means to connect to the universal mind any time you want to. You connect through your third eye with a beam of energy that is like a golden thread of light. Through this thread you can send and receive all the knowledge of the Universe.

> **Soul Stories**
>
> Barbara really liked the third eye self-hypnotic technique. She used it for many different reasons. When she had a health issue, she not only worked with her doctors but also felt the healing energies of the universal mind helping heal her body. The doctors were amazed at her recovery.

When you are ready, take a deep relaxing breath, and slowly exhale. Continue to breathe slowly as you shift your focus to your third eye. You may be aware of many things going on around you, and you will hear the phone if it rings, or people talking or traffic going by. At the same time you will be aware of the many muscles in your body. If one of them becomes stiff, you may relax it, and as you do, you may relax yourself even more.

The goal of this self-hypnotic exercise is to count yourself down from five to zero to a place deep in your unconscious mind where you are connected to your universal mind and your belief. You do not need to visualize to go to this place in your mind. If you do see it in your mind's eye, you can use this method to travel out on the golden thread to places such as the Akashic Records. You are now ready to begin counting down to the center of your unconscious mind.

   ◆ FIVE. Continue to breathe slowly in and out as you feel yourself beginning to go deeper and deeper downward, looking forward to going to the depths of your unconscious mind. With each breath you are relaxing more and more and sinking deeper and deeper.

   ◆ FOUR. You feel yourself going deeper into hypnosis as you focus on your third eye and look forward to your connection to the golden thread of the universe. With each breath you relax more and more. You may imagine a relaxing color surrounding you if you are visual. You may feel the positive energy of the universe beginning to flow through your body.

   ◆ THREE. You may feel yourself sinking deeper and deeper into your unconscious mind. You are relaxing more and more as you feel the energy from the golden thread of the universe spreading. You may look forward to the peace and love of the Universe as it flows into your body.

   ◆ TWO. You are sinking deeper and deeper into your self-hypnotic trance as you feel the universal energy flowing into your body through the golden thread of the universe. You are getting closer and closer to this very special place deep in your unconscious mind. You may suggest to yourself that when you reach zero you will be connected to the golden thread of the universe through your third eye. You may communicate with your belief and the universal mind. You will feel the peaceful energy of the universe surrounding you and protecting you.

   ◆ ONE. You are almost there. You are going deeper and deeper into hypnosis as you connect to the golden thread of universal energy. On the next number you will feel yourself in the center of your unconscious mind where you can connect to the universal mind. Breathe in and out slowly and allow yourself to continue to feel relaxed and positive as you prepare to experience the connection to your universal mind.

◆ ZERO. You are now at the center of your unconscious mind. You feel so comfortable and relaxed as you look forward to experiencing the peace and love of the universe. Take some time to enjoy this wonderful feeling. You may feel in tune and balanced with the universal mind as you open yourself to communicate with your belief and the universe. Let yourself be open to the knowledge and wisdom of the universe.

You may spend as much time as you want in this positive and relaxing place in your unconscious mind. If you have thoughts that you want to send to the universal mind, you may do so. If you are looking for an answer to a question, you may send it out and let yourself be open for the reply that may come now or at some time in the future.

Suggest to yourself that you may visit this special place deep in your unconscious mind anytime you want or need to. Give yourself a special word or touch that will help you anchor this special place so that you may return or instantly feel connected no matter where you are.

When you are ready, you may count yourself back up to consciousness.

> **Ageless Insights**
>
> You can experience a calm and relaxed feeling while you are fully awake by focusing on your third eye. You will always be fully aware of what you are doing at the time, but you can experience feeling positive, relaxed, and calm as you connect to your third eye and your unconscious and universal minds.

◆ ONE. You are beginning to start your journey back to your conscious mind. Continue to breathe slowly in and out and feel the positive energy of the universal mind. Your body is filled with this positive energy.

◆ TWO. You are continuing to come back to the surface. Your journey back is relaxing and peaceful as you reflect on the insights of your universal and unconscious minds. You feel very calm and peaceful.

◆ THREE. You feel the energy of the universe slowly bringing you back to the surface of your conscious mind. You continue to breathe slowly in and out as you journey upward.

◆ FOUR. You are getting closer and closer to the surface of your conscious mind. The next number will bring you there. Take a deep breath, slowly exhale, and come back to consciousness.

◆ FIVE. You are fully awake. You may relax your third eye connection and slowly open your eyes. You feel calm, relaxed, and filled with the positive energy of the universe. Take as long as you want to reflect on your journey to the special place deep in your unconscious mind. You may reflect on the insights you gained on your journey and make some notes to help guide you when you return.

The more you practice either one or both of the exercises in this chapter, the more your mind will be prepared to experience a past life regression. The more you learn to accept and trust the information that your mind gives you, the easier it will be to explore your past lives. Remember, all you have to do is take a deep breath and open your eyes to come back to the surface of your mind whenever you are experiencing a self-hypnotic trance.

The Least You Need to Know

- ◆ The more you learn to relax your mind, the easier it will be to experience self-hypnosis.

- ◆ When you experience a positive relaxing memory through your five senses, you will relax even more.

- ◆ If you establish a specific routine to experience self-hypnosis, you will automatically begin to enter your relaxing trance.

- ◆ It is not necessary to be visual to develop a technique to enter a self-hypnotic trance.

- ◆ The more you develop and practice your own technique, the better prepared you will be to experience past life regressions.

Chapter 10

A Visit to a Past Life Regression Specialist

In This Chapter

- ◆ What to expect when you visit a past life regression specialist
- ◆ Portions of three past life regression transcripts
- ◆ Discovering the origins of Mary's seashells
- ◆ Visiting ancient Hawaii with Nora
- ◆ Examining the root of Malcolm's fears

In this chapter, you will read the transcripts of three past life regressions that were done by a professional hypnotist specializing in past life regression. Even though the facilitator is trained to guide his subjects into a state of trance that will help them enter a past life, as you progress through this book, you will be able to accomplish the same thing yourself.

All hypnosis is, after all, self-hypnosis. The hypnotist does not have the power to create a trance; only you have that power. You will read how three people like yourself were able to enter a past life regression and benefit from the experience.

What Should You Expect?

Many people who want to experience a past life have read or heard about others who have already done it. The subject may have a set idea in their mind of what the regression will be like, and they come into a hypnotist's office with expectations that they hope to accomplish. Some may want to just have the experience of a regression, while others are looking for specific answers that they hope will provide enlightenment on a certain situation in their life.

Try to keep an open mind. If your expectations are too focused, you may miss the real purpose of the past life regression. You could be expecting an insight to occur in a certain way and when it doesn't, you focus on what you didn't want when you could have been open to what you needed.

Words to Remember

A **past life regression specialist** is someone who has been trained to assist and interpret your past life regression experience. The training may be recognized by acceptance to an organization such as IBRT, the International Board for Regression Therapy.

It is good to have an idea of what you would like to learn when you visit a *past life regression specialist*. However, you also want to be prepared to go with whatever takes place during the regression. There will be plenty of time later to analyze the experience.

Always check on the credentials of a professional past life regression specialist. That includes inquiring about the person's training, certifications, and even talking to his or her previous clients.

Ask if you can bring a friend to videotape your regression, or ask the past life regression specialist to tape the induction for you when you are being induced into your hypnotic trance. Sometimes they do this, and sometimes they turn the tape on after the induction has been completed. This is done to save tape space for the regression information. If you supply a video camera, the tape usually lasts a minimum of two hours, which should be plenty of time to get the induction also.

The better prepared you are, the better the chance for a positive past life regression experience. You may want to give the specialist a written list of some of your past life interests.

One of the biggest disappointments to a client when experiencing a regression is the failure in their own mind to enter a deep hypnotic trance. Many good and successful past life regression trances are not as deep as you might think. The specialist is trained to observe every expression, every movement, and hear every word or phrase the client uses during the regression. That is the benefit of videotape as you get to see yourself offer clues about your past life that you did not realize you were giving.

It's okay to imagine the answers to the questions you are asked, even if you consider yourself completely awake. The specialist can actually help your imagination become a mind reality experience if you will let him or her. The answers you give lead to more questions, which are designed to help you enter into a light and perhaps eventually, a deeper, hypnotic trance. The specialist will focus on your image strengths to help you shift your view into the hologram that is contained in your unconscious mind.

Soul Stories

Christi came for a past life regression filled with hope that it would be an exciting experience. She was very worried about being able to relax. She confided that she was not very good at it. She began to get some images, but she constantly analyzed what she was doing and convinced herself that she was not really getting a past life image. Then she saw a figure being chased by men with guns, and remembered that a psychic had told her she was a child in World War II who was able to escape from the Gestapo. No wonder she has had trouble relaxing in her current life!

The more you let yourself go with the flow, the better the possibility of your having a successful past life regression. Remember that there is no scientific proof up to this point that indicates that you are in fact having a past life experience. You are ultimately responsible for interpreting what took place.

After you finish your regression, you may want to make some notes about your experience. The regression specialist may give you the suggestion that every time you listen to the tape of your experience, you will remember more details. You can use the tape as a work tape to help you actually go into a trance and allow you to focus on the images you experienced during your regression. Each time you go over it, you may be able to fill in details that you missed previously.

A past life regression usually lasts no more than an hour. The entire office visit with pre- and post-talks can last from an hour and a half to two hours. Follow-up visits usually take a little less time as the specialist is already acquainted with how your mind produces images.

Let's look now at how the experience went for one past life regression subject.

Mary's Past Life Regression

Mary recently became aware that she had psychic gifts. She wanted to go back in time to understand the meaning of seashells that she was given when she was a little girl.

The following transcript is a portion of a past life regression she experienced in hopes of gaining some answers to her quest. It begins with a pre-induction talk with the past life regression specialist (abbreviated PLS in the transcripts) about Mary's goals for the session.

Mary: I have three seashells that were given to my mother [by a lady] to give to me as a small child. My mother cleaned her house. I never had the opportunity to meet this lady. [The shells] are approximately 150 years old. I don't believe in coincidence. [Ever since Mary received the shells, she believed that they had been given to her for a specific reason.]

PLS: *[after hypnotic induction]* Now go back to an image, an image perhaps of when the shells might have been held before. Can you see that and picture that image?

Mary: I am standing on an ocean shore dressed in a white shirt.

PLS: Allow yourself to feel that person standing on the shore. What does the hair feel like?

Mary: It's long.

PLS: What is the temperature there?

Mary: It's cold. I'm chilly.

PLS: Okay, but you don't need to feel that chilliness right now. Is that okay? Feel the warmth and love of the universe. Can you feel that? Experience just a little bit of the chill. Are there any sounds there?

Mary: I can hear the ocean.

PLS: How does the ocean sound?

Mary: Calm.

Words to Remember

Detachment is the ability to observe, or even experience, a potentially upsetting image with little or no emotional feeling. It's not possible for everyone to detach from his or her imagery, but detachment from an image provides a way to view it without emotional trauma.

PLS: And the temperature is cool. Are there any smells there?

Mary: I can smell the salt water.

PLS: Take a good deep smell of that salt water for a moment. How is your mood—your feelings?

Mary: I know I am going to die.

PLS: You know you are going to die. How do you feel?

Mary: I'm okay with that.

PLS: Let's go back for a moment in the life of this person to a significant point of time. Go back to a more pleasant memory. What's happening now? Describe what's happening in that memory.

Mary: I'm in a cave. It's black.

PLS: What's the temperature there?

Mary: Damp and cool. And I'm getting cold and frightened, and I'm burying the shells.

PLS: You are burying the shells. Why are you burying the shells?

Mary: Because then they can't have them?

PLS: Who can't have them?

Mary: I don't know.

PLS: Let's go back to see who is looking for the shells.

Mary: I'm back on the shoreline, and I'm looking out to the ocean. Somebody's coming on a horse.

PLS: Can you turn around and look at that person?

Mary: I won't turn around.

PLS: Then step back and watch the scene. What do you see?

Mary: He kills me.

PLS: But before he kills you, let's go back and just describe him.

Mary: He has armor on.

PLS: He has armor on. What does his horse look like?

Mary: It has armor on [its] feet.

PLS: And how many [people] are there?

Mary: Just him.

PLS: Was he looking specifically for you?

Mary: Um hum.

PLS: Where were the shells buried?

Mary: They are in the cave in the mountain.

PLS: How far away is the mountain from the seashore?

Mary: Not very far. He doesn't know that.

PLS: He doesn't know that. Did he say anything to you?

Mary: No. He just wanted me dead.

PLS: He just wanted you dead. Why did he want you dead?

Mary: Because I know.

PLS: What do you know?

Mary: Too much.

PLS: How is it that you know everything?

Mary: When I'm quiet, I listen and I learn.

PLS: When you're quiet, you listen and you learn. And what did you learn? What did you learn that he did not want you to know?

Mary: There was somebody that he looked up to, and I knew that.

PLS: You knew that. Go back to that time. Who was the person that he looked up to?

Mary: He was very high, and he was a teacher.

PLS: He was high, and he was a teacher. What was that man's name? What was he called?

Ageless Insights

It can take time and patience to get all of a name. In a normal regression the specialist would keep coming back to the subject, hoping to deepen the image and get more clues.

Mary: It began with a D.

PLS: What was the man's name that owned the sword and the suit of armor?

Mary: I don't know.

PLS: What is your name? You can hear people calling you that. What is it?

Mary: I can hear the voices, but I can't hear anything.

PLS: Okay, you may turn the voices up or go closer to them. Where are the voices coming from?

Mary: There is this party, a room, and we are in a party before it started.

PLS: Before what started?

Mary: Before all the craziness.

PLS: Was it a happy time?

Mary: Um hum.

PLS: What were you there for?

Mary: I was there for the party?

PLS: And what did you look like?

Mary: I was in my 20s. I had long hair. It just all happened so fast.

PLS: Explain what happened after that.

Mary: I took the shells from the man because the other man wanted them.

PLS: And what was the significance of these shells?

Mary: Peace and hope.

PLS: Did he do anything in particular with the shells?

Mary: He would hold them, and he would say that he would know from the shells.

PLS: How well did you know him before?

Mary: I knew him well. The man that killed him I think was my husband.

PLS: Who was your husband?

Mary: The man that killed him.

PLS: Go back to that point of time before and tell me what is taking place there?

Mary: The man that has the shells is sitting, and we are all celebrating with him, and my husband was the law. And he killed him, and I knew.

PLS: You knew?

Mary: I knew that my husband did it.

PLS: And so then you went …

Mary: He told me to take the shells.

PLS: The man?

Mary: Yes. He told me to take them and hide them.

PLS: Why?

Mary: Because.

PLS: When you took them, did you feel anything from the shells while you had them?

Mary: Well, I felt love. I felt love for the shells.

PLS: And how long did you have the shells?

Mary: Not very long. I had to hide them fast.

PLS: If you look at the theme of this life, and you review it, what were your last thoughts of this lifetime?

Mary: I saved the shells, and he can't have them, and he can't touch them, and if I die, I know he won't have them.

PLS: Now reviewing this and looking at that whole life theme, what is the theme of that life that you can know?

Mary: I just feel that there is knowledge in the shells.

PLS: Could you experience the knowledge that he knew back then and now become the keeper of the shells so that you may find the magic that might have been there?

Mary: There is a light that comes directly from the sky.

PLS: Who did you recognize from that life, or was there anyone that you recognize from that life that would be in this life?

Mary: I couldn't see the face of my husband.

PLS: And how did the older man, the wise man, hold his shells? Can you see that?

Mary: He placed them on a blanket in front of him.

PLS: Did different shells mean different things?

Mary: I don't know.

PLS: So now ask if it would be okay for you to do the same thing.

Mary: I think now it is okay.

PLS: Will he be willing to guide you?

Mary: Yes.

PLS: So he will be willing to be one of your guides?

Mary: Yes.

PLS: And how often should one consult the shells?

Mary: I don't know. When it's time.

PLS: How will he come to you?

Mary: He will come to me. He will speak to me, and I will know him.

PLS: Through a signal?

Mary: Yes. I will know. I will feel him.

This is only a portion of Mary's past life regression. She was able to learn about her shells and she was able to meet the wise man of her past that will be one of her guides in her present lifetime. Now she can meditate on the shells and visions that come into her head providing insights. She can also communicate with the wise man through trance states and ask him for guidance in the decisions she needs to make about her life. Mary's past life experience gave her a renewed confidence to deal with problems that she has in this life.

Nora's Past Life Regression

Nora had never experienced a past life regression before and didn't have any particular expectations of what she would find when she went back. The past life regression specialist suggested that she go to the lifetime that would be the most important for her to visit relating to her current life. After she entered a light trance state, she began to get an image in her mind.

PLS: Where are you?

Nora: The coast of Hawaii.

PLS: Where are you looking at the coast from?

Nora: From a part of the land that projects out of the water.

PLS: And what time of day or night is it?

Nora: It's quiet time, either morning or evening.

PLS: How close to the water are you?

Nora: Right at the water's edge.

PLS: Can you hear the sounds of the water?

Nora: The water is quite slow, just a little bit of lapping.

PLS: Are there any other sounds that you can hear?

Nora: There is a bit of wind in the trees. It is very still.

PLS: Very still. What is the feeling there?

Nora: Peaceful.

PLS: So you feel peaceful. Okay, are there any smells that go along with this?

Nora: Ocean smell, sort of rich smells, maybe fruit.

PLS: Is this an enjoyable smell?

Nora: Yes.

PLS: How clear is the picture you are seeing?

Nora: I can see details. At least I can imagine individual trees on the beach.

PLS: What does the sand feel like?

Nora: It's very warm. It's very fine.

PLS: Can you feel the water?

Nora: It's very warm.

PLS: Now for the moment, look down at your feet and describe what you see.

Nora: They are bare, and they are in the water. They are brown, very tan. Outdoor feet. They don't wear shoes much.

PLS: For a moment, allow yourself to feel your hair in your mind.

Nora: It is very long.

PLS: What is the thickness of it, the coarseness?

Nora: It's quite thick but sort of fine, not real coarse.

PLS: And what are you wearing?

Nora: Kind of a simple covering, a piece of cloth.

PLS: And how comfortable does that feel?

Nora: Good.

PLS: Is there anyone else there besides you? Look around.

Nora: Well, initially I didn't think there was, but I can imagine there could be some-one sitting right next to me.

PLS: Can you see that person?

Nora: It's dark. I can't see that person. I can feel them.

PLS: How old?

Nora: I want to say old, old, old.

PLS: How are they dressed?

Nora: I don't think they are.

PLS: Now in this scene with this person, how do you communicate with that person?

Nora: Hum. With touch.

PLS: And what does the touch feel like from that other person?

Nora: Like an ape of some kind. Human, primate.

PLS: Now how does that ape feel to you?

Nora: Hairy.

PLS: Can you step back for a moment now and see the two of you together?

Nora: Yes. It's a woman and an ape.

PLS: Describe what you see on the beach as far as what might indicate what is there.

Nora: The beach is fairly wide, expansive sand. It stretches off to the left of the coast. There are some rocky outcroppings. There are some palm trees. Small bushes, shrubs.

PLS: Let's go to where the woman lives.

Nora: Back into the trees. A hut definitely surrounded by trees of the forest.

PLS: What kind of conditions does she live in?

Nora: Very simple. Wood structure, leaves, branches, poles, supports. Very small.

 Soul Stories

This regression revealed that Nora was chosen to go to the island to learn secrets from the ape-man and to communicate without speaking. After a period of time she was brought back to her island where she put her knowledge to use with her tribe.

Nora's regression experience continued on for some time. It established that she had been sent by her tribe to the other island to learn the secrets of the ancient ape so that she would be able to use these secrets to help her people when she returned. The main lesson for Nora was to be able to communicate through the unspoken language of the ancient ape. She felt that bringing this ability into her current life would allow her to better understand what others were saying when they had trouble expressing themselves. This excerpt should help you understand the importance of imagery. Nora was able to gain some insights into her Hawaiian lifetime that she began applying to her present life almost immediately after the regression.

Malcolm's Past Life Regression

Malcolm has had feelings of confinement and claustrophobia through his adult life. He wanted to go back and find the roots to these emotions. It was decided to use an *affect-bridge regression* technique that would move him back through his current life and before, using a hypnotic trance.

Words to Remember

An **affect-bridge regression** technique takes the subject back through their life to events that relate to a specific emotion. As they regress, they may transfer the emotion to a similar emotion that they experienced earlier. In a past life regression they bridge back to another lifetime which has images with the same or similar emotions.

Malcolm: I'm a teenager, and I'm working in a crawl space in the house that my family has, and I'm doing some electrical wiring. The crawl space is about three feet wide and really, really tight. I remember lying on my back with a flashlight making an electrical connection, and suddenly there was a crash or a snap as if the floor above me was crashing down upon me. I had a moment of panic, which is the first time I can remember doing so.

PLS: Take the sound of the floor crashing down upon you back to an imaginary image where the same feeling was there before. Can you experience it? Go back to a similar moment when the feeling of that first panic was learned.

Malcolm: Well, I remember being younger and being on vacation with my parents. We were down at Lake Chattanooga and went to these caves. They had a place called "Fat Man's Squeeze" where two huge boulders were really close together. You had to squeeze through them. I remember feeling that if the rock had shifted, it could be really gruesome.

PLS: Let's imagine a time and a thought when someone might have been stuck.

Malcolm: I'm getting an image of an old method of torture. I don't know if it has to do with the time of the Inquisition where you were laid down and had a board put on top of you. On top of the board they piled rocks.

Karmic Cautions

Malcolm was having trouble visualizing, and he is very visual. The past life specialist asked him to go back to an image where he could see as well as feel. He was able to visualize a man in charge of a crew constructing buildings. When you have trouble visualizing, just go with another one of your image senses.

PLS: Imagine what it would have been like to be there. Can you feel the board?

Malcolm: I can even go further than that. I can hear like ribs starting to crack.

PLS: Take it back to before the person was being crushed to see what he was doing to cause him to be crushed.

Malcolm: He was called a heretic. He was in charge of a crew building buildings of stone.

PLS: How did they hold the buildings together?

Malcolm: They had a mortar of fine sand that took forever to cure up.

PLS: What was the architecture of those buildings like?

Malcolm: The buildings are kind of boxy. What I'm getting about the guy is he is some kind of a teacher.

PLS: What does it feel like to be there, to be that teacher?

Malcolm: He's a flake. He knows they are watching, and yet he has deep convictions.

PLS: Who is watching him?

Malcolm: The Church. It's a terrible time of Inquisition. He is more mathematical than scientific. His theories don't jive with the Church's position. He observed that Galileo's didn't regarding the rotation of the earth.

PLS: How did he become elevated to being a teacher?

Malcolm: It was obvious in his small town that he could explain things in a simple way that others could not. For example, when someone needed to lift up a cart, he would design a fulcrum and a lever and show them where to put the fulcrum for the maximum advantage.

PLS: When did he first become at odds with the Church?

Malcolm: He had a copy of a first publishing of Galileo to explain retrograde motion of the planet. Everyone could observe with a telescope, but no one could explain it. This guy understood it and took Galileo's notes even further. The Church felt he was on a path to take the earth out of the center of the universe.

PLS: When was he arrested?

Malcolm: It was outside his classroom by a small armed guard. He was put in a cell for a day or so and then they called for him to denounce Galileo's theories, and he refused. They set a date for his execution, and they crushed him to death.

PLS: Now relate how he felt when he died to how you feel about confinement and claustrophobia in your current life?

Malcolm: He actually blacked out before he died from lack of oxygen.

Malcolm was able to relate the times in this life when he felt tightness of breath to times when he is frustrated about not being able to share his knowledge with people who will listen. He was able to relate the sounds and feelings of his past lives to the present and break the pattern of his old fear.

Malcolm, Nora, and Mary all benefited from their past life regressions and found ways of using the knowledge gained to help resolve situations in their current life.

The Least You Need to Know

- ◆ Every past life regression experience is different.

- ◆ It is not necessary to enter a deep trance to be successful.

- ◆ Go with your first image without analyzing it until after the regression.

- ◆ Keep an open mind, because what you experience may not be what you expected.

- ◆ Be aware of the many small image details in a past life regression.

Part  3

Preparing for the Adventure

It's time to begin to prepare for the journey into your past. Now that you have been to detective school you know how to start looking for clues about your soul's memory. In fact, you may already have a lot of the pieces of your past life puzzle laid out.

You have read about other experiences and may wonder if you, too, will be able to regress into your past. You will consider what a regression will be like as you prepare for your own. You will also learn how your belief is an important part of your travel.

In this part you will begin to spread out your puzzle so that you can decide what pieces you want to look for in your past to help complete the picture. There may be an unresolved karma, an old fear, or a soul mate connection. It's time to create a travel plan and pack the tools you will need to take on your journey back to your past lives.

What Is a Past Life Regression Like?

In This Chapter

- ◆ Going with the flow of your images
- ◆ Can you get stuck in the past?
- ◆ What will you be like after your regression?
- ◆ How imagination helps the regression experience

One day Debbie decided to go to the movies by herself. She chose one that had a very intense theme. As she watched she was drawn deeper and deeper into the plot. The movie ended, and Debbie left the theater in a daze. She wandered the parking lot in a state of confusion, and it took a period of time before she remembered where she had parked her car.

When Stravinsky's *Rite of Spring* premiered in Paris, the music was so powerful that the audience spilled into the streets in a daze after the performance had ended.

A past life regression can be like attending a powerful performance. Although the experience is different for everyone, this chapter explains more about what you can expect.

What Will You Experience?

Now that you've had the opportunity to read about how others experience a past life regression, you may wonder what the subject felt like while they were in their trance. The answer is simple. Your experience will be different than anyone else's.

Many factors enter into a past life regression. Your state of focus can change each time you have an experience. It is possible that your mind could be cluttered with day-to-day business at one time, while another time you may be totally relaxed and focused on the experience. You could feel differently each time emotionally, physically, or spiritually. There may be interruptions that were not anticipated that could interrupt your focus.

You may start a regression with an expectation of what you are going to or should experience only to end the session disappointed with the outcome. You may have a specific time period or place that you want to visit, only to go someplace completely different. You may have read about, heard of, or observed a past life regression that was particularly dramatic. It could have touched on famous characters in history or had an unbelievable outcome.

Soul Stories

Chris participated in a past life regression as a guest in an old house. Several others were there at the same time who had vivid experiences and were able to describe them to the group after they finished. Unfortunately, Chris had a different experience. It seems that the old house had a spirit living in it that chose to communicate with her during her regression. All she experienced was a contact by the ghost.

Your first regression image may be in a traumatic situation, and it is important for you to be able to move yourself out of it just as a past life regression specialist would. You will learn to ground and protect yourself before you have your first past life regression. This sounds much more serious than it is. Grounding means that you will be able to have an experience without getting totally caught up in an image that might be negative for you. Protected means that you are in balance between what you experience and your belief so that you will not have an unsettling regression.

The way that you process with your five senses (see Chapter 8) will have a big impact on your past life regression experience. Because your mental DNA is different than anyone else's, you will have an image experience that no one except yourself will have. You can expect that you will recall past life information in the same manner as you do a comfortable memory in your mind. If you image visually, you should be able to see your past life experience. You may be able to step back and watch it, or you may be able to step into and see what you are experiencing. You may be able to do both or neither.

As discussed in Chapter 8, a regression specialist would identify a subject's image strengths before a regression starts. He would then be able to ask questions related to their mental DNA that he knows the subject could respond to. It would probably do no good to ask a visual question of a nonvisual subject. Both the specialist and the subject could become frustrated and disappointed by the experience.

All your other senses work in the same manner as your visual sense. If you have a strong smell sense, it can help you to gather valuable information in that regression about the lifetime you are visiting. The more you understand how you can use your senses, the more confidence you will have in your ability to experience and collect information during a past life regression.

> **Ageless Insights**
>
> The more you practice your self-hypnotic image trances, the more you can sharpen your focus on your strong senses. At first you may have to remind yourself to see, hear, feel, taste, and smell in your mind. You may need to practice a bit to sharpen your sense imagery. Every time you work on your technique, you will become more confident and comfortable with it.

A strong sense experience can also help deepen your trance state. That was one of the goals of the special place self-hypnosis technique. You practiced entering your comfort zone and imaging through each of your five senses to help you focus with a higher intensity on the experience. The more your image experience intensifies, the easier it is for you to step into the reality of the experience. A self-hypnotic trance is an altered state of reality. It is possible to change your reality so that your image experience becomes your reality. When that happens, you are in a deep state of self-hypnosis.

And remember: The less you expect to experience in regression, the more open you will be to what you will actually experience. If you are looking for something specific, you may pass by something that is very important. In fact, the littlest clue could be very important as you put the pieces of a past life together. Something that you may have dismissed may eventually turn out to be the missing link. Of course, you may collect some information that does not fit into your past life regression. At the same, time even that information may be very important to something else that you are looking for or need to know.

The more you can allow yourself to accept that every past life regression is important, the more open you will be to understanding the lessons that may be there for you to learn. There are no failures. There are no ways to do it wrong as long as the experience is one that has a positive outcome.

It is not necessary to gather all the information in one session. Many times the regression images will continue to surface in your conscious mind long after the trance has ended. More information may come up to the surface through your dreams or thoughts at most any time. The best thing that you can do is to think of it as an adventure, and a past life regression has the potential to be just that, a great adventure.

Is It Possible to Get Stuck in the Past?

As you'll recall from Chapter 1, the television show *Soap* had a story line one season about a character who became trapped in a past life. It was very funny to watch him try to adjust to a culture that was much further advanced than he was accustomed to. This character stayed stuck for several episodes of the show.

So could this happen to you? The answer is no, you won't get stuck in a past life. You may have an experience that is so strong that when you come back to conscious reality it can take you a few moments to adjust. This is no different than being absorbed in a good movie, a play, or a good book. Have you ever had the experience of becoming so focused on what you were reading or watching that you shifted your reality to the experience? If you have, you know that sometimes when you are jerked back to conscious reality, you still continue to focus on the other image for a moment as well as your actual surroundings.

This same feeling can happen after you have experienced a deep trance state during a post-hypnotic regression. This is why it is important for you to come back to your conscious mind slowly so that you can easily make the adjustment back to your conscious reality. It is a good idea for you to plan to give yourself some time to reflect on your experience and get accustomed to your surroundings again.

It is also possible to continue an intense past life experience for a period of time after the regression. It is always important for you to suggest to yourself that you will come back to the surface of your conscious mind refreshed and relaxed and in a positive mood. This way you will be more open to letting your past life regression slowly make its way into your conscious mind at a pace that is comfortable and positive for you.

It is very important that if you are receiving treatment or counseling from a professional you discuss your goal of a past life regression experience before you try the process. Some people have such an extreme ability to be influenced by suggestions that it is easy for them to lose track of reality. That is not the goal of this book. It is good for you to always know where you are on some level. Once you are comfortable with that, you are free to experience the altered reality of self-hypnotic trance for a past life regression without the fear that you will be trapped somewhere in the past.

The experience of a past life regression is sort of like wandering around in woods that you are slightly familiar with. It is very easy to get turned around if you are not paying attention, and yet the woods are not so large that you won't be able to find your way out in a reasonable time. Then again, if you had a compass with you, you could wander around and be confident that you could always find your way out. If you have a tendency to get lost in your mind, then you will want to be sure of your ability to come back to the surface of your conscious mind and know where you are. The more you practice your self-hypnosis, the more you will know and trust your ability to return to your conscious mind.

It is always important to know where you are physically, mentally, and spiritually. People who get lost in their minds can lose track of reality. You might compare it to a war veteran who was so traumatized in battle that when he hears a car backfire, he instantly shifts his reality to a memory still playing in his unconscious mind. Once the veteran has focused on that reality, he will continue to do so until the battle trance has run its course.

Fear and phobia trances can work the same way. Some of them can last for days, weeks, and even years. All this time the conscious mind is powerless to change the course of the trance.

There is no more danger of getting stuck in a past life then there is getting stuck in this life. By understanding and grounding yourself in normal reality, you will have the opportunity to experience the reality of a past life without the fear of being stuck there. It is just like going to the movies, only they are in your mind.

> **Ageless Insights**
>
> Some people actually live in a past life trance. They may realize where they are, but they have compelling images that they cannot explain that flow from their soul's memory. If they are able to understand these images when they first start, they can stop a trance by pulling back and focusing on something that keeps their mind in the present rather than in the past.

After the Past Life Regression

So what will you be like when you return from your past life regression adventure? What are you like after you have read a book, or gone to a play or a movie? A great many different elements can influence your response to that question.

The quality of the work in a book or play and your interest in the subject may affect your response to the material that you have experienced. If it is done well, you may be drawn into the material even if you did not have an initial strong interest in it. You can actually become mesmerized or hypnotized by a good presentation. You will shift your focus and become totally absorbed in the subject, remaining in your trance state until the presentation is over or until something interrupts you. When that happens, you sometimes need a few moments to regain your balance and come back to your normal reality.

A past life regression therapist believes that you can change for the better after regression. They help you sift through the image material that you have just experienced so that you may gain a different perspective on a situation that needs to be clarified in this lifetime. The goal of the therapeutic session is to resolve a past life memory that keeps resurfacing through your unconscious mind. Once you can understand the surfacing images, you can resolve them and move forward in your mind to other more positive and productive images. When you have done this, there is a good possibility that you will have a different outlook about your life. Yes, you may change from your regression experience.

Keep in mind that when someone who is unqualified tries to do therapy, the results can be harmful to the subject. An old trauma may be brought up to the surface of the conscious mind, and an untrained person will not know how to deal with it. Leading the subject to imagine a reality that never really existed can create what are called "false memories." An untrained person could also jump to the wrong conclusion about the meaning of a regression.

Soul Stories

Donna had been plagued her whole life by a dream that made no sense to her. It always had the same content and the same character. It was no one she could identify. She experienced a hypnotic regression that put her inside her dream, where she determined that the character was actually herself in a past life. The awareness of her relationship to her dream helped her resolve some issues in her present life, and she never had the dream again. Donna's life changed for the better after her past life regression.

Then again, you may have read a book that changed your life. There may have been just one piece of information that became your motivation for change. Was it what you read that changed you, or did the book unlock the knowledge that was already inside you? What if you had not read the book or paid attention to its message? Would you have eventually found another source to provide you with the insights to bring about your change? Only you know the answer to that.

The experiences of reading a book, of going to the movies or a play, can relate to experiencing a past life regression. You may be profoundly changed after your regression, or you may come away from it disappointed. The more you are prepared, the better the opportunity for a positive experience that will encourage you to have more.

You can prepare by reviewing and practicing the exercises in this book up to this point and those that are still to follow before you experience your first past life regression. Not only will the exercises help you with your regression, they will also help you become more relaxed in general. The more you are able to relax your conscious mind and escape your daily stress, the better prepared you will be for the adventures that lay ahead for you.

> **CAUTION**
>
> **Karmic Cautions**
>
> It might take more than one past life regression to bring about your desired change. Sometimes the information collected is confusing and not complete. Don't be discouraged if this happens to you. The more patience you have, the better the chance is that you will find the answers to what you are looking for and to perhaps help you change.

Experiencing or Just Imagining?

It is not uncommon for someone who is going to experience a past life regression for the first time to wonder if they will really be having a past life recall or if they are making the whole thing up. That is a good question, and many times the subject will supply his or her own answer.

Mental images come from *imagination*. They may be made up of a single memory or a composite of different memories. Remember in Chapter 9 how you found your relaxed comfortable image in your mind? You experienced a positive memory through seeing, hearing, feeling, tasting, and smelling. To do this, you entered a self-hypnotic trance that helped you to enhance and strengthen your images. When you did this, you were using your imagination, or memory recall, to put you back in your mind to your special place. You were also able to physically experience what your mind was imaging.

> **Words to Remember**
>
> Part of the *Webster's Dictionary* definition for **imagination** is, "the power of the mind to reproduce images or concepts stored in the memory." Consider that definition with the exercises you have been doing to help you identify and use your five different sense images to recall positive memories from your unconscious mind.

When you had this experience, you were able to shift your focus from the reality of the moment to the reality of your memory. You might say that imagination includes the use of the images that you recall from your unconscious mind. So were you experiencing or imagining? It just might be all the same thing.

During a past life regression the real question may not be whether or not you were imagining, but "What is the source of your imagination?" Where did the images in your imagination come from? Were they from something that you read, saw, heard, or otherwise experienced in your current lifetime?

Sometimes these questions are difficult to answer. You may not have a conscious recall of something that you heard, saw, or experienced during your life, but it is possible that your unconscious mind does. That is the nature of something that does not have readily provable facts. Just because it seems real does not necessarily make it real. At the same time, if there is no way of proving it to be true, there is also no way of proving it to be untrue. It is a reality that only the person who experiences a past life regression can answer, and it is possible that even they may not know for sure.

One past life regression session may not provide enough information to make a determination, even if you wanted it to. Sometimes a lot of information surfaces all at once, and the images themselves can be unclear. Think of the experience as similar to an event you may have just witnessed that you will be asked to report on. If you give this report right after you have witnessed it, you may be a little fuzzy about what took place. It often takes some time for the unconscious mind to process the information for it to be recalled accurately.

A witness to a crime can offer more vivid details several months after the event rather than right afterward. The term used for hypnotic memory recall is "memory revivication." However, hypnotic enhanced memory recall has come under great debate by the legal system. Why? Lawyers and experts question whether witness recall is real or imagined. No one really knows what the unconscious mind really knows.

You may want to have several past life regressions on the same lifetime so that you can bring out details that can be historically researched. You will be given ideas in a future chapter about what to look for during regression. It may be possible to establish a link with your regression recall to actual events before you were born.

Each of you will experience your regression differently and at different depth levels of hypnotic trance. Some of you will be able to visit your special place in such a deep trance that you will lose all awareness of your present surroundings. Others of you will have just a mild experience, perhaps recall a pleasant memory, but never lose track of your conscious reality.

The real benefit of experiencing a past life regression with someone else watching you is that they will see and hear you express things that you may not be aware of. Better yet, have someone else videotape the regression so that you can watch yourself afterward. When you watch the replay, you may be able to decide if you were experiencing more than you thought during your regression.

CAUTION **Karmic Cautions** _____

There are many depths of self-hypnotic trance, from a light daydream to somnambulism. You don't have to be in a deep trance to have a productive past life regression. All you need to do is just let the images flow whether you are aware of them or not. If you spend much of your time during a regression analyzing whether or not you are imagining what you are reporting on, you may miss much of the information that is coming up from your unconscious mind.

One of the best ways to prepare for your past life regression is to practice your imagination. The more you become comfortable with the way you recall your images in your five senses, the easier it will be to have a positive regression, no matter how deeply you enter a self-hypnotic trance. This is why it is important for you to establish a regular relaxation routine so that you will be prepared to let your imagination take over. The better you can imagine, the stronger your regression experience will be.

The Least You Need to Know

- Every past life regression will be a different experience.

- You will not get stuck in a past life.

- Returning from a past life experience can be the same as going to a movie, watching a video, or finishing a good book.

- You may find that you will improve your life through the insights gained from a past life regression.

- It is not necessary to determine if the regression was real or imagined to experience positive benefits from it.

Chapter 12

The Karma Club

In This Chapter

- ◆ How past karma can catch up with you
- ◆ Identifying karmic cycles
- ◆ The connection to soul mates
- ◆ The roots of your fears and phobias
- ◆ Do you know where your aches and pains come from?

Have you ever found yourself stuck on a highway rotary? Perhaps you drove around and around, not knowing where to exit. You may have tried to get off and taken the wrong road. Your only recourse was to turn around and start over again.

You were caught in a cycle that went around and around because you didn't know how to exit correctly. It may have taken you some time to learn the correct route to get to your destination.

Likewise, until you learn the correct route to resolving your leftover karma, you will continue to cruise the highway rotary of your mind. Identifying and plotting the correct route through the karma of your past lives will help you chart your course for your soul's journey through your current lifetime.

Your Past Lives Can Catch Up with You

You learned in the first chapter that you may be constantly dealing with karma or left-over issues from your past lives. You also know that it is your choice or free will as to how you will resolve these issues. Of course, you may not even be consciously aware of some of your karma. You may not have looked at your life situations from this perspective. This is a good chapter for you to start looking at some of the clutter in your life that may have come from unresolved situations in a past life.

Once you become aware of the possibility that you have karma, you will begin to examine some of your life situations differently. Remember the idea of two different views. If you are stuck in just one view, that is all you will see until you have the opportunity to get a different perspective. The second view is the other perspective. As you know, this is what happens when you enter a hypnotic trance. You shift from one focus to another. In this case, the second focus is the chance for you to gain a different view on a situation in your life by examining it from a past life experience.

Now we're back to your willingness to imagine again. It's not necessary to do a deep self-hypnotic past life regression to benefit from examining a situation from the view-point of unresolved karma. All you have to do is take a moment and imagine. It may help you to imagine how you would respond to a situation if it had happened during a different lifetime.

The first step is to consider the multitude of past situations in your life that may have resulted from karma from a past life. There are several different types of karma that you can identify. Remember, karma is unfinished business from a past life that resulted from a missed opportunity to follow your soul's purpose and the lessons in that lifetime. Karma is the result from your or someone else's (or even a group of people's) choice to exercise the right of free will and not follow soul lessons.

The first questions you may wish to ask yourself are, "When did I first become aware of my situation? When did I first see it, hear it, feel it, taste it, and smell it?" You may find many different things that bring out an emotion in you that can't easily be explained—a picture or a certain selection of music, a feeling, or the touch of a specific material. It could be a certain food or smell that creates an emotion in you that is not easily resolved.

If you think about it, every thought you have is related to an image. Some of these images can be explained in terms of your memory recall and others can't. The key to identifying karma is a reaction to a situation or image that is not normal. It could be a heightened attraction or repulsion to someone or something.

Ask yourself when and where you first learned to react that way, and it will automatically open the door for the possibility of a past life connection. This is especially true if there is no plausible explanation in your current life as to why you or someone else would react that way. The reaction had to be learned somewhere. It gives you an excuse to consider the possibility beyond one view.

Soul Stories _____

June had been trying to stop smoking without success for quite a while. There was something about the habit that she could not shake, and she didn't understand why she couldn't. Finally, she tried a past life regression. She learned that as a Native American in a past life, tobacco had a special spiritual meaning to her. She had used it to communicate with the spirit guides of that lifetime. Currently, she had a great many worries, and smoking always gave her a momentary sense of relief. Once she was able to understand her connection to tobacco, she was able to substitute a different, less dangerous habit to help her deal with her stress.

For a moment, think of a relationship or emotional feeling in your life that has no plausible explanation. Perhaps it is one that you have been trying to understand. It may be a good topic for you to consider when you pick a destination for a past life regression. When you seriously start to think about it, ask yourself the following questions and make notes that may eventually help you in a regression:

◆ When was I first aware of this situation?

◆ Does this situation relate or connect to others?

◆ What are my strongest images relating to this situation?

◆ Is this situation currently positive or negative for me?

◆ In my five different senses, how do I react positively?

◆ In my five different senses, how do I react negatively?

◆ What else about this situation can I relate to a past life karma?

How did you make out? Could you identify a possible karma? Maybe some of your karmic images are so powerful that it's hard for you to examine them rationally. If that's the case, a good way to do this is to view them from your comfort zone, which you can enter with your self-hypnotic trance to bring you to your special place (see Chapter 9). From there, you can get a different perspective of the situation in a less emotional and more detached manner. You may be able to step back and run the images you want to examine like a movie in your mind. Then you may be able to determine a possible karmic connection to them.

Does Your Life Run in Cycles?

One of the most common past life karmas is the continuing of a situation that started during one of your other *life cycles*. It is a lesson that you get a chance to work on again if you choose to. If you don't, it will keep coming up again and again during your soul's journey.

Words to Remember

A **life cycle** is a theme or situation that keeps coming up or happening over and over again. Many times these conditions or situations start out full of hope and end up with your swearing never to do it or get involved again. Unfortunately, the bad memory does not last for long, and before you know it, you are immersed back in the same old karmic conditions.

Once you start the old pattern again, you actually enter a type of trance that impedes your conscious mind from making rational decisions. Like any other trance, it will continue until something or someone breaks your focus so that you are able to get a second view of the situation. Does this sound familiar to you? You're back to considering the concept of two different views or focuses again. That sounds like a cycle itself, doesn't it?

A life cycle trance is one that starts at the beginning of the cycle. It can begin innocently and simply, and before you know it, you're hooked again. A cycle is often connected to a bad habit such as smoking, over-eating, or stress. It's possible to stop the habit for a period of time, but unless the *reason* for the habit is addressed, it may be only a matter of time until the habit trance starts its cycle all over again.

Can you identify a possible karma in your life that runs through cycles? It may surface in one of many different ways. Some of them may be very powerful and disrupt your life, while others could only result in a slight aggravation. It is an aggravation that after a while you begin to anticipate before the cycle actually begins again. Simple and less severe karma can relate to different seasons and how they affect you. Most everyone knows someone who goes through a mood change during a specific season of the year. A normally happy individual may go through a period of depression before they suddenly emerge from their mood as if nothing had happened. Some people require counseling to help them deal with their problems, while others just weather their mood change, knowing that it will eventually improve.

Of course, many mood changes are related to situations that have occurred earlier in the person's life. Holidays and other dates or events that have sad memories can plunge someone back into the emotions that are connected to the actual time that the event happened. What has happened is that the person has shifted their focus from the present onto an event in the past. When this happens, they enter a memory trance that puts them back to that time again rather than being able to move forward in their current reality. At this point the trance runs its course until it ends or is interrupted and the person is able to refocus on their current life.

Soul Stories

Terri had several failed marriages and relationships with people whom her friends and family described as "losers." She would invest time, money, and energy into relationships, only to feel that she could never do enough. When the relationship failed, she always felt it was her fault. In a past life regression, she found she had been the mother of a large family who had been left by her husband. She worked so hard to provide for her children that she became sick and died. The guilt Terri felt in that life had transferred into her present life as the need to again provide for her children. Each relationship was a part of her need to provide, encourage, and nourish someone she unconsciously related to as one of her lost children.

As I mentioned in Chapter 10, a past life specialist may use an affect-bridge regression to take you back into a past life to help identify a cyclic pattern that has happened in not only this lifetime but in others as well. You will learn more about this technique in Chapter 16. It can take you through the cycle of the karma in your current life and then work it backward into other lifetimes. By doing this, you have the opportunity to return to the karma's source so you can break the cycle and create a new positive direction in the future using your new past knowledge to resolve the old situations.

A cycle that involves relationships usually begins with the prospect of one that will last forever. Often, one of the parties will see something in the other that they hope to change. They know that they can help their partner reach their potential, one that perhaps others do not see. Once a relationship like this has started, the optimistic member fails to see potential problems until it is too late. By then, the other member has taken control and has succeeded in bringing the other one down to their level. They are now trapped and will continue to be until something finally causes them to break free.

As you give it some thought and read on in the chapter, you may identify one or more karmas in your life that are cyclic in nature. If you can, make some notes that you may want to refer to when you prepare for your past life regression. You might want to try your relaxation exercise to help you consider the possibility of karma from a place in your mind that is comfortable for you.

Do You Have Soul Mates?

A soul mate is someone you have been together with before in at least one or more lifetimes. Your souls have an unconscious connection that has been carried over into your current lifetimes. You feel that you know each other like a book. You may have the same likes and dislikes. You may even be able to finish each other's sentences. Sometimes you may know someone else too well. You may see something in that person that has been carried over from a past experience when both your characters in the karma play had different roles. The experience during that lifetime was so powerful that deep inside of you the connection to the old play still exists.

Do you have a soul mate? Ask yourself the following questions:

◆ Have you ever met someone for the first time who you felt you had known all your life?

◆ Have you ever felt an unexplainable attraction to someone?

◆ Do you have a friend who feels like a sister or brother?

◆ Have you ever met someone you instantly disliked for no particular reason?

Although most people think of a soul mate in only positive terms, a soul mate attraction can also be dangerous. It's possible that a past life relationship may not be appropriate in this lifetime. If you had a lover or were married in the past, it may not be in the plan for this time around. Perhaps you know someone who threw caution to the wind and was drawn into a relationship that spelled disaster from the beginning. Just as you can feel an instant dislike for someone from a past life, an instant attraction can also be so powerful that you cannot separate the different lifetimes. Remember that the roles in the play change from lifetime to lifetime even though the players may remain the same.

Sometimes the attraction is not for a specific soul mate, but for a physical similarity. For instance, a man could have had a wonderful relationship with someone in a past life with beautiful blond hair. His emotional memories of the hair are so powerful in his unconscious mind that he spends much of his time searching for someone who has the same physical description. Of course not everyone he finds turns out to be his soul mate from the past. This physical attraction could also be for size, height, and even the sound of a voice.

Ageless Insights

Not every soul mate connection from the past is wrong for this lifetime. Some souls who were together before are reunited in this lifetime to resolve or continue their roles from the past. For those soul mates who are fortunate enough to reestablish this connection in a lifetime where it is part of the plan, the journey together can be fulfilling and totally in tune with their souls' purpose.

Psychic Edgar Cayce had a very strong attachment for his secretary, Gladys Davis. Through his readings on her past lives it was determined that the two of them had been together before in many different lifetimes. In this lifetime, however, despite their bond, Edgar remained faithful to his wife, Gertrude Cayce. He was able to overcome his karmic attraction and focus on continuation of the work that he and his secretary had begun many lifetimes before.

Take a moment to think about your family members and friends as if they were in a different relationship with you. Perhaps you have a child who feels more like a brother, sister, or a parent to you. You may feel closer to a friend than you do a family member. It could be that this person was a part of your family in a past life. At the same time, you may have someone close to you that deep down you see as a rival rather than family or a friend. There is no plausible explanation for the feeling, and yet it still exists no matter how hard you try to rationalize.

Have you identified at least one relationship with a friend or family member that you would like to understand better? If so, you may want to make some notes and keep them handy when you are ready to do some past life regression research. You can also apply the same concept to casual acquaintances or even strangers you have a gut feeling about being connected to in the past.

Unexplained Fears and Phobias

Past life karma can also be connected to a fear, phobia, or even an unexplainable health problem. Some of these may only be minor, and some others may be serious. A condition from the past can manifest itself again from an unconscious soul memory that is triggered by a situation or event that occurs. It could be a single experience that is triggered by participating in or observing something that relates to a past memory.

Soul Stories

John has an extreme fear of heights. He even has trouble handling steep stairways. When he thinks he is in a precarious position, he starts to sweat, his knees feel like rubber, and he freezes in place. He can't even watch a similar situation on television. In a hypnotic regression he focused on an image that was formed from a past life memory. He saw himself climbing a treacherous mountain path, and as he neared a particularly dangerous area, his feet slipped out from under him. He could not stop himself and slid several hundred feet to his death. When John was able to understand the roots of his fear, he was able to function in high places.

A birthmark on your body might indicate a continuation of a condition that started in a past life. It could be a mark with a special symbol that could actually be researched to determine its origins. Some cultures would look for a child with similar markings after their leader died, believing they would find him again. Other birthmarks can continue the scar from a wound suffered in a past life.

The seeds of your fear or phobia could have been planted in your subconscious mind earlier in your life, or you could have been born with a memory that developed into a phobia as you encountered similar situations. Phobias often have their first onset during the teen years. Interestingly enough, the teen years are also the time that people often become aware of their psychic abilities. Children are much more open to natural trance and can be caught off-guard when the unconscious mind sends up a response to an earlier experience long since forgotten by the conscious mind.

Most people have a fear or a phobia to some extent. Can you identify one or more in yourself? If you can, this might be something that you will want to examine through a past life regression. As you can see, there are enough regression ideas in this chapter to keep you busy working on resolving your past life karmas.

Mysterious Aches and Pains

Ann had been bothered most of her life by a pain in one of her shoulders. It was always there, a deep dull ache as if something had penetrated right to the bone. She had been to many doctors and specialists looking for relief. She finally turned to past life regression for the answer. Ann was taken back to colonial times when Indians invaded her home, a cabin at the edge of the wilderness. She was shot in the shoulder by an arrow that went all the way to the bone. To top it off, the cabin was set on fire, and she burned to death. When she woke up from the regression, she revealed that she had never been able to stand hot temperatures. She not only understood the pain in her shoulder, but also her extreme discomfort in hot weather.

> **CAUTION**
>
> **Karmic Cautions**
>
> Do you have any mysterious aches and pains or other medical conditions, such as asthma, that the doctors can find no reason for? You may have been told that it's all in your mind and maybe it is—deep in your unconscious mind. The condition could very well be an incident from a past life that has manifested itself for you to deal with again.

For Ann, getting to the root of her problem meant that she was now free to resolve her pain and intolerance to heat by bringing a positive memory of before the tragic event in her past life forward into her conscious mind. She could now remember what it was like to live pain-free, and her pain was greatly reduced. However, because it was most severe when she was stressed, her goal now is to use self-hypnosis to keep herself calm, positive, and relaxed, and thus eliminate the pain.

It is always important to remember that a past life regression is not a substitute for medicine. It does not mean that you can go to a past life to cure an actual physical condition that requires medical treatment. This being said, it is also possible that an insight gained from researching a medical condition in a past life may help modern medicine bring about healing in a shorter time. If you have any thoughts about doing a past life regression with the objective of gaining knowledge that can help provide a cure for a present medical condition, check with your doctor first.

You may gain an understanding of your present life situations by experiencing a past life regression. You can try out any of your ideas when you are ready to begin. Adventure awaits as you learn to work with your leftover karma through past life regressions. In Chapter 21 you will have an opportunity to study the karma that you have found in your past lives and learn how you can resolve it.

The Least You Need to Know

◆ You may have a lot of karma from your past lives.

◆ Karma may come and go in specific cycles.

◆ It's possible to recognize a soul mate from a past life.

◆ Some of your fears and phobias may have their roots in a past life.

◆ Unexplained medical conditions may begin in a past life.

Chapter 13

Keeping Yourself Grounded

In This Chapter

- ◆ The importance of being grounded in your inborn belief system
- ◆ What it means to be in balance
- ◆ Do you have angels, guides, or other beings watching over you?
- ◆ A self-hypnosis grounding exercise

When Richard was in his teens, he discovered an article about past life regression. He and a friend decided it would be fun to try it. They found a book with instructions for hypnotic trances.

His friend easily hypnotized Richard, and he slipped into a deep trance. He went back to a past life and suddenly began to cry when he encountered something very traumatic. His friend was totally unprepared and panicked. Fortunately, Richard brought himself out of his trance. The experience left both boys shaken because they were not prepared for what they encountered. They were out of balance and ungrounded.

When you are totally prepared to travel into your past, you can experience the journey with the assurance that whatever insights come to surface in your conscious mind through your imagery, you will be able to relate them to your current life. When someone is not prepared, they can get out of balance when they encounter something unplanned. The best plan is to plan for everything and nothing so that you will not be thrown off-balance.

Travel Insurance: Understanding Your Internal Belief System

How do you protect your assets when you travel? Do you carry cash? If so, do you keep it all together or do you hide it in several places? Do you carry credit or debit cards? Do you take travelers checks? If you are in a foreign country, do you convert all or some of your funds to their currency?

What kind of trip insurance do you carry, if any? Perhaps you are willing to take the gamble that nothing will go wrong and that you will save money by taking the risk that everything will go just fine on your trip. Perhaps you are the type who worries about everything that can go wrong and overprepares by purchasing too much insurance.

There are many different things for you to consider when you decide on your travel insurance. There is the trip itself. If something happens and you have to cancel it, you may be out the money you paid and have nothing to show for it. You may want to insure your vehicle for damage and repair. You may want to insure some of the items you take with you. The more you plan for insuring your trip, the more at ease your mind can be when you start to travel.

There are several things that you can do to help ensure that your travel back into a past life regression will go successfully. You have already taken the first steps by identifying your mental DNA, developing your self-hypnosis trance technique, and using it to help you find your special relaxing places in your mind. You also now know the importance of letting yourself imagine in your five different senses so that you can shift your focus into the reality of your unconscious mind. The next step is to develop an understanding of your *internal belief system* and confidence in your conscious reality to ensure that your past life regression will be a positive experience. I'll discuss this more in a moment.

Words to Remember

Your **internal belief system** is the set of values that you were born with. Everything you do or think about is compared to this. Many people choose to listen to their ego or their internal voice for self-gain instead of what they believe in their heart.

You are a product of a combination of different influences. You inherit certain physical and mental traits such as size and color and different sensory strengths such as a photographic memory and perfect pitch. The environment in which you were raised also influences you. Your parents and others can make a large contribution to your character development and to the values that you were born with. These often do not relate to the other influences you have experienced. The feeling may be as simple as knowing that there is something more to life and a deep passion to go in a direction that is different from what would seem normal for other members of your family. The values from a past life could make you feel out of place in your present lifetime.

If you have ever had nightmares related to a past life or a disturbing dream, you know that they can be very unsettling. At the same time, if you can detach yourself from the nightmare or dream, you may be able to figure out the reason you had it. The same thing could happen when and after you experience a past life regression.

A regression specialist will have given you an "escape route" in case something traumatic surfaces while you are in a hypnotic trance. That could be permission for you to come out of trance in case you feel uncomfortable. If you know that you can always come back to your conscious mind, you are more likely to allow yourself to enter a deeper trance state than if you were worried about facing a potentially unpleasant situation. The regression specialist will watch your physiology to determine signs of discomfort and distress. He or she will know how to move you away from something that is unpleasant and yet at the same time let you experience just enough of the negativity to help you produce an image of your past life regression.

The regression specialist also usually gives the client permission to open their eyes and come out of their hypnotic trance anytime they want or need to. This helps diminish any fear that they will be stuck in a past life while having a traumatic experience. Knowing that you can change your past life travel plans is part of your insurance package that the experience will have a positive result no matter where you go.

Soul Stories

Jack went to a hypnotist who was not formally trained in past life regression but was familiar enough to be able to help him go back to a time during the Middle Ages. The hypnotist moved Jack into a battle scene where he was hit in the shoulder by a lance. He suddenly cried out, experiencing great pain from his wound. His reaction was so traumatic that the hypnotist panicked and immediately brought him out of his trance. He did not give Jack the option of examining the relationship between his past life and current one. It was a very frustrating experience for Jack.

Also included in your insurance package is the ability to keep yourself balanced between the past and the present, a secure feeling that you are in tune with your belief and that your journey will be protected and guided by your team from the other side, your guides, angels, or other spirit beings. This type of travel insurance only requires the patience to practice your self-hypnosis trance technique, and you will be covered on your journey into the past.

Keep Your Balance

One of the most important ingredients for a successful past life regression is your ability to keep yourself focused and in balance. Being in balance means that you are spiritually, emotionally, and physically ready to experience the adventure. Perhaps a good way to explain balance is to use part of a hypnosis suggestibility test as an example. A hypnotist often uses one or more suggestibility tests to determine how well a client for hypnosis follows suggestions and can experience what they imagine. The subject is given a series of suggestions, such as imagining the feeling of heaviness in their eyelids or lightness in their arms. The better the subject responds to the suggestions, the more likely they are to enter a deeper hypnotic state.

To try a suggestibility test, stand up (if it is comfortable for you) with your feet together and your arms down at your sides. Take a deep breath, exhale, and close your eyes. Now for a moment imagine that you are standing on a plank of wood, sort of like a diving board, that is two inches thick, a foot wide, and is suspended a foot off the ground. As you feel this plank under your feet, you are aware of how it is secure but bouncing a little up and down, up and down. You know that you are only a foot off the ground, and the board is nice and wide as you feel its gentle spring bouncing up and down.

Now imagine that you are 10 feet off the ground standing on the same plank. You can still feel it gently bounce up and down, but you are now aware that you are 10 feet up in the air. You may even be able to feel the wind and see the ground below as you gently bounce up and down. It is the same plank, but it is higher up in the air.

Now imagine being on the same plank moved to 50 feet off the ground. You can feel more air stirring around you as you bounce up and down, up and down. You can look around and see many things from 50 feet up. You feel yourself balancing as you gently bounce up and down in the breeze. Now you may come back to the ground and become aware of the surface that you are standing on. Take a deep relaxing breath, exhale, and open your eyes.

The object of this exercise was to see if you would feel any difference in the three images that you were asked to focus on. If you let yourself experience what you were asked to imagine, you may have felt differently when you were at each level of the plank. The reality is that there was no difference. If you were able to experience these sensations, it means that you have an active imagination and are a good candidate for hypnosis. At the same time, if you felt no sensations, it does not mean that you would not be a good subject. You may be an observer rather than an experiencer.

If you can easily imagine an experience, such as when you watch a movie or read a book, you can probably step into the story so well that it almost seems real to you.

Some people have such a powerful past life experience that for a period of time emotions come through that can overpower the rational conscious mind. If you are unprepared to handle images such as these, the effects of an unpleasant experience can last much longer. It can also greatly diminish your interest in having another past life regression. The result can be missed opportunities for getting back in tune with your life purpose.

Soul Stories

Gretchen was unprepared for the powerful images she experienced after she easily regressed into a past lifetime. She was working with someone who was not trained for what occurred next. All of a sudden she was running for her life. As the end came near, she began to panic. Her whole body stiffened with fear, and she pulled herself out of the trance. The feeling of panic was still there as she gasped for breath and sobbed hysterically. The person guiding the regression did not know what to do to calm her down, and the experience stayed with both of them for a long time afterwards.

Part of the balance that you are looking for in this lifetime could very well hinge on your understanding of the lessons of your past lives. As you learned in Chapter 12, each time you resolve a past life karma you help to balance your present journey. If you are not prepared to experience and resolve the karma of your past, it will follow you into your future.

Another very important step to take before you embark on a past life regression is to make sure that your internal and external guidance systems are balanced and grounded. We will talk about that next. It's also important for you to help your physical body get and stay in tune and in balance. You are the amplifier for the messages that flow from your unconscious mind. If you are out of balance, you may not be able to interpret the lessons of your past.

Include Your Belief

Your internal belief system—your core set of values—is one of the most important elements of keeping yourself grounded and balanced, not only during a past life regression, but also in most aspects of your life. One of the reasons you are probably reading this book is because a part of you believes that there is something beyond your daily existence. As you know, that view may be difficult to express to your friends and family. As you become comfortable with what you already know deep inside your soul's memory, the more you will begin to believe in your connections to the past.

It's easy to get off balance when trying to work with your internal belief system and other people's beliefs. Many religions and their followers are not very tolerant of beliefs different than their own. In their eyes, if you don't follow the rules of their religion, you risk the possibility of damnation in hell. That form of intimidation can make it difficult to break away or try out other religious philosophies. The more you are pulled by conflicting beliefs about past life reincarnation, the more you are drawn away from your own internal belief. This conflict can keep you off-balance or ungrounded.

Your internal belief can communicate with you through your unconscious mind. It can send up messages to you in one or more of your five sense images. In other words, you may get a feeling, a taste, a smell, a voice, or a visual message. The message can come from the universal mind, an angel, spirit guide, or a deceased relative or friend. Your inner guidance can reach you when you are awake or through your dreams when you are sleeping. If you are open to your inner belief, you will be guided to make the right decisions in your life, including how you will use the knowledge that you gain from your past life regressions.

Soul Stories

Listening to your inner belief system can be life-saving. This belief is a part of intuition, or what your soul knows. Rachel really wanted to attend a party that all her friends were going to. At the same time she knew that she needed to complete a homework assignment. She agonized over making the decision until she listened to her inner self. The message was to stay home. Her friends were in a serious car accident, and if she had gone with them to the party, she would have been in the middle of it.

You can ask your belief system for guidance on many things, including help to get you in balance with your soul's purpose. An answer may come right away, or it may take a little time. It may come in any of the five sense images, or it may come from an outside source. It may also come when you are sleeping, either from a dream or a feeling you have when you wake up. The more you are in tune with your inner belief, the more you are prepared to visit your past.

Being comfortable, balanced, and grounded in your belief system does not mean that you are able to define what it is to anyone else. Most people actually cannot. Those who absolutely think they know what they believe in may not be flexible enough to make adjustments when something different surfaces. So if you are unsure, that is really okay. The main concept of staying balanced and grounded is that deep inside you know there is something to help guide you on your soul's journey. At the end of this chapter is a self-hypnotic exercise that will help you.

Once you learn to trust and are comfortable with your inner belief, regardless of how you define it, you will be able to keep yourself balanced and grounded. You will be prepared for any images that might come through while you are experiencing a past life regression with the knowledge that it is there to help you progress along your life map. That feeling can go with you all the time anywhere you go as long as you stay in tune and connected to your belief system.

Include Your Guides or Angels

Besides your belief system, you also have a guidance system that travels with you throughout your life journey. Many people choose not to use it even though it is always available. It can materialize in many different forms and ways. It is a part of your soul connection, and you have been developing it over many lifetimes. Your psychic or intuitive gifts are a part of this rich heritage. You may not realize all of them yet, but a past life regression is a good way to discover them and bring them up-to-date in this life.

Psychic Edgar Cayce said that there are two types of realities—manifest and unmanifest. Manifest reality is all that everyone has the ability to see, touch, hear, taste, and smell about him or her. Unmanifest reality is that which is also real but is not acknowledged by most other people. You can experience a reality in the nature of your external guidance system, which is composed of angels, spirits, guides, and other unseen elements that are a part of your daily life. Your guidance system will appear to you in the way that you can accept it if you choose to.

Even though your external guidance is different from your belief, it can still communicate to you in your mind as well as in your dreams. It can also get the message to you through someone else, or even from electronic media such as the radio or television. You may have someone tell you exactly what you were thinking about. You will usually hear, feel, see, taste, or smell something more than once. When that happens, your guidance system is trying to tell you something. It's time to pay attention!

Ageless Insights _____

Your guides can take many forms. They may represent ancient connections to your soul. They may be old souls that have finished their earthly life cycles and are now there to watch over you as you continue yours. They may represent one or more cultures from your past lives. They may even be animals or other beings. Whatever form they take, their main job is to help you as you continue on your soul's journey.

An angel may be someone who was with you on the earth plane before they passed over. It could be a deceased relative or a friend. They have come back to keep an eye on you if you will let them. Some people are so closed to that possibility that they miss all the clues their angels have given them. You may be aware that something is watching out for you, but you have no idea who it is. That's okay. Just believing in the possibility that something is there can be a great comfort to you in many aspects of your life, including exploring your past lives.

You could actually do a regression to find out when you first became associated with your guides. You can also go back in time to reconnect with some of your psychic abilities. You can also visit a psychic who specializes in talking with the other side to help you identify who your angels might be. Once you are confident that there is something with you that is unmanifest to most people, you can experience a past life regression with the knowledge that you are being looked after and protected.

Karmic Cautions

Some people may not be open to the view that angels, guides, or other beings exist. Don't expect others to believe you if you tell them about your imaginary friends. You may not want to tell everyone about your beliefs.

You may communicate directly with your universal mind or God for guidance and protection. You could say that you are just bypassing the middlemen, your guides and angels. You can also use all of the above, your internal and external and universal minds all at the same time. The more you feel grounded, in balance, and protected, the freer you will be to explore the unconscious regions of your mind.

A Ground-Level Exercise

Now it's time to add something more to your self-hypnotic trance technique. This exercise will take you a step beyond your comfort zone and put you in touch with your guidance and belief systems. Once you are comfortable and confident in this self-hypnotic induction, you will be ready to start planning your first past life regression. Just as with the exercises before this one, the more you practice, the more you will become proficient at using it. You may want to memorize, record, or have someone read to you the following self-hypnotic induction. Find a place where others will not interrupt you while you are trying it.

If you are ready, you may get comfortable and loosen your clothing. Take a deep breath, slowly exhale, and continue to do so as you let your eyes focus on the center of your forehead. If you can imagine a relaxing smell, do it as you let yourself prepare to count downward from five to zero to the special place in your unconscious mind. With each breath you are relaxing more and more.

You may begin to feel the connection through the center of your forehead to a peaceful flow of energy that is connected to the guides, angels, or other beings who are there to watch over you. You may feel the peace and love of the universe entering and surrounding your body as you slowly count yourself five to zero, downward into your self-hypnotic trance. You are feeling so comfortable and relaxed as you feel the energy begin to flow over and through you.

◆ FIVE. You are beginning to start your countdown to your special place where you will feel the peaceful and loving energy of the universe surrounding and protecting you. You can feel it slowly spreading down over your head to your shoulders. With each breath, you relax more and more.

◆ FOUR. You are going deeper and deeper. You can feel the peaceful and loving energy spreading all the way down over your arms to your fingers. Your inner and outer guidance systems are there with you as they work with your belief to help you feel balanced, protected, and grounded. With each count you are going deeper and deeper into hypnosis.

◆ THREE. You can now feel the peaceful and loving energy of the universe spreading all the way down to your waist. You have many muscles. Some of them are stiff, and some of them are relaxed. Every time you feel a muscle stiffen up you may relax it, which will help you relax more and more. You can feel yourself sinking deeper and deeper with each breath you take. You are feeling so relaxed and comfortable.

◆ TWO. You are getting closer and closer to your special place deep in your unconscious mind where you will feel totally connected to your belief and guidance systems. You can feel the universal energy spreading all the way down to your knees. You are relaxing more and more and feel the peaceful energy of the universe and your guidance systems watching over and protecting you. With each breath you are going deeper and deeper.

◆ ONE. You are almost there. The peaceful and loving energy is flowing all the way down to your ankles. You are going deeper and deeper with each relaxing breath you take. In a moment you will be all the way down to zero. You will be in your special place deep in your unconscious mind. When you get there, you may feel the peaceful energy flowing over, around, and through your entire body. You will be in balance, grounded and protected by the universal mind, and you will be open to the intuitive energies of the universe connected with you. You will feel your guides, angels, or other beings with you, watching over and protecting you. You will be open to their guidance.

◆ ZERO. You may now feel yourself totally immersed in the peaceful and loving flow of universal energy. You are in your special place deep in your unconscious mind. You feel in balance and grounded by your guides, angels, or beings. You may ask them to help watch over you in every aspect of your life. If you have something that you need help or guidance with, you may ask them for their assistance. Let yourself feel grounded in universal love as you prepare to experience a past life regression that will help you be in tune with your soul's journey. You feel comfortable and ready to have a positive experience when you journey into your past.

You will continue to feel safe and grounded after you count yourself back up to the surface of your conscious mind. You can easily come back to this grounded state every time you experience your self-hypnotic trance. When you're ready, you may count yourself back up to consciousness.

◆ ONE. Continue to breath slowly.

◆ TWO. You are coming slowly back to the surface feeling grounded and in balance.

◆ THREE. You are halfway back.

◆ FOUR. You are almost there. On the next number you make take a deep breath and exhale, open your eyes, and come back to your conscious mind.

◆ FIVE. You are all the way back, grounded and in balance with your belief and guidance systems. The more you practice this technique, the easier it will be to slip into a grounded and relaxing self-hypnotic trance.

The Least You Need to Know

◆ You were born with your belief system already inside you.

◆ Unless you are properly grounded in your belief, it is easy to get out of balance during a past life regression.

◆ You are balanced when you are in tune with your belief and guidance systems.

◆ You have guides, angels, or other beings who watch out for you if you choose to acknowledge and accept them.

◆ Practicing your self-hypnosis grounding technique will help prepare you for any kind of past life regression experience.

Chapter 14

Creating a Travel Plan

In This Chapter

- ◆ Choosing a destination for your past life regression
- ◆ What to look for in your past lives
- ◆ Traveling alone or with the help of a partner
- ◆ Tools that can help you gather information during your regression
- ◆ How long do you want to spend at your destination?

How do you plan when you prepare to go on a trip? Perhaps you are used to going places often and keep a bag of essentials packed and ready. Maybe you seldom travel, and when you do, you find that there are items you wished you had remembered. How much detail do you put into planning?

Do you spend days developing a checklist, or do you put together a rough idea of your plans and hope that you have included everything? Do you make your own trip plans, or do you depend on a travel agency to handle the details? Do you go on package tours, or do you customize your plans to meet your own interests?

Now it's time to start planning your first past life regression. Of course, you may already have naturally been regressing. You have had the opportunity in previous chapters to examine what can influence you from your past lives through your interests, relationships, and even your dreams. Past lives can spill over into virtually every aspect of your current life.

Where Do You Want to Go?

Just as you would prepare for any trip, doing the same for a past life regression can help give you the best opportunity for a positive and fulfilling experience. Usually you travel to a destination for a specific purpose. It may be because of an interest, work, or for relaxation. Many of you combine business and pleasure. The same can be true for a past life regression. You may have a destination that you enjoy or would like to go to currently. Perhaps you would like to go there during a different time period. You can examine the culture, try the foods, experience the music and art or any other thing that you want to. You can immerse yourself in that time in all of your senses, stepping into the imagery of your mind.

Soul Stories

Dean Bennett has a passion for the wilderness. In his book *The Forgotten Nature of New England* (see Appendix B) he identified and visited every place in that region that still remains untouched from the time before the white man first explored it. He literally put himself in a trance and regressed hundreds of years. The reader has a chance to do the same through his descriptive writing.

You may want to visit a specific location, a certain time period, or investigate a culture. You may want to understand a feeling about someone in history whom you have been interested in. You may have done a lot of research already and wonder if you will get any new insights or just make up a regression experience using the information you already have.

Start with a pad of paper (or the computer) and make a list of the places that you would like to visit during a past life regression. You may have several or only one. You may not have any place at the moment that you feel you want to visit. You may have a destination that you do not want to regress to. If you do, make a note of it, but find a place for your first experience that looks like it would be really neat to visit. Just like the special place in your mind, if you are comfortable in your first past life trip, you may be encouraged to continue your regressions.

To get an idea of where you'd like to visit during a past life regression, ask yourself the following questions:

◆ **What place or places in the world would you really like to visit?** Maybe you have visited there several times and feel a special connection to it beyond this current lifetime. You may feel at home again when you are there. It could be somewhere you have never been but have always had a special place in your heart for. You may have read or studied about it. You may have already imagined being there in your mind.

◆ **Is the location you want to visit real or imaginary?** Perhaps the special relaxing place in your unconscious mind is also your regression destination. Bruce always imagined an old farm in Canada with a small apple orchard. When he was a boy, he would drift off in his daydreams and play under the fruit trees. This imaginary place influenced him as an adult to develop his own small backyard orchard. Caring for his trees became a way of briefly leaving the stresses of the world behind. It is the place that he wanted to regress to.

◆ **Is your choice of destination one that you visit in your dreams?** Perhaps you have had a dream of a specific location throughout your life. If you have, you may want to investigate it in a past life regression. So your destinations may come from a real place, an imaginary place, or a dream. These possible destinations may come from your childhood or be somewhere that you have not consciously thought of before. It doesn't make any difference as long as it's a place that seems like an interesting travel destination.

What to Look For

Maybe your reason for visiting a place is to determine where you first learned an emotion, ability, or an interest. It may be to understand a relationship with one or more other people who may be family, friends, or casual acquaintances. Ask yourself a few simple questions to help define what you want to look for in a past life regression:

◆ **What feelings have you had in your life that you would like to know where you first learned them?** These feelings could be something that you long for. It may be the sense that a part of your life is incomplete without understanding why you have those emotions deep inside of you. You may have a feeling of belonging or not belonging, or of being in sync or out of sync with your current place in the world.

◆ **What emotions that are normally out of character for you do you experience from time to time?** These feelings may be triggered by music or other sounds, smells, food, or pictures. You may find yourself suddenly reacting in a way that you did not anticipate. If this is the case, make a note of it as a part of your checklist of something to look for in your travels.

◆ **Do you want to investigate the history of some of your relationships through past life regressions?** You may have one or more friends or family members that you know you have been with before in different roles. It may be an attraction to someone that goes beyond normal. If this is so, add relationships to your list of things you are looking for.

You may want to go back and connect with the roots of an artistic or athletic ability. You might want to use a regression to enhance your natural, born ability. You could look for a connection with psychic talent from another lifetime.

Kelly went to a past life regression specialist with a specific list of what she wanted to experience during her session. Much to her disappointment, her soul and her unconscious mind had other ideas as to her travel destination. She wound up someplace completely different than she wanted. At the same time, this was the place she *needed* to go.

It's also possible that you don't have an idea yet of anything that you might want to research in a past life regression. In that case, perhaps you could regress to a time when you can apply what you learn to your current life situation. Remember that your soul will already have an agenda for you to investigate that your conscious mind may not yet be aware of. Just the fact that you are reading this book indicates that there is something in one of your past lives that will be helpful for you to learn now. You will have an opportunity in Chapter 17 to review your final preparations.

> **Ageless Insights**
>
> You may feel that you and someone else are soul mates. You know that you've been together before. If so, you can plan to investigate your relationships in one or more past lives. The result may be insights into your current feelings about this person. Be sure to make note of the relationships that you want to investigate in one or more other lifetimes.

Traveling Alone or with a Partner?

Do you like to go places by yourself or with other people? Perhaps you enjoy taking a tour with a whole group of people. If so, you'll want to check out Chapter 24 on having a past life regression party. Right now, though, let's consider whether you would go alone or with someone else.

The first few times you try a past life regression you may want to consider working with a partner by taking turns being the *subject* and the *operator*. There are several positive reasons for doing this. If you have someone who might be interested, you can read this book together and compare how your minds are the same and different. You can help each other practice relaxation and self-hypnosis techniques before you have your first regressions.

> **Words to Remember**
>
> In hypnosis terms, the **subject** is the person who is experiencing a trance state, and the **operator** is the person who is guiding the hypnosis session. The operator's assignment is to ask questions that will help produce the desired information from a regression session. The operator is also a valuable witness to the event.

Besides having the support of someone else when you do a past life regression, a partner can sometimes give you more insights into your experience. They can watch your facial expressions and body language and run a recorder or video camera to capture your regression for you to hear or watch later.

If you are working with someone, you both may come up with some good ideas for questions to ask and directions to go during your regression. Together you can develop a script that will help guide you. Chapter 16 will talk more about scripts. In the meantime you can make notes about what you would like your partner to help you look for in your travels. You can decide if you want to record and playback questions you want to ask yourself, or have someone else read them. If you have a partner, he or she may also be able to ask questions about your responses during the regression that will clarify your answers.

Psychic Edgar Cayce used someone to conduct his self-hypnotic trance sessions. He would first put himself into hypnosis and then open up to questions about the subject he was doing a reading for. In the beginning, sometimes the people who conducted the sessions would experiment with him to test his abilities or gain information for themselves. Finally his wife, Gertrude, became the one who conducted the readings while his secretary, Gladys, transcribed the information.

Another benefit of having a partner is to help you move out of any past life images that might be unsettling. It's good to have them available to remind you that you can open your eyes and come back to your conscious mind if you want to. Sometimes, if your partner is psychic, they may be able to actually see into your regression images and remember things that you forgot to note during and after your trance.

It may not be an option for you to work with someone else, or even if you do, after a few sessions, you may want to continue the work by yourself. That's okay. You will probably approach the session differently by yourself than with someone else. You may choose to record your induction and the script for your past life regression or memorize it and talk to yourself internally or out loud during your session. You can experience the regression in silence, or you can verbally describe and record the details of your travel.

You may choose to use a form of automatic writing to experience your past life regression. This means that you would place yourself in front of your computer or sit comfortably with a pen or pencil in your hand poised and ready to write on a piece of paper. Once you have induced yourself into your self-hypnotic trance, you can suggest that you will begin to let your fingers write down the images that come from your unconscious mind.

> **Karmic Cautions** _____
>
> Past life regression specialists have a lot of training and are experts in guiding their clients into their past lives for both discovery and therapeutic reasons. This book is not designed to provide the education to become a professional, and your regression sessions are not meant to take the place of any serious issues you may have in solving the karma of your past. At the same time, this can be an exciting adventure for you and your partner.

Have you decided whether or not you want to travel alone? If you want a partner, have you approached them yet? If not, now is the time to do it. If you are traveling alone, then you are one step closer to beginning your journey.

Tools to Bring with You

Now that you have made some notes about where you want to travel and what you would like to experience, you may want to consider what other tools are workable for you. A couple of the tools you have already heard about. They are the tape or video recorders to capture any reaction, either verbal or physical, to the images you encounter during your regression. You also can use automatic writing, which I discussed in the previous section.

Another potential tool to help you get unconscious soul memories is the pendulum, which is a weight such as a crystal, a pendant, or anything that can dangle from a chain or string. It could be as simple as a washer on the end of a string or as intricate as a gold watch on a chain. You may have heard of the word *mesmerize*, which means "to hypnotize." Anton Mesmer (1734–1815) is often associated with using a dangling watch or pendulum to induce a hypnotic trance. This technique, actually developed later on, is still called "mesmerizing."

The use of the pendulum is a form of psychic knowing called dowsing. Dowsing is the ancient art of divination, or determining information through one of several different devices controlled by the unconscious and universal minds of the individual holding them. Dowsing tools include "Y" rods or sticks, "L" rods, bobbers, and the pendulum. For those of you who would like to learn more about dowsing, visit www.dowsers.org on the Internet.

If you want to try using a pendulum, find something you already have or make something simple that is light enough to hold comfortably between your thumb and first finger and yet heavy enough to swing freely in different directions. Once you have selected your pendulum, try holding the string, chain, or cord with the thumb and first finger of either one of your hands. Let the weight dangle about six to eight inches and hold it out in front of you about a foot to eighteen inches in front of your face with your hand at eye level.

Now ask the pendulum to show you the direction of "yes" and watch what happens. It could start moving in one of several directions, swinging back and forth from side to side, moving toward and away from you, or rotating clockwise or counterclockwise. It may start very slowly, or it may become very active right away. If it doesn't respond, don't worry. Practice concentrating on it moving in a direction that you choose. Then ask it to go in a different direction. When you have accomplished this, ask the pendulum to come to a stop. Did it work for you?

Once you get comfortable with the movement of your pendulum and have found the direction of yes, ask it to show you no. Each time you try dowsing with a pendulum, yes and no may be different movements. Therefore, you will want to go through this procedure whenever you begin to dowse. When you have established this, ask the pendulum if you can receive answers from your soul memories regarding the past life information you are looking for.

Obviously you will need to ask questions that can be answered with yes and no answers.

If you have a partner, you can prepare a list of questions for them to ask you. If that is the case, or even if you are alone and use a video camera, you can answer with your eyes closed, letting the pendulum go its own way. You can ask your questions out loud or silently. Dowsing may be a useful tool for you to take with you in your past life travels.

Ageless Insights

The real benefit of using a pendulum in conjunction with a past life regression is to help you get information that you are having trouble imaging otherwise. For instance, if you felt that you had lived in a specific location or time, and you could find no information through normal regression, you could use the pendulum as a tool to answer your questions.

You may want to use music or other sounds to help you go back in time. For instance, you may have the feeling that you lived during a time where music from that period was important to you. Playing some period background selections may help you deepen your regression trance. Certain sounds such as the ocean may help bring you back to a lifetime connected with the nearness of water. Smells, tastes, visual images, and even something you might wear may also prove to be useful tools in helping you regress into one or more of your past lives.

How Long Should You Spend There?

What is the right length of time to spend experiencing a past life regression? The answer is that there is no exact amount of time, but at first, generally no more than a half hour to an hour. Each time will vary according to the level of trance you achieve and the amount and clarity of the information images that you experience.

The most important thing is that you are comfortable in the time you spend there during and after the regression. You might want to come back and revisit an uncomfortable situation after you get used to the images that you are experiencing. When you do this, you are actually desensitizing the impact of the images so that each time you are able to work with them a little more easily. You can even choose different views of the same images to make the experience easier.

Remember that your regression may be similar to going to the movies or reading a good book. There may be times when you feel all the emotions that are going on in the story. Have you ever been so involved that your heart rate speeds up, your hands become sweaty, or you feel the sadness or happiness of the characters? If you have a health condition where you are not supposed to become excited, you should check with your doctor first to make sure that a regression experience will be all right for you.

> **Karmic Cautions** _____
>
> Prolonged periods of intense emotional feelings can be unhealthy for you. Your physical, mental, and spiritual bodies can all be impacted. Edgar Cayce was told by a reading of his own health that he needed to cut back on his self-hypnotic trance time near the end of his life, but by then he had become much in demand, and it was impossible to keep up with the requests. He ended up with health problems that are thought to have shortened his life. This does not mean that you will experience the same exertion as Cayce did, but it's always wise to be aware of your own health condition.

Some people who go into a deep self-hypnotic regression may experience some physical discomfort during and afterward. Feeling cool or cold is fairly common. This can result from being very relaxed and staying in one position for a period of time. If it occurs during the regression and is because of an image that is being experienced at that time, you or your partner can make a suggestion to feel warm. You can also move away from that image to a warmer one.

If you consistently have a problem with being cold during or after a regression, you may want to have a blanket over you or ready to cover you if you need it. You can also address the temperature problem in the suggestions you use in your script. Tell yourself that you will be warm and comfortable as you relax in your deep trance and that you will wake up calm, comfortable, warm, and relaxed. Once you get used to your routine, then you will be prepared for temperature changes while and after you travel.

Another sensation that may be experienced during but especially after your past life regression is that of heaviness in all or part of your body. You may feel as if you gained 50 pounds while you were away. This result may stem from the depth of your self-hypnotic trance. If you use words such as *sinking* and *deeper*, you may wake up with these feelings if you do not remove them when you come back to the surface of your conscious mind. Other feelings such as lightheadedness, dizziness, or even nausea can result from past life images while you are in deep trance.

It's important to be able to move away from these images without taking the feelings with you. A death scene can also bring a regression to a close if you are uncomfortable with the images you encounter. Again, it's always important to feel confident that you will be able to come back to the surface of your conscious mind any time you want. All of these factors will influence the length of time that you travel back in time.

If you are using automatic writing, you may be able to spend a little longer in trance. In fact, you may even be able to break up your session by moving about or sipping some tea, etc. and going right back into your regression when you start again. The more you let yourself experiment with past life regression, the better you will understand the right length of time for you to travel in your mind. Just remember to focus on your current life when you are not in a regression trance. It is sometimes easy to forget the reality of the moment.

The Least You Need to Know

◆ You can choose your destination, but be prepared for changes in travel plans.

◆ You can define what you want to look for by considering the feelings and abilities that you currently experience.

◆ Working with a partner can help you gather and record your information.

◆ Many different tools are available to help you delve into your soul's memory.

◆ You can expect your regression to vary in time length.

What to Do When You Get There

In This Chapter

◆ Using your mental DNA in your past life regression

◆ Getting used to the experience

◆ Brushing up on your detective skills

◆ The characters in your regression

◆ The themes of your past lives

At one time or another almost everyone has imagined what it would be like to be a detective and solve a mystery. Public interest has even led to the development of mystery dinner theaters where the audience participates in determining who did it. Some of the most popular television shows are about detectives or invite the audience to be a part of the hunt for the criminals. *America's Most Wanted* and *Unsolved Mysteries* are two examples of these types of shows.

Well, now you have a chance to take a crash course in gathering evidence. It's time to get yourself ready to start piecing together the clues of your past lives. You are becoming the expert detective of your own soul as you prod its memory and search for evidence of your past.

Put Your Mental DNA to Use

The more you understand your mental DNA, the better you will become at recognizing the clues from your own images of the past. This simple review of your five senses, discussed in detail in Chapter 8, will remind you of the way your mind works and how to use that knowledge to gather information that your unconscious mind reveals about your soul memories that you might otherwise miss. It's often impossible to gather all the clues at first. Your unconscious mind records images in its memory that your conscious mind is not aware of. This will be the same for you when you go back into a past life. The way you experience the event will be different from anyone else's.

Your visual sense is usually one of your strongest senses. The way you see the events of your past will determine how many details you can recall. If you are very visual and can retain the images in your unconscious mind, they will always be there to revisit once your conscious mind is aware of them. A visual person has the ability to supply a great many details.

Ageless Insights

It's easy to tell if a visual author has written a book. Sometimes they set the scene so vividly that you begin to wish they would just get to the point rather than focus on the background details. For the visual reader, however, these graphic descriptions help transport them into the story. You may have this same ability to report on the scenes in your past lives.

If you are not a strong visual person, you can anticipate that you will not see the vivid details from your past life regressions. You may, however, be just as vivid in one or more of the other sense images. Remember that there are two different ways of being visual. The first is by detaching yourself from the image as if you were watching it from a distance or on a screen. Your other senses do not come into play as much from this vantage point. The other type of visual image is experiential, where you find yourself fully involved in your past life experience. A partner can be a big help here as they can ask you what you are doing and how you feel. By yourself, you may have to rely on how you remember the experience afterward.

How well you can hear sounds in your past life regression is also very important. If you can, you will have the ability to listen to conversations that may take place and be able to repeat them so that they can be recorded for later evidence. You may be able to gather information from different sounds such as running water or wind. You may be able to hear a battle as it is fought or music as it plays out in your past life. There are so many clues that can be gathered if you have the gift of hearing what your unconscious mind is remembering from your soul's memories.

Feelings and emotional images are also a great source of clues. Temperatures and the touch of something in your regression can help deepen your trance. A past life regression specialist often uses the kinesthetic sense for just that purpose. They may spend a lot of time on small details at first to help sharpen the focus on the regression images. Once this is done, the subject can easily be moved around throughout that lifetime.

Perhaps you can put yourself in the mind of a character from a soul memory of your past and rediscover how you thought in another lifetime. Sometimes the smallest clue that is not understood at the moment will mean a great deal later on as you solve your regression mystery.

Imagine that you could sit down to a 2,000-year-old meal. If you have a good sense of taste or smell, you can. All you have to do is step back into the regression scene and experience it. You can take in the aromas and textures as you describe in as many sense images as you have what is taking place around you. The more you use your natural mental DNA in your past life regression, the better the opportunity to collect a vast amount of clues about the mysteries of your soul.

> **CAUTION**
>
> **Karmic Cautions**
>
> Chances are you will not be able to produce clues in all five of your senses. If you focus on the senses that are weakest for you, you may get frustrated with the regression process. If you go with your strengths and trust them, you should have much more satisfying results. There is no one who knows your mental DNA better than you.

Just Allow Yourself to Experience

Remember, you may not be able to experience images in some of your senses. You may become discouraged when you try to follow the method of someone who uses images in senses that are not strong for you. It is usually developed around the way their mental DNA works and not the way yours does. That doesn't mean that you will not be able to experience exactly like someone else, but the message is to be true to your own way of imaging.

A good detective will just collect the data and then mull it over, constantly comparing and working at fitting the pieces of his case together. Perhaps you have seen an investigation scene in a movie where the detectives have a large board and are constantly arranging and rearranging the information they collect. As you compile your own notes, you will be doing the same thing.

Remember, if you don't get all the information you want the first time, you can go back. There is no need to try and force clues to the surface of your mind before they are ready. At first you may gather a great many details within a very small range of imagery. If that is all you have to work with at the time, then work with it. Each time you regress, you may bring out a little more. Always be on the lookout for a new piece of information that you might discover.

Experiencing a past life regression is like going to a movie, only it's in your mind. To a certain extent you are at the mercy of your soul. The images that play in front of you may be pleasant or unpleasant, happy or sad, funny or serious, and even provoke you into examining a part of your life and your beliefs. You can stay or leave your theater any time you want.

You do have another option that a movie doesn't. You can change your scenes, come in for a close-up, or pull back for a broad view. You can use all of your senses. You cannot rewrite the play that is your soul, but you can look at it from many angles and perspectives.

If you have ever acted in a play, you know what getting into character means. Many of the great movie stars spend months preparing for a role. They study the history of the character whom they are going to play and even begin to imagine what it would be like to be that person. They change the way they speak, their hair, and may even gain or lose weight. When they finally act out their role onscreen they are totally experiencing what it is like to be the person whom they are portraying. You are the actor in your own play. The more you get into the characters of your past, the more you will go with the experiences of your soul.

As you probably know, some movies start slow, and just as in a good book, it takes time to set the scenes for the plot. You may have wanted to get up and leave, but for some reason you stayed. After all, it costs a lot of money to go to the movies today. You may have gritted your teeth and decided to tough it out. As you continued to watch, suddenly you found yourself engrossed in the story. By the end you forgot how you felt about it in the beginning. Again, you may want to enter a past life regression with the expectation that the story may take some time to get going. The more you are willing to just go with the experience, the better the chance of your getting your money's worth out of your performance.

You Can Be a Detective in Your Own Mind

Are you ready to be a detective? If you are, how do you begin to collect the clues to your case? Of course, you already have gotten started. You have been going to detective school as you have been reading this book. You have begun making notes and deciding on possible areas to investigate. You are almost ready to visit your first scene. Now is the time to make a checklist that will help you gather the information that you seek.

" " **Soul Stories**

Patty wanted to do a past life regression to learn about a health issue she had. She came out surrounded with purple, and dark symbols were coming through the color passing into her body. The regression took her back to when the purple was inside of her—back when Jesus was alive. As a follower, she was filled with spiritual guidance, represented by the color purple, the symbol of her healing abilities. Before she was crucified, she lost her faith and the color. Her regression showed her how she could reconnect with her faith again and visualize the healing color purple entering her body and pushing out the negative symbols. This imagery provided a way for her to use her mind to help her doctors promote healing of her blood disorder.

When you experience a past life regression, what are you going to look for first? You already have an idea from your notes. Are you comfortable with the way you image in all your five senses? You may want to start collecting your information through the sense that you are the most sure of. For instance, if you are visual, start with what you can see. Make as many mental notes as possible, or have your partner ask you for visual descriptions. If you rely on your hearing or feeling senses, start with them. If you are strong in more than one sense, after you have focused your first images, move to your other senses and report or make notes on what you are experiencing.

Start with a small area or view. Collect as many details from that place as possible before moving on. This technique actually will help you deepen your self-hypnotic trance as you sharpen your focus on your regression experience. Be patient and go with what you are experiencing. You may not even go beyond this spot in your first regression.

Do you remember a television show called *Columbo?* The main character was a detective dressed in a rumpled trench coat who came across as unsophisticated and bumbling. The criminal often dismissed Columbo's ability to solve the case, and yet the detective would keep coming back and reasking question upon question until the culprit was tricked into admitting guilt. You may think you miss a great many details at first. Be patient, and like Columbo, keep coming back and asking more questions until you have solved the case.

Detectives often take photos of the crime scene. They can study the photos to help them look for visual clues they may have missed when they were first investigating. They spend hours pouring over the evidence, trying out different scenarios in their minds. When they have a new idea, they look for more clues in that direction. They are using a thought process called *divergent thinking* as compared to *convergent thinking*.

Words to Remember

Convergent thinking means that you focus on only one objective and continually work toward reaching it. The problem with this is that if you reach a dead end, you are stuck and have no place to go. **Divergent thinking** means that when you get stuck, you begin to look for other directions to take. It may seem to you that you are going sideways or backward, but eventually you will find a way to go beyond where you were. In the meantime, the convergent thinker has given up.

Some detectives will stay on a case for years, long after others have given up and even forgotten about it. They may have files filled with clues, or perhaps there was little evidence to gather at first. As they continue to let their unconscious mind work, even if they are busy on another case, there is always action taking place. They may wake up with an idea that surfaced to their conscious mind. Now they plug it into their investigation. It may help them move forward, or it may not, but sooner or later they will be back on their case with a renewed vigor.

Your unconscious mind will do the same thing after your past life regression. It will take the pieces of information collected and play with them while your conscious mind is occupied with something else. Something that may not make sense at first will begin to make sense as you keep the files on your past lives open. Keep your note pad or recorder with you ready to make a note of the ideas your unconscious mind sends up to you.

Soul Stories

Many people who experience a past life regression continue to fill in details of their experience long afterward. Sometimes the details don't seem to fit, as in John's case. At first, the dates he discovered during his regression conflicted with his own time of birth. He later realized he was tapping into a different past life than he had thought, and everything finally made sense to him.

If you have even a little artistic skill, make sketches of what you encounter in your regressions. Just as with your other observations, focus on the scene that is the easiest at first. Put in as many details as possible. You are, in effect, making a composite sketch of what you are witnessing. Once you have the basics down, you can always go back and sketch in more information. Think of the flow of your unconscious information like priming a water pump. In order to get the water going, you have to put a little bit back in the line first. Always have a little bit of information to work with in your regression that will help get the information flowing again. The more it's used, the easier it becomes to start it again the next time you look for clues.

Study the Cast of Characters

A good detective not only takes note of the scene but of the different characters that are encountered during the investigation. Profiles are developed on each one. What is each character's personality type? How do they think? What are their habits? What are their interests and likes and dislikes? There are many questions you can ask about each of the characters you encounter in your past life regressions. You might begin with who, what, when, where, and why:

◆ WHO are the characters that you want to profile? Are they someone that you recognize from dreams or other images from your unconscious mind? You will want to gain as much information as possible on their relationship to other characters in your regression, if there are others. Who is the most important character you encounter?

◆ WHAT are their physical descriptions and their approximate ages? What are their personalities? What do you see them doing? What do you hear them saying? What are their emotions? What do they smell and taste? What is their role in your regression? What is their relationship to you, or are any of them related to you in a past life?

◆ WHEN do the characters live in your regression? Can you determine the time period? If you are able to follow the main character through that lifetime, when does something significant happen that relates to that life or to your life today? In your character profiles, you can communicate verbally with your partner or to your recorder. You can sketch their likeness, and also recall your experience later. Your unconscious mind will work on the material while you are concentrating on other things.

◆ WHERE are your characters located during your regression? Get the best description that you can. Remember to consider all these questions with all five of your senses, using the strongest one first. You may want to ask yourself where the personality of the main character in your regression fits into your life.

◆ WHY are the characters that you are profiling important to the case you are working on? How do they relate to your life? It is possible that at first you will find a character popping up who seems to be unrelated to what you are working on. If this happens, just collect all the information and have it ready to review when and where you think it will fit.

Another popular crime detection television show is *Profiler*. The main character uses a combination of research and psychic intuition to put her in the mind of the one she is trying to apprehend. You have the opportunity to do the same when you experience a regression. You can put yourself in the mind of the character in your past life. You can feel as they felt and apply the knowledge to help you solve the case of your soul's lives.

Ageless Insights

Look for similarities in different characters in more than one lifetime. Remember the principles of karma: Unresolved business will keep coming back until the lessons are learned. You may be able to trace the karma from one lifetime to another following the similarities in the different characters that you come in contact with during your regressions.

It may be possible for you to put yourself in the mind of more than one character in a lifetime. How can that be? It means that you may be able to draw upon the past life memories of other souls besides your own. This is sometimes referred to as collective unconsciousness—the place in the universe where it is believed all thoughts and experiences from the past are recorded. You'll recall from Chapter 4 that Edgar Cayce called this the Akashic Records. You'll learn more about this in Chapter 20 after you have experienced your first past life regression. If you encounter this situation before then, just go with the experience and collect the information.

Everything you observe about the characters in your past can be important clues, as well as anything you experience through their eyes. Every piece of the puzzle that you can collect and have ready and waiting to put in place when its position is recognized will help you gain a better understanding of your soul's purpose. Remember that all the pieces might not fit right away, and all of the characters may not seem to relate, but chances are that they will sooner or later.

Follow the Story's Theme Wherever It Goes

Every one of you will have different reasons for wanting to investigate your past lives. You may have a pressing need to discover something in your past that relates to you now and the route your life will take in the future, or you may have only a casual interest in finding out about your past. You may be considering studying the techniques of past life regression for the purpose of becoming a past life regression specialist as a part of your vocational work.

You may not want to invest a lot of time and energy into investigating your past lives. You really can go at your own speed. There may be periods in your life when you can devote more time to studying your past, or you may be pulled in many different directions. You can start and stop any time you want. Just remember that the better you make notes or record your regression sessions, the easier it will be to get back on the track of your soul's history when you begin again.

Good detective work takes time, energy, and patience. It takes the willingness to follow leads wherever they go. There might be many dead ends before something is discovered that advances the case forward. Even then the path may seem to dry up, and the detective is back to square one. Sometimes it seems as if the case will never be solved. Just as in a busy life, a detective may be working on more than one case at a time. Priorities need to be established.

Have you ever seen the plate-balancing vaudeville act? The goal is for the performer to twirl a plate fast enough on a stick so that it will stay balanced and not slow down, fall off, and crash to the floor. He is supposed to balance up to 10 or more plates on sticks. The trick starts easily enough, but by the time they are all spinning, the performer is racing back and forth trying to keep them all going at once. You may feel the same way about your life. You are the plate-balancer, and it is hard to see everything at once, including your past lives.

> **Karmic Cautions**
>
> The themes of your past lives can relate to the karma or unfinished business that you have the opportunity to resolve during this lifetime. The karma itself may interfere with giving you the time and energy to solve it. In other words, you may be so caught up in your life play that you don't realize that the same theme is playing itself over again.

Consider for a moment the benefit of taking a little time each day to experience a relaxation exercise as you have practiced in this book. It could be an instant one, or one that takes a few minutes. It could be just before going to bed or the first thing in the morning. Go to your favorite place in your mind.

This is the time to think about your past lives and how they may relate to your present life. It only takes a moment, and you may ask your belief to supply you with more clues after your conscious mind has gone on to the other happenings in your life. If you consider doing this, you are actually staying with the theme of your soul's path. Your unconscious mind will then help bring you the insights when it is time for you to make note of them.

The Least You Need to Know

- ◆ Use your mental DNA image strengths to help gather regression information.
- ◆ Let yourself experience whatever takes place during a past life regression.
- ◆ Imagine that you are the detective on your own past life case.
- ◆ Every character you encounter may be important.
- ◆ Stick with the regression themes during and after the experience.

Part 4

Going Through the Window

Okay, mind detectives, it's time to open the window and enter into the experience. You've finished your training and you are ready for your first encounter with the past. Before you go, you'll be given some important dialogue to help you enter the scene.

You will go back in time and meet the characters in your past life adventures. You will use your skills and ability to image to collect important clues. When you return from your research in the field, you will organize and analyze the material you have just retrieved. You may decide to revisit the same location to look for more past life clues.

You will learn about one of the most important past life regression stories of the twentieth century and how to decide what is truth or fiction in your own case. Get ready. It's time to lift the veil and step through the window into your past.

Chapter 16

Past Life Regression Scripts

In This Chapter

◆ Reading about your past lives in the library of your unconscious mind

◆ Going to a movie theater that features a memory of your soul in your unconscious mind

◆ Watching a television program about a past life in your unconscious mind

◆ Learning to count yourself back in time

◆ Tracing a feeling to where you first experienced it

◆ Which regression technique works best for you?

In this chapter you will find several different ways to experience your past life regression. As you read each section you can decide which technique you want to try first. You probably already have a tendency toward one or another.

Do you often go to the library, the movies, or watch television? If you do, with a little self-hypnosis you should feel right at home traveling back in time. If you start by imagining something you enjoy doing, it will make it easier for you to experience the images you encounter during your past life regression. In other words, any way that you are already comfortable imagining a story is okay for you.

You can adapt any of the following scripts to fit your own way of regressing. Each time you try one out, you can continue to make adjustments to it. Eventually you will probably be able to reduce your induction time as you learn to relax and enter your self-hypnotic trance. Each technique is a vehicle for helping you enter and achieve a past life regression.

Going to the Library

Do you go to the *library* for research or for pleasure? Do you have a home library? Perhaps you like to read in bed or a favorite chair. If you do, and it is possible, that may be a good place to experience your past life regression. If being there is impossible, you may be able to remember a positive reading experience and imagine going there in your mind to use a library regression induction. If you are ready, you may give the library regression technique a try.

Words to Remember

Your definition of a **library** may be totally different than anyone else's. It could be a real place or one that you imagine in your unconscious mind. You may find that you have one book of your soul's memories or a series of books, each featuring one of your past lives.

Find a comfortable place where you will not be interrupted. If you are working alone, you may want to record and play back the induction, or if you have a partner, you may have them read it to you. You can rewrite it to fit the way you relax and imagine. Start in with your relaxation exercise and include your belief and guides to help you with the direction in which you will travel. Just read the following induction without fully experiencing it to see how it might work for you in the next chapter.

Take a deep breath and slowly exhale. Do this a couple more times. Let your eyes go out of focus as you slowly breathe in and out. You may be aware that there are many muscles throughout your entire body. Some of them are stiff, and some of them are relaxed already. Every time you relax a muscle, you may feel yourself relaxing more and more. For a moment imagine what it is like to be in your special comfortable place deep inside your unconscious mind. Slowly breathe in, and as you do, feel the experience of being there with all your five different senses.

In a few moments you may begin counting slowly downward from five to zero. When you get to zero, you will be in a very special library deep in your unconscious mind. This library is filled with many different volumes of books. Each one is about a special past life that your soul has experienced. When you get there, you may select one that is appropriate for your past life regression. If you want, you may ask your guides or angels for help in choosing the right one. You feel very relaxed and comfortable as you prepare to start counting backward into a deep self-hypnotic regression trance in the library of your mind. You may feel and hold the book if you want to and let it open to the right page.

You may end your past life regression at any time by taking a deep breath, exhaling, opening your eyes, and coming back to the surface of your conscious mind. Tell yourself that you may always have a positive experience even though you may witness things that might seem negative. You will come back to the surface of your conscious mind relaxed, refreshed, and comfortable, whether you choose to stop early or finish your regression. All the information you find in the books of your past lives can be used positively as you learn more about the journey of your soul. If you are ready to go to the library of your mind, you may now close your eyes, take a deep relaxing breath, exhale, and begin to count yourself down.

- ◆ FIVE. You can feel yourself sinking deeper and deeper into your relaxing self-hypnotic trance. You are beginning your journey to the library of your unconscious mind. You are going deeper and deeper, and relaxing more and more.

- ◆ FOUR. You are now going farther down and getting closer and closer to the library of your unconscious mind. You are relaxing more and more as you slowly breathe in and out. You feel very comfortable and look forward to choosing a volume of your past life stories.

- ◆ THREE. You are now halfway there. You are going deeper and deeper into hypnosis. You feel the library getting closer and closer. You are very comfortable and relaxed.

- ◆ TWO. Breathe slowly in and out as you go deeper and deeper. You look forward to entering the library of your unconscious mind. In a few moments you will be there. You are only two steps away.

- ◆ ONE. You are almost there. You feel relaxed and comfortable and surrounded by your belief, your guides, and your angels. You feel warm and positive and ready to select a volume on one of your past lives. Now count slowly from five to zero and let yourself go into a deep, relaxing self-hypnotic trance. Five, four, three, two, and one.

- ◆ ZERO. You are now in the library of your unconscious mind. Using your five senses, let yourself become comfortable with your surroundings. You may see the books, feel them, and even smell the material they are made of. Take a moment to select a volume and hold it in your hands.

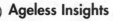

Ageless Insights

When you open your book and start to read, you may see the images of the story. You can step into the minds of one or more of the characters. You may experience your story in all of your five senses. You can re-read any part of the story you want.

You are now ready to open a book on one of your past lives. You know that any time you need or want you can always close the book, take a deep breath, exhale, open your eyes, and come back to the surface of your conscious mind, calm, relaxed, and feeling positive about your regression experience.

This is a sample script that you can use for your library regression. The next portion, your actual past life regression, will be in the next chapter. The more prepared you are before you experience your regression, the better the chances are that it will be positive and productive.

Movies of Your Mind

If you like to go to the movies, you may want to consider using a movie theater of the mind induction for your past life regression. The beginning relaxation exercise and countdown procedure will be about the same as the library induction. Here is a sample of how you would create and use this type of self-hypnotic induction.

Once you are relaxed and comfortable, you may begin counting downward from five to zero. When you get to zero, you will be in the movie theater of your unconscious mind. You will be able to experience the film that you select about one of your past lives in all of your five different senses.

You will notice that this is a very special movie theater. You can watch the action or you can step into the play and experience what it's like to be one or more of the characters. You can change the view by zooming in or out, turn the sound up and down, and even experience the smells and tastes of the movie of your past life regression.

Any time you need to or want to, you can stop the movie, take a deep breath, exhale, and come back to your conscious mind feeling relaxed and positive. You can always turn down disturbing sounds and move forward beyond a scene that might disturb you. You are in charge of your own movie in your unconscious mind.

Every time you go to the movie theater of your unconscious mind you can select a different film or one that you have seen before. You can replay them as many times as you want. Each time you will notice something that you may have overlooked before.

I Saw It on TV

Another effective technique to help you regress into a past life is to watch television in your unconscious mind. This is the same concept as going to the movies, but you will imagine a television instead. If you frequently watch television, this might be a more natural way for you to visit a past life.

Again, just as with the other regressions, you would experience a basic relaxation exercise to begin your self-hypnotic induction. You will count yourself down from five to zero and when you get to your unconscious trance level, you will imagine that you are watching a television set. It could be your own TV, or it could be the big screen one that you wished you had for watching your past life program.

You may choose a comfortable chair or a bed for the regression experience. You can actually be there when you do your regression or you can imagine the feeling of being there. Imagining something familiar to you like a television is a good way to help deepen your self-hypnotic trance.

If for any reason you need or want to turn off your past life television program, you can push the off button in your mind, take a deep breath, exhale, open your eyes, and come back to the surface of your conscious mind, relaxed and positive. You can always change a scene or turn down the volume and other senses whenever you are uncomfortable with your regression experience.

When you count yourself down to zero, you may feel the control "zapper" in your hand. This control is special. You can turn your volume up and down, as well as alter the images in your other senses. You can zoom in and out for the best view. You can turn the emotions up and down and feel the temperature and textures in your past life program. You can also enhance the smells and tastes that are in your regression, stop the action, and replay it any time you want.

When you are ready, you may select the proper channel to watch the program on a past life of yours. Just imagine that you can feel the controls in your hand. Relax and enjoy a program featuring one of your past lives.

You may like to watch videotapes or DVDs on your television set. If you do, you can combine the library and television techniques. You may go to the video library of your

> **Soul Stories**
>
> Tim was an avid television viewer. He even imagined watching a favorite program when he was trying to go to sleep at night. He would just turn the set on in his mind and enjoy his show until he fell asleep. It was a natural way for him to experience a past life regression. He especially liked using the controls to help him enhance his images from his unconscious mind.

unconscious mind and select the past life album to watch. Just put it in, take the controls in your hand, and start the program. You will be able to work the controls of your regression the same way as in the television method.

You may have a home theater—a special place where you can get the experience that you would when you go to the movies. You may have a great sound system, a big screen, and comfortable chairs. You may even have the smell of fresh, popped popcorn. You can imagine such a place deep in your unconscious mind if you want to. You can combine any of these techniques to create the one that works the best for you.

Going Backward in Time

Another technique to help you go into past life regression is to count yourself back into a different lifetime. In this induction you would journey through your unconscious mind to a place where the memory of your soul is kept. You could look your past up in the Akashic Book of Records, you can update the old book to a contemporary computer system, or you can just step into a past life experience. As in the other methods, you can mix and match to find the best one for you. The key is to be patient and go with the experience.

In this countdown you would use different wording than in the earlier inductions in this chapter. Always start by getting comfortable and connecting to your belief, your guides, or angels, to ask for the right assistance in your past life regression. Concentrate on your breathing as you focus on your third eye to begin your self-hypnotic trance induction.

At zero you will be at the place where the records of your soul are kept. You always know that any time you want or need to you can take a deep breath, exhale, open your eyes, and come back to the surface of your conscious mind, relaxed, comfortable, and positive about your regression experience. We'll pick the count up at five.

◆ FIVE. You are beginning to slowly count yourself backward from five to zero. With each count you will go farther and farther back to before your current lifetime to another life that will help you where you are at the moment. With each count, you will feel yourself going farther and farther back, feeling relaxed, comfortable, and positive about your past life regression experience.

◆ FOUR. You may feel yourself going back before you were born, journeying out into the universal mind and to the place where the records of your soul are kept. When you reach zero, you will step into a past life that is the right one for you to experience at this moment. You feel yourself going back and back through time.

- THREE. You are going back farther and farther. You are halfway there as you continue to slowly breathe in and out. You are relaxed and comfortable and looking forward to your regression experience.

- TWO. You may have the sensation of floating out of your body as you go back in time. It is a positive feeling, and you feel safe and secure. When you reach zero, you will be able to experience your past life in all of your five senses. You can review and move around in your past life to collect the right information to assist you in this lifetime.

- ONE. You are almost there. You will be able to step into a past life image at zero. You will be able to experience it in all your senses. You can move out of any image that is uncomfortable. The records of your soul are now ready to show you your past.

- ZERO. You are now at a place deep within your mind that is comfortable and relaxing. Your unconscious mind is open to the memories of your soul.

Once you have reached your destination, take some time to adjust to your surroundings. Use your five senses to help deepen your focus. The next chapter will provide the actual past life portion of your script. You can rewrite these samples to fit your own goals.

Soul Stories

Marilyn started her past life regression in a place that was absolutely black. She couldn't see anything. At first she thought there wasn't anything to see, but the past life specialist who was guiding her asked her to put her hand out and feel around her. She felt the rough texture of wood surrounding her. She was in a crate, and as she got closer to the side of the crate, she could see out between the cracks. She was then moved in her past life to a point before she entered the crate. From there her regression was very informative. She had been kidnapped and was being moved to a place where she was eventually sold as a slave.

If your destination is the Akashic Records, after you have arrived, you can use the same concept as the library induction by opening the book to the right lifetime. You might find yourself in a hall with one or more doors. If you do, ask that the right door for your past life regression be opened for you. You may find yourself in a place with modern or futuristic electronics. These can work just as well for you by letting the past life information and experiences take place in a way that is positive and right for you. Sometimes your original concepts may transfer to another way of regressing. If that is the case, just go with the experience.

Where Did That Feeling Come From?

An affect-bridge past life regression is a method that takes an emotion, a relationship, a phobia or fear, or even an ache or pain backward through your life into past lifetimes that had related situations. You can go directly into a past life after the induction or you can regress the feelings of what you want to investigate backward in your current life first, and then back into a past life. It's possible that an affect-bridge regression could take you back through more than one lifetime. You may find that you have had an unresolved karma for quite a while.

To regress into a past life, you can use any of the earlier techniques I mentioned in this chapter, such as the library, the movie theater, or the television. The affect-bridge regression takes you back through a series of images that all relate to a specific physical feeling or emotion. To start, you would experience your relaxation exercise and count yourself down to zero. You will suggest to yourself while you are counting backward that when you get to zero, you will select a lifetime with the information that you are looking for relating to the situation in your current life.

Karmic Cautions

During the regression, some of the feelings you're investigating may be intense or unpleasant, such as a fear or phobia. If so, suggest to yourself that you only experience enough of the unpleasantness to help you find its roots in one of your past lives. You can tune up or down any of your five sense images to help you get the best focus in your regression.

The induction is a little more complicated if you are following the feelings back through this lifetime to a past one. If you remember Malcolm's regression in Chapter 10, he traced his fear of tight places back through his current lifetime to where it began in the Middle Ages. He went to a regression specialist because he had an uncomfortable feeling in his chest from time to time. The specialist bridged him back to several incidents in his life when he had felt that sensation. One was under his parent's old house in a tight place, and another was trying to squeeze between two big rocks. These helped bridge him back to a lifetime where he died being crushed to death with heavy stones.

You will do your basic relaxation induction and count down from five to zero. You may suggest to yourself that when you get to zero, you will be able to bridge your feelings back over your life to your earliest unconscious memory. From there you will bridge it back into a past life that relates to your feelings, and you can use your most comfortable past life regression access method. Don't forget to suggest to yourself that you can always end a past life regression any time you want by taking a breath, exhaling, opening your eyes, and coming back to your conscious mind, relaxed and positive.

Here is an idea for a script that you might use after you have counted yourself down to zero. Think of a time within the past few months when you have had an experience related to the subject that you are researching. Then think of another one within the past year. Now go back a couple years. After you have found one, go back five years. You may think of something else besides your original subject that may be related. If you do, you may want to continue with this new one.

Go back to a memory from about 10 years ago. When you have recalled one, you may go back even farther. Work your way back to the earliest unconscious memory about your regression subject or a related memory. Once you have done this, go back beyond to another lifetime that is related to the reason that you are regressing. You can experience it in the way that is the most comfortable for you.

Choosing the Route That Works Best for You

These are some potential past life regression techniques. It is now time for you to consider which you feel will be the best for you because you know yourself better than anyone else. Now is an excellent time to review the different ideas and try them out in your mind. You may ask yourself which one, if any, feels like it would be the best and most productive for you.

Without going back into a past life regression, use your self-hypnotic trance to imagine watching television, going to a movie, or reading a book. Determine which of the images are the strongest for you. Don't forget to try them out in all your five different senses. Remember, the more you practice, the easier it will be to step into your unconscious mind when you experience regression.

Once you get comfortable with the route to your past lives that is best for you, you will be able to get to your destination much faster. You can develop an anchor to assist you in reentering your trance state. At that time you can go directly to the regression technique that produces the clearest images from your unconscious mind.

Ageless Insights

You may want to design your own induction for experiencing your past lives that is completely different from those listed in this chapter. That is perfectly okay. The main goal is to get you into a self-hypnotic trance that will produce a positive past life experience for you.

The Least You Need to Know

◆ If you are an avid reader, the library technique might be right for you.

◆ Going to the movies is a natural way to watch a film of one of your past lives.

◆ A television program in your unconscious mind is a good way to regress.

◆ You can count yourself back in time.

◆ An affect-bridge regression follows a feeling backward to its beginning.

◆ Experiment with all the techniques to choose the route that's the best for you.

17

Back to the Past: Time for Travel

In This Chapter

- ◆ A review on using self-hypnosis to help you experience your past life regression
- ◆ Deciding how and where you want to go
- ◆ Trying out the television technique
- ◆ Time to experience a past life regression!
- ◆ Coming back to consciousness

You've done all the preparation; it's finally time to try a past life regression. Have you ever waited a long time for something to happen? All along you may have been anticipating and imagining what the experience will be like. Finally the day arrives.

Usually when you are waiting, you develop a certain expectation of what the experience will be like when it happens. That can set you up for a major disappointment when things don't go as you had anticipated. This could easily happen in your past life regression.

The more you give yourself permission to let the regression experience take a natural course into your soul's memory, the better the chance of you not being disappointed. Each of you will have a different adventure and experience in your own way. Have a good journey!

Will Hypnosis Work?

Now that you're actually ready to experience a past life regression, do you think that you will be able to induce yourself into a self-hypnotic trance? Hopefully you have already found that you can experience hypnosis. Just to help make sure that you feel confident in your ability to go into a trance, let's review how to put your script together.

You started with learning to relax. You can do this easily with slow breathing. Next you can focus on your third eye as you let yourself slip into a light and comfortable trance. If you can do this much, hypnosis can work for you. You may never go any deeper than this trance level. That's okay as long as you are willing to go along with what you imagine. In fact, the imagination itself can help you enter into a deeper trance. Just let yourself go with whatever takes place. Wait until later to analyze it.

Words to Remember

A *fantasy prone personality* is someone who imagines a great deal in his or her mind. They are the type that a stage show hypnotist hopes to attract to the show because they are easily hypnotized. They actually are in a trance when they imagine, which is most of the time.

The more you practice relaxing and focusing on your third eye, the easier it will be to enter a self-hypnotic trance the next time. Some people are naturally adept at going into a trance. In fact, there is a term for them. They are called *fantasy prone personalities*.

You have learned how to use a hypnotic trance to visit a special place in your unconscious mind. And you learned about your mental DNA and how to determine your strengths and weaknesses. The more you are comfortable and trust them, the better the chance for a productive regression.

You have learned that hypnosis is not dangerous and that you can easily come out of your trance state by taking a deep breath, exhaling, opening your eyes, and coming back to the surface of your conscious mind. You also know that if you believe in your inner and outer guidance systems, they are there with you when you have your regression experience. Your angels or guides may play a part in picking the place that you visit in your past. You can also feel the universe surrounding you with peace and love when you go back in time.

You know how to count yourself down to zero, going deeper and deeper into your trance on each count. This does not mean that you will be unaware of sounds around you. You would hear if someone spoke to you or if the phone rang. Remember that hypnosis is not sleep, but a heightened state of focus. It is this focus that helps guide you into your past life regression.

Finally, a good way to begin your past life regression is to get permission from your unconscious mind after you have counted yourself down to zero. Ask this mind to signal when it is all right to begin by letting one of your thumbs or fingers float upward into the air. Let yourself feel it rise. That by itself is a good indication that hypnosis is working for you as you experience a past life regression.

Ageless Insights _____

You will want to decide which type of regression you want to use and have a general destination or goal in mind. Ideally, you should have a recording device ready to turn on before you start. The advantage of a video recorder is that it can record for two hours or more, whereas a cassette tape will need to be changed if you are taping the whole session. Seeing a video replay may also prove to you that hypnosis does work.

Check Your Final Preparations for Your Journey

Have you decided where you want to go first? It is very important to establish goals for your regression session. In previous chapters, you considered how to determine what your travel priorities are. If you are facilitating your own regression, you will want to have them clearly in your mind, or have made a recording to follow as an induction.

Hopefully you have been making notes as suggested while you have been reading throughout this book. If you are working with a partner, you can write your script together. The more details you have for planning your trip, the easier it will go when you are ready for your regression.

It's best to start with one specific destination rather than several. Keep it simple at first. As you get used to experiencing regressions, it will be much easier to get to where you want in a much shorter time. At the same time, be prepared to take a detour. You may go someplace you hadn't planned on visiting. If you don't arrive at the destination you are looking for, don't be disappointed. Some people are expecting to have a perfect regression and get instant satisfaction when they go back in time. Wherever you go, you are usually there for a specific purpose. However, your destination may be someplace unknown. You may just want to have the experience without picking a specific place to find out what it is like to regress into a past life. That is a great reason in itself.

Have you composed your past life regression script yet? You've been doing it all along. It is the language that will help get you to your destination. Once you are there, you are free to examine and experience your past lives in the way that your imagery works best for you. In other words, you are in charge of what takes place whether you have a partner or not. You may not consciously be as much aware of your experiences when you work with a partner as you would if you regress yourself. That doesn't mean the information will be any better either way. You can still have the same insights by yourself.

Soul Stories

When Diane videotaped her past life regression, she was totally unprepared for what she watched afterward. She had wanted to go back and examine a closeness she had always felt with a relative who died before she was born. She found that the relative was herself during the lifetime that she visited. She was under hypnosis so deeply that she had no conscious knowledge when she came out of her trance of what had taken place during her experience. She was amazed at what she saw as she watched herself turn into her distant relative.

To get to where you want to go, follow these steps:

1. Relax, count yourself down from five to zero, and suggest that you are going deeper into self-hypnosis with each count.

2. When you reach zero, use the technique that is best for you to start your past life regression.

3. Take time to focus on your first image in all your five senses, using your strongest first.

4. Step into your regression experience if you can and remember that you can move in and out, forward or back.

5. Begin to look for important pieces of information in that lifetime that relate to your present lifetime.

6. Follow that life through to its end and examine the last thoughts and feelings that your character had that they might have taken with them into other lifetimes, including your current life.

7. Finally, review the theme of that lifetime, look for the people there who might be in your life now in the same or different relationships, and understand how the new knowledge of this past life can help you in a positive way after the regression.

Most stories have a general theme to them. So does a past life. The theme may be the opportunity to resolve karma, or to advance the soul's purpose. As I mentioned in Chapter 15, one of your goals in a regression is to understand how the theme of that lifetime may relate to your current lifetime.

These steps will be illustrated in the sample script coming up. It's time to begin counting back in time. Are you ready to begin?

Begin Your Trance

This script will use the television method (see Chapter 16) to help you experience a past life regression. Remember that you can integrate any technique into your own script that works best for you. You can record it or have your partner read it to you if you wish. If you think you might want to sketch or draw, you should have paper and pencil ready. If you are ready, find a comfortable place to begin.

Take a deep breath of air and slowly exhale. Continue doing this as you feel your body beginning to relax. With each breath you may relax more and more. There are many muscles throughout your body, and some are tight and some are loose. Every time you loosen a stiff muscle, you may relax more and more. You may from time to time hear different sounds such as traffic or talking as you experience your past life regression. If you do, that is all right. You may hear them, but you do not need to focus on them. You may focus on your third eye and the peaceful and loving energy of the universe.

As you continue to slowly breathe in and out, you may feel yourself relaxing more and more. You may feel the peaceful and loving energy of the universe beginning to flow through your body and surround you. You feel connected with your belief and your inner and outer guidance systems. Your guides and angels are with you, watching over and protecting you. You feel positive, safe, and secure. You know that any time you want, you may always take a deep breath, exhale, open your eyes, and come back to the surface of your conscious mind, feeling positive and relaxed.

In a few moments, you may slowly start counting down from five to zero. As you do, you will go deeper and deeper into a relaxing and peaceful self-hypnotic trance with each count. If you are ready, it is time to let yourself begin to experience your self-hypnotic trance.

Ageless Insights

Notice that many words such as *relax* are repeated over and over. There is a purpose for that. Each time you say or hear them, let yourself relax a little more. Repeating the words helps your unconscious mind accept their meaning.

- FIVE. If your eyes have not closed yet, you may let them close now. Continue to breathe slowly in and out as you begin to feel yourself going into a relaxing and positive hypnotic trance. You may focus on your special place as you count downward and experience your positive images in all of your five senses. With each image you will experience them stronger and stronger as you feel so relaxed and comfortable. In a moment you will go even deeper and deeper as you reach the next number.

- FOUR. You may imagine many positive images of your special place as you go even deeper and deeper into hypnosis. You can see, hear, feel, taste, and smell the images as they float upward from your unconscious mind. With each breath you relax more and more. You are looking forward to reaching zero and holding the controls to the television program about one of your past lives. You are prepared and will remember the images shown to you about your soul's memories. If you are looking for specific information, you will let yourself be open to the experience, believing that the knowledge you will gain will help you understand what you are looking for, especially as it relates to your life now. It is time for the next number.

- THREE. You are going deeper and deeper into self-hypnosis. You look forward to your past life regression. With each breath your body is relaxing more and more. You can feel the positive love and energy of the universe surrounding you as you continue your journey into your unconscious mind and the memories of your soul. In a short while you will be able to view and experience a past life with all your different senses. You may ask that the right information come to you as you step into your past. You are prepared to go with the program that is selected for you, and you will collect the information that will give you the clues to the questions that you would like answered. You are now ready for the next number.

- TWO. You are going deeper and deeper into hypnosis as you continue to breathe slowly in and out. You are getting very close to the place in your unconscious mind where you will view and experience your past life program. You are more and more focused on the images of your special place and will easily be able to focus on the program of your past life. You feel calm, comfortable, relaxed, and ready to experience your past life regression. You know that you are prepared and open to your past life experience.

- ONE. You are almost totally connected with your unconscious mind and ready for your past life regression. You can feel yourself going deeper and deeper into hypnosis. You will continue to go deeper as you experience your past life regression. Your focus on your past life images will become stronger and stronger. You even have a control on your remote to help sharpen them. You feel relaxed and very positive about your regression. You may now count totally back down to zero and experience deep hypnosis.

◆ FIVE. FOUR. THREE. TWO. ONE. ZERO. You are now connected and in tune with your unconscious mind. You may ask one of your thumbs or fingers to raise up in the air when your unconscious mind indicates that it is ready for you to experience your past life regression. You may feel it floating upward. When it has shown that your unconscious mind is ready, you may begin.

Imagine that you have a television remote control in your hands. You can see and feel the different buttons that let you fast forward through or review any image you want, turn up or down the intensity of any of your five senses, step in and out of the images, and stop your program any time you want.

Travel Time!

Focus on the television screen deep in your unconscious mind and select the correct channel for your past life program. Let an image come into your mind. It may be out of focus at first, but if you let yourself go with the experience, it will become clearer and clearer.

What is the first thing that you experience? Which of your senses are you using? Take plenty of time and let your focus become clearer and clearer. If you are recording or working with a partner, you may speak out loud and describe what you are seeing.

If you are not getting a strong image, you may let yourself begin to experience in all your senses. You many answer any questions out loud and clearly. What does it feel like? What is the temperature? What is your mood? Can you reach out and touch anything? Are there any smells? Can you hear any sounds? If so, what are they? Where are they coming from? Do you have any tastes in your mouth? Are you comfortable there? What can you see? If there is no picture, can you see colors or energies? How clear is your visual image? What else can you collect for information from the first images of your past life regression?

Once you have found an image, look around and describe what you see. Slowly shift your focus to different views of this image. Ask your unconscious mind to show you what is important for you to note. Now place yourself in the image. What does it feel like to be there? What are your emotions? What is the temperature? What time of day or night is it? What do you hear? What can you smell? Are there any tastes in your mouth?

CAUTION **Karmic Cautions**

Don't get discouraged if you are still having trouble getting images. Use your controls to move yourself forward in your soul's memory to where you will be able to experience the program that's right for you. You will continue to go deeper and deeper into hypnosis as the images become clearer in your past life regression. Focus on the information and images that are correct for you.

Can you feel yourself there? What position are you in? What does the nearest surface feel like? Now feel your hair. How long is it? What is its texture? Can you feel something under your feet? Are you wearing shoes? Are you wearing clothes? If so, what is the fabric like? What is the style?

If you can do it, change your view of the past life television program from experiencing to watching. You may describe the scene you are watching. Now is the time to draw or sketch if you want to. You may open your eyes to see the paper you are putting your image on. Remember that you can zoom in or out and stop the action or review it if you want.

When you are ready, move the program forward to an important event in that life that may have a connection to yours. Take your time and let the images flow until they stop at the right place. You may now step in and out of the images as you want to gather the information that can give you insights into your past life. Remember to use all your different senses for the strongest images.

If you are searching for something or someone specific, focus on that part of your past life program, and let the action stop at the right places. Look for a theme in this program that relates to your life. Take note of all the different characters that are in your past life program. The longer your regression lasts, the more focused on your past you will become. If at any time you want to focus more and clear up your images, suggest to yourself that as you count slowly from five to zero, you will focus more and more, and the image will become clearer and clearer on each number.

When you are ready, fast-forward your program to the end of the life that you have been viewing. How did the person die? What were their last thoughts? Did they leave anything unresolved in that lifetime that resulted in karma in your life? How did they feel about their life as a whole?

Soul Stories

Marie always had the feeling that there was something missing in her life. It was as if she was grieving a family member that she never had. She discovered that in a past life she had died before she was able to raise her child. In this life though, she realized that her child was an elderly aunt who she had taken care of before she had died. With this revelation, she could resolve the karma of her past and feel her current life was complete.

Now go back and review the whole lifetime and look for the theme that emerged. Look for the relationships your character had with others. Can you recognize any of them in your lifetime now? If so, how are the roles the same or different? What could you learn from a relationship in your past life that could give you insights into your current life? You will be able to remember more details from your past life regression after you have come back to the surface of your conscious mind and every time you refer to the notes or tapes you make about your experience.

Finally, is there anything else at the moment that could be helpful to you to watch or experience while you are still visiting this past life? When you are ready, it is time to come back to your conscious mind.

Coming Back to the Present

You may now turn off your television program in your unconscious mind. If you have had the sensation of leaving your body, you may now gently float back and become aware that you are totally connected with your mind, body, and soul. Take a few moments to enjoy the relaxed and peaceful feeling that you have created while you are still in your deep hypnotic trance. In a moment you will begin to count back up to consciousness.

◆ ONE. You are beginning your journey back to the surface of your conscious mind. You continue to breathe in and out, feeling very relaxed and comfortable. At five you will come back to the surface of your conscious mind relaxed and feeling very positive. You will be able to remember more and more of your past life regression as you reflect on your experience.

◆ TWO. You are continuing your journey back. You are breathing in and out at a very relaxed and comfortable pace. You feel positive about your regression experience. You are slowly coming out of your deep hypnotic trance back to the surface of your conscious mind.

◆ THREE. You are halfway there. You are becoming aware of your body. Any heaviness you may have felt is returning back to normal. You can feel the warmth of the peace and love of the universe flowing through your body. You feel positive and very relaxed. With each breath you continue to come back to conscious awareness.

◆ FOUR. You are getting closer to the surface. Feel the warmth and positive energy of the universe flowing through your body. You are slowly and comfortably coming out of your hypnotic trance. Your body is back to normal. You feel very good as you slowly breathe in and out.

◆ FIVE. You have almost returned to the surface of your conscious mind. At the next number you will be all the way back. You can feel the peaceful and loving energy of the universe flowing through your body, and it will stay with you after you are totally awake. You are warm and comfortable, feeling very positive about your past life regression experience. If you are ready, take a deep breath, exhale, slowly open your eyes, and come back to the level of your conscious mind.

You are now back to the surface. You are fully awake feeling relaxed, comfortable, and very positive. You continue to feel the peaceful and loving energy of the universe flow through your body. You may take a few moments to let yourself adjust to being back to consciousness. Take a few moments to let yourself reflect on your past life regression. You will remember more of the details every time you review them.

The Least You Need to Know

- Self-hypnosis helps you regress into a past life.

- The more prepared you are for your regression, the better opportunity you have for an informative experience.

- After you have reached zero, ask permission from your unconscious mind to begin your regression.

- A good way to get permission is to let a thumb or finger rise into the air when you are ready to regress.

- You will continue to fill in the blanks of your past life regression after you have returned to the surface of your conscious mind.

Chapter 18

What Just Happened?

In This Chapter

♦ Collecting your impressions of your past life regression

♦ Sorting through any confusion

♦ Did you go to the place you wanted to go or the place you needed to go?

♦ Taking notes on your past life regression

♦ Keeping a past life journal

Now that you've had the opportunity to try a past life regression, your head may be spinning with everything that you encountered on your travels. In this chapter, you'll take a moment to catch your breath and collect your thoughts.

The post-regression wrap-up is a very important part of your experience. It is your chance to capture the information while it is still fresh in your mind. Some facts will begin to fade from your conscious mind very quickly while others will take some time to surface. Start with what is freshest in your memory.

Collecting Your Thoughts

Take a little time to let yourself adjust to the real world again. Continue to breathe slowly in and out, and enjoy being in a relaxed state. You were given the suggestion that you would continue to feel positive effects of the peaceful and loving energy of the universe flowing through your body after you counted back to consciousness.

Coming back from a past life regression is much like waking up from a nap in which you have been dreaming. That dream may still be buzzing around in your head. If that's the case, just come back to reality at a nice slow pace that is comfortable for you. You may feel sleepy, or you may feel full of energy. You may even drift in and out of a partial sleep state. Everyone responds a little differently after they have experienced a past life regression.

Your eyes may not react well to full light when you first come back. If you find this to be true, you can always use softer lighting in the future. If the light is too harsh, just close your eyes again and slowly make the transition back to full vision. You can even use candlelight, which will not only help with your return to consciousness, but provide a nice relaxing focus when you are first entering your self-hypnotic trance.

Ageless Insights

A person may come back from a past life regression in a very relaxed state, especially if he's in a deep enough trance so that he's not yet consciously aware of what he has just experienced. The self-hypnosis can be very relaxing for anyone who has forgotten how to put himself at ease. You may not be quite so affected because you have been learning how to relax throughout this book.

How do you feel physically? Do you feel heaviness anywhere in your body? If you do, take a moment and count yourself back from three to zero and suggest that when you come back to three your body will come back to its normal weight again. This heaviness effect, as well as other sensations, can result from being in a deep hypnotic trance. Just the word *deeper* may suggest heaviness. If you did not count yourself back down, you would still come back to your normal sensations in a short period of time.

Do you have any other physical sensations? You may feel tightness in your third eye area from being connected to the universal flow. You may feel a slight buzz in your head. If you experienced something in your past life, you may have that sensation for a short period of time when you awaken. You might have been very cold or very hot and are still continuing to feel it a little. You might be thirsty. You may want to reflect over a soothing cup of tea or something else that refreshes you after your journey.

During his regression Arthur went to a lifetime where he had had his hands severed from his body. He did not die as a result of the accident, but he did resent not having hands for the rest of that lifetime. There were things that he could not do in his life now, such as playing piano, that seemed to be affecting his unconscious memory. He brought forward the memory of what it was like when his hands were still attached, and right after he came out of his regression, he reported that his wrists stung as if his hands had been sewn back on.

If you are cold when you come back to the surface, cover yourself with a blanket or warm clothing. Turn off air conditioning or fans if it is too cold, or turn up the heat if it is during the colder part of the year. The important thing is for you to feel comfortable.

How do you feel mentally? What were your first emotions when you came back from your regression? It is possible to carry over some of the emotions felt during your past life regression. You may feel empathy for the person you were in your past, especially if it was a trying life. The result could be a lingering feeling of sadness or loneliness. If this happens, take a few moments to feel the peaceful and loving energy of the universe and send some back to your soul's memory to help old scars heal.

How do you feel spiritually? Did any of your past life experiences challenge how you believe? Was what you encountered so powerful that it could affect you in a life-changing way? Perhaps you were given the opportunity to begin a new and much more positive and spiritual way of life after your regression. Then again, you may have felt nothing physically, mentally, or spiritually from your journey into your past.

It Can Be Confusing at First

Now that you're back from your first past life adventure, what was it like? You may not be sure what just happened. That is the case when someone is in a deep hypnotic trance. In a stage show, a good subject can be totally unaware at first of what they have just done while in a state of hypnosis. They may wake up to find their face covered with Band-Aids, or minus their shoes. Part of the fun for the audience is telling them what they did. The hypnotist often gives them a post-hypnotic suggestion that they will remember everything they did within an hour after the demonstration has finished.

It's not uncommon to come out of a past life regression trance remembering only bits and pieces of the experience that just took place. The deeper in trance you go, the less you are apt to remember when you come back to your conscious mind. The fragmented images that you do recall can cause you to feel disoriented for a short period of time. As you continue to do past life regressions, you will find it much easier to come back to your conscious mind more in balance. It is also possible that you will be able to go deeper into your hypnotic trance as you become comfortable with the regression process.

Think of coming out of your regression trance as looking into a snow globe that has a scene inside. When you shake it, you can't see the scene because the globe fills with snowlike particles. When the snowstorm subsides, you are able to see the picture once more. When you come out of trance, you may be staring into the blizzard of information inside your mind. It, too, will settle in time.

Confusion can result when your regression goes differently than you had planned. You may have been so focused on where you wanted to go and what you expected to learn, that you missed what was actually taking place in your regression. If you rehearsed in your mind what you expected, you might not have wanted to accept what you experienced. Did you go with the experience?

Were you worried or anxious about your past life regression? If you were, you may not have allowed yourself to relax and trust your imagination to take over. Your conscious mind may not have turned itself off the whole time. It is not uncommon to be a little anxious about the unknown, no matter how much you have prepared. Remember that you are still learning the skills of regressing into the past. There is no such thing as a perfect past life regression because there will always be something else that you may wish you had looked for while you were there. That's the incentive to go back again.

Karmic Cautions

Certain physical, mental, or spiritual conditions in your life may prevent you from totally focusing on your regression. Perhaps you have a cold, or got some bad news before your regression. There are always issues—both known and unknown—that can interfere with your ability to enter a deep trance. These conditions can lead to disappointment if the experience doesn't go as well as you had expected.

You may have encountered something that you weren't expecting that was very unsettling to you. You may still have a disturbing image that was brought back with you into your conscious mind. The more you work with your belief to help you resolve your past, the better the possibilities to melt away any negative image. Remember to surround yourself with the peace and loving energy of the universe.

Did You Go Where You Wanted to Go?

Cathy read a book on past life regression and visited a specialist with a list of where she wanted to go and what she expected to gain from her visit to her past. She easily went into a trance and back in time. She went to a different place than she had expected and was disappointed with her experience. She failed to see that what was placed in front of her could have helped resolve karma in her current life.

Did you travel to the destination in your past life regression that you had hoped to go, or, like Cathy, did you take a detour? If you changed destinations in the middle of your trip, how did you react to the change of plans? Did it bother or confuse you? If so, how? This is an excellent time to consider all aspects that you encountered during your travel into your past. You will consider what to do with your thoughts in the next two sections of this chapter.

You may have wound up exactly where you wanted to go. If you did, congratulations! Most of this section deals with the regression experiences that may have taken a detour. It is good for you to read it because every regression trip is different. Everyone takes a regression destination detour at one time or another.

Were you disappointed in your past life regression destination? If so, how? Take some time and think about what you may have learned in the place that you wound up. Perhaps the real reason you went there is not apparent yet. As the dust settles, you may get a different perspective of your regression experience.

You may have had your goal very well defined, and yet you were not able to get to where you wanted to go because of *tunnel vision*. In the meantime, you may not have taken note of what was actually happening around you during your regression.

There is only one view while you are in a tunnel. Remember the concept of the hologram? It is two different images that are contained in one picture. Shift it one way, and then shift it to another angle. Did you consider two different views when you regressed back to your destination? If not, the next time you might want to remind yourself to go with the destination you wind up at and analyze the experience later.

> **Words to Remember**
>
> **Tunnel vision** happens when you focus so narrowly that it is like looking through a tunnel. All you can see out the other side is the area in front of the opening. The farther away you are, the smaller your actual view is. It's impossible to see anything that is placed outside of that field of vision.

It doesn't really matter where you went. It's what you might have experienced and learned in that location that is important. Even though you may be disappointed, you may have gotten more than you thought out of your regression. Rather than trying to decide that right after you come back, give it some time before you critique the results.

Part of the unique challenge in a past life regression is to collect the clues from your past and relate them to aspects of your life now. The more open you are to examining what you have experienced, the more you will find all kinds of information that are pieces of your soul's puzzle. Any destination or past life experience is an opportunity to gain more insight into the memories stored in the record of your soul.

> **Soul Stories**
>
> Julie decided to focus her research on one of her past lives. Over a period of several months, she regressed 25 times to the same lifetime. Each time she went back she gathered more pieces of her puzzle until she had researched just about every aspect of her soul's memory. The more she regressed, the easier it was for her to make the transition between the past and the present. She was able to come back to her conscious mind relaxed, refreshed, and ready to rejoin the world around her.

Making Notes

Did you prepare to make notes right after your past life regression experience? Just as soon as you have adjusted to being back to your conscious level and have collected your thoughts, you'll want to make a record of your first impressions of your journey. You can do this in several different ways. If you recorded the trip, you can capture your first impressions easily. Another way is to write down your thoughts. A laptop can be ready to go so that you hardly have to move after you have come back from your regression.

You may not be able to remember graphic details right after your experience. Just write down what you remember at the moment and fill in more impressions later. How do the different characters relate to each other and you, not only in your past life but in your current one? After you've described the actors in your story, review them to see if you missed any details.

Write down your answers to the following who, what, when, where, and why questions to help you collect your past life data:

◆ **Who did you meet in your past life?** Were there other characters present? How many different ones can you describe? Start with ones that you have the best images of. Remember to note sights, sounds, feelings, touches, smells, and tastes. Look around for as many details as possible.

◆ **What was the big picture?** Once you have figured this out, zero in on the little picture. Describe the clearest image that you can remember. In other words, get down as much information as possible. You may change some of your first impressions, as you get farther away from your regression experience. If you don't make notes in the first place, you might forget some of the information after a few days.

◆ **When was your past life?** Can you figure out what time period in history you went back to? One of the values of describing the characters and their dress is that you may be able to research the fashions to help give you a concept. If you are unsure of the time period, you may want to dowse your unconscious mind for an answer. Just pick your tool and follow the directions in Chapter 14. Count the dates backward in larger numbers at first, such as a hundred years if the date is back far enough, or 10-year increments if it is not as far back in time. Finally you can count back in single years when you get close.

◆ **Where did you regress to?** Can you recognize the location? What kind of physical description of your destination or destinations can you give? How does the landscape appear? Is it in the country or a more populated area? There are many different things that you can note about your surroundings. Are there any landmarks that you can describe—mountains, oceans? Perhaps you can get enough information so that you can research the location. Just note anything that comes to mind. You can sort it out later.

You may recognize the country that you went to but not the specific location. Any information that you can recall such as street signs, names of businesses, house numbers, or other researchable clues can help solve your case. It is important to remember that your information right after you come back from your past life regression may not be totally accurate. Write it down anyway. The more you investigate in the future, the more defined and accurate your information will become.

> **Soul Stories**
>
> Jack was unsure of the time he had regressed to. The house in his images could have been 200 years old, but the scene he was experiencing may have been only 40 years ago. As he searched the house, he described the kitchen in detail and eventually found a calendar on a wall. The date was May 1923. The kitchen also had appliances that matched that time period.

You may have heard and remembered conversations or other sounds that can help you identify where you went. Again, it's possible to recall only part of what you heard. You may have nearly the right sound but not defined enough to recognize it yet. Your unconscious mind will continue to work on the information after you have turned your attention to something else. Don't be surprised if you wake up one morning with a clearer perspective of what you had been trying to piece together.

You can also use your pendulum to dowse a map to help narrow down the location that you visited (see Chapter 14). Ask the pendulum to show you the direction of "yes." When that has been defined, ask which direction is "no." Next ask your unconscious mind for permission to ask for the location and wait for the answer from the pendulum. Permission is usually asked for as a way of respecting the power of the unconscious mind and its connection to your soul memories. Not everyone follows that step in dowsing. When you are ready, hold the pendulum over the map of the general location where you think you traveled to and narrow down the area until your unconscious mind has found the correct spot.

◆ **Why did you go back to this specific past life?** Could you find a theme to your past life regression that relates to your life now? If you think you know what it may be, make a note of it. Can you understand the connection you currently have to the past? Is there any information from your regression that can make a positive difference to you as you go forward in your life? Jot down any ideas relating to the purpose of your visit to the past that you might have when you come back to the surface of your conscious mind.

Keeping a Journal

Do you have enough information to start keeping a journal yet? If you were able to answer all the questions in the last section, you may already have a lot of material to start with. Now you have the challenge of organizing the material you have collected. Your next goal is to develop a way to manage and add to your growing quantity of past life information.

You may already have started a journal relating to your past lives as suggested when you were learning about the connections that you have to the past without even consciously knowing it. If you have one, you can add your recently gathered information to what you have already started. This may, however, be an excellent time to start a new journal that you can add your previously gathered information to.

Your journal should not only include the notes from past life regressions but also have a provision for daily insights that may surface after you have experienced a past life. You will probably find yourself thinking about your regression experience quite often. As you do, your unconscious mind will be comparing the information that has been deposited in it independently from your conscious mind. These insights may surface at any time while you are awake or sleeping. A small note pad or a portable tape recorder can serve to store the information until you can transfer it into your journal.

CAUTION

Karmic Cautions

So far you probably have material on just one life-time. Imagine what it will be like when you have several different lifetimes to keep track of at the same time! A journal of past life material will make it easier to organize your information. It's crucial to start out on the right foot so that you won't get confused with additional information as you continue to visit your past lives.

Your journal can serve as a way to develop goals for your next past life regression session. The more you become comfortable with visiting your past, the easier it will be to decide what you want to learn from your next session. The next chapter will consider how you can sift through the data you keep in your journal and help you develop future regression goals.

It's a good idea to have a loose-leaf binder if you are producing a hard copy of your journal. That way you can move the information to the appropriate places. If you are making entries into a computer program, make sure you date each entry so that you can keep track of the chronological order in which you gather your material. Always remember to keep copies and back up all your journal information if you're working on a computer.

Keep a record of each past life regression you experience. Include what your pre-regression goals were, and what your first impressions were after you came back to your conscious mind. Leave room to add more insights as they come to you and what you would like to learn from this life in future regressions. Make sure that you note any dreams about your regression that you might have as well as spontaneous insights.

As you add more regressions and more past lives, keep them in chronological order. You may want to construct a flow chart to help you track the movement of your soul through different reincarnations. This could be a simple map to help follow the sequence of events of one or more past lives and might use symbols to depict persons, places, occupations, and other details. Make sure you leave plenty of space at first so that you have room to fill in the gaps as you retrieve the information from your unconscious mind.

You should have a place for character profiles from your past and how they may relate to your present life. You may want to have a place to note the theme of that life and any possible karma you may have encountered. If you sketched any of what you saw, keep a copy of it in your journal.

Keep a record of the relationships and themes that span more than one lifetime. Look for past life abilities or strengths that may be utilized in your current lifetime. Also make note of weaknesses that could have carried over into your present. Finally, try to choose a time that is convenient for you to review your journal and possibly write in it on a daily basis.

The Least You Need to Know

- ◆ Always take some time to collect your thoughts and readjust after you experience a past life regression.

- ◆ Don't be surprised if all the past life regression material you have collected is confusing at first.

- ◆ If you didn't go where you expected, you may have gone where you were supposed to go.

- ◆ Always keep good notes after your regression.

- ◆ An accurate and organized past life regression journal can help you sort through your clues from the past.

Chapter 19

Making Sense of What You've Learned

In This Chapter

- ◆ Organizing your past life data
- ◆ Did you collect all the information you wanted to?
- ◆ Revisiting past lives
- ◆ Filling in the details
- ◆ Make a research project out of your past life experience

When Julie decided that she wanted to research one of her past lives, she systematically set up a plan to gather her information and developed goals for each one of her regressions. She not only tape-recorded each session, she transcribed the notes and kept a journal of all the data she collected. She also made sketches and maps of the locations that she visited in her past life.

She developed dates and names. Finally, she went to the place that she had been to through her unconscious mind. There she found evidence to support the data she collected during her regressions. She knew she was in the right place when she found landmarks she had only seen in her mind.

You may also have a mystery to research from your past life regression. This chapter will help you organize your data. Now is the time, right after a past life regression, to make plans for your next adventure, either back in time or to investigate the facts you have already collected.

Sifting Through the Data

Now that you have experienced a past life regression and collected a whole lot of data, what are you going to do with it? If you are like most people, you will get excited about something for a period of time and then either lose interest or be pulled away to work on something else. When you get involved with a research project such as looking into your past, it would be nice to be able to devote all your time to it. That, however, is usually impossible to do. Once you get away from it, it is harder to get motivated to begin again. Every time you get back to something you have not touched in a while, you usually have to spend quite a bit of time trying to remember what you did before. The further away you get, the harder it is to begin again. At the same time, though, it's good to take a break every so often.

But even when you are unable to devote yourself to researching your past lives as much as you would like, you really are doing something. That something is what your unconscious mind continues to work on while you are consciously occupied with other things. In other words, you can continue to research your past lives while it seems as if you are doing nothing about them. Remembering this will help you not to get discouraged when your time is otherwise occupied. Your unconscious mind can send up information at any time and will help you keep a mental focus on the history of your soul and how it may impact your current life.

As I mentioned in the previous chapter, the benefit of keeping a journal is that you will have a good record of what you have researched so far. When you have a moment to review your regression material or jot down more thoughts and insights, a well-organized journal can make it much easier. You might find a few minutes each day to reflect on your regression project. Establishing a routine in your daily activities can help keep you on track.

The first step in sifting through your past life data is to determine how you want to continue researching your project. What part of your regression do you want to focus on? When you have answered that question, you can select just the data gathered so far on that portion of your regression. It might be a character who you want to learn more about. It could be a geographic location or a certain time period. You may want to further examine a relationship, a fear, or a talent.

That doesn't mean you should discard the rest of the data that you are not using at the moment. They are all pieces of the puzzle of the journey of your soul. Just like putting together a jigsaw puzzle, you may want to put the pieces that are the sky or the border together first. Once you have done that, you go to work on another section until the key pieces that link the whole thing together are found.

> **Karmic Cautions**
>
> If for some reason you didn't get much data from your past life regression, that is actually material in itself. Keep a record in your journal even when the experience did not reveal much of what you think is past life material. Noting what went wrong will help you come up with a different strategy for your next regression. It could be that your nonexperience will make more sense to you as you continue researching your past.

You may also have a lot of data that looks unusable. Just keep it filed in your journal in a place where you can review it from time to time. You are the detective, and every clue could be the one that breaks the case. Hopefully you are having fun with your regression project and you do feel like a detective! The more you mull the data over in your conscious mind, the more active you keep the investigation into your past lives.

If you have your information on tapes or video, you or someone else will want to get much of the material down in your journal. That way you can review it, make notes on what you want to do next, and then re-listen to the whole recording to help refresh your memory. You may even want to use self-hypnosis to suggest to yourself that when you hear it again, more details of your regression will become clearer to you. Of course, this will give you more data to record in your journal.

Was One Visit Enough?

Perhaps you got enough information with just one visit to one of your past lives so that you do not feel the need to go there again. If this is the case, you can move on to a different lifetime if you want. You can always revisit a specific past life anytime in the future. You may want to follow a theme or karma through more than one lifetime.

Even if it takes you a while to get back to your past life research, you will be prepared to start right in again. You may have a whole binder full of information before you finish your project. At the same time, just as in researching your family genealogy— the study of family history—the genealogy of your soul will always have something more to be learned.

It is very possible that you will want to get to know yourself in a past life better than you did on your first visit. Now is the time to begin to plan to return. Make notes on what you would like to learn next about your soul's memory. Your reasons could include focusing in on the theme of the life, studying either yourself in the past or other characters in the story, visiting a specific location to gather as much historical information as possible, or digging deeper into a past life situation.

> **Ageless Insights**
>
> You may discover all kinds of relatives from your past lives when you regress. Your family tree may recycle itself and look pretty confusing when you try to chart it out. You may find that your mother in this life was your daughter in a past life, or that a good friend in this life was a brother in the past.

Check your regression notes when you are making your return travel plans. Were you happy with the method you used last time? If you were, you can certainly use it again. Even if it was successful, you might want to regress differently the next time just to compare which method works best. You might want to go to the movies (see Chapter 16), or you could try going to the Akashic Records (see Chapters 4 and 16). You may also want to make up a regression technique for yourself.

Whatever method works best for you, it's a good idea to wait a couple of days before you revisit a past life. One reason is that you may not have processed all the information you gathered on your previous visit yet. Some of the material in your unconscious mind will take a while to work its way to the surface. Unless you are clear on the images you have already received, it could cloud the picture even more if you go back too soon.

Another reason to wait is that a regression can use up a lot of your energy. Even though you are in a relaxing trance, there is still a lot that is coming through you. It is good to re-energize your mind, body, and spirit before you take off again. You may sleep a little restlessly the first night or two after a past life regression. That is because there is a lot of processing going on in your unconscious mind, and your dream state is one of the ways that it works its way into your conscious.

Were there things that you would do differently this time? Make two lists. The first should include everything you liked about your first regression, including the induction, the regression itself, and the quality of images you experienced during the process. Make note of all that went well so you can include them in your next regression. The second list should include what you did *not* like about your regression. Try to break the information down so that you can focus in on the things that didn't work.

Now consider what you would do to change it this time. It could be that your physical location was uncomfortable and made it hard to enter a trance. You may be working with a partner who is not quite fitting into your regression plan. If that is the case, you might want to change partners or go it alone. Perhaps you tried your regression by yourself and it didn't work out, so you may want to look for someone to assist you in your next regression. (See Chapter 14 for tips on working alone or with a partner.)

Ageless Insights _____

When you revisit a past life, you take the things that you liked that worked for you and add the ideas that you think will help you strengthen your regression trance the next time. Don't include the things that didn't work for you the last time. Keep a record of this in your journal. You will find that it may take a few different regressions before you finally develop the method that works best for you. Even after doing all that, each journey into the past will take its own route.

After you have put together your approach to your next past life regression, let yourself relax and try the concept out in your mind. Remember, it's good to allow yourself a few days to process all the information you have collected. You can imagine what it would be like so that you can look for potential glitches in your plan before you actually go. If you find something that doesn't seem to fit, you can readjust it. Now try that out in your mind. Once you are comfortable with the way you will approach your next regression, make plans in a few days to get ready to go again.

Going Back Again

You may find that the more you go back, the easier it will be to get there. An induction that could take between five and ten minutes can probably be reduced to at least half that time. Eventually you may be able to get comfortable, take a deep breath, exhale, focus on your third eye, and go directly into a past life regression. Be patient. If you keep practicing, it will happen for you.

If you are ready, find your comfortable place. Prepare your partner if you have one, and have all your recording equipment ready to go. Have your regression script, with your goals clearly thought out, and any other material that will help you gather your past life information. It is still a good idea to take your time going into your trance. At the end of your regression session, suggest to yourself that on your next visit you will enter your trance state at a faster rate.

Take a deep breath and exhale. Focus on your third eye and let your body relax. Feel the peace and love of the universe begin to flow into your body as you prepare to count yourself down to zero when you will be connected with your unconscious mind. When you reach zero, you will begin your journey back into the past life that you want to visit. With each count downward you will go deeper and deeper in hypnosis. As you go deeper, you will feel more and more relaxed and comfortable.

◆ FIVE. You continue to breathe slowly in and out as you go deeper and deeper into hypnosis. As you relax more and more, you will go deeper and deeper.

◆ FOUR. You are going into your trance at a very comfortable and relaxing pace. You look forward to connecting again to your unconscious mind and to the memories of your soul.

◆ THREE. You are relaxing more and more as you go deeper and deeper into hypnosis. You continue to breathe slowly in and out while the muscles in your entire body relax. You will soon be stepping back into the world of your soul memories.

◆ TWO. You are getting closer and closer to entering your past life again. When you get to zero you will be ready to step into your past and experience it in all your senses. The images you will have will be even clearer than the last time you regressed. Images that were confusing before will be very clear, and you will understand them this time as you reach the destination deep in your unconscious mind.

◆ ONE. When you reach the next level, you will be in a deep hypnotic trance. You will be very calm and relaxed as you journey to your past life. It is time to count all the way down to zero and your deep hypnotic trance connecting you to your past.

◆ FIVE. FOUR. THREE. TWO. ONE. ZERO. Enjoy your relaxed and comfortable state of hypnosis for a moment before you journey into your past. Suggest to yourself that every time you enter into your self-hypnotic trance to go back into your past that you will be able to easily get to this state of relaxation deep in your unconscious mind in less time. The moment you start your induction you will feel yourself slipping into your deep trance. You may always go at a pace that is comfortable and positive for you.

Soul Stories

David gathered a lot of past life material after his first regression. As he started to sort through it he found that all the dates didn't correspond with what he had imagined, so he decided to go back again. This time he suggested that the images would be clearer than before. He was able to resolve his confusion from the previous regression and put together a time frame that made sense.

When you are ready, let yourself focus back into your past life regression. If you are returning to a place you have been before, bring the images into your unconscious mind using the technique that works best for you. Focus on something that is comfortable and positive from your previous experience. Let yourself become reoriented to being in your past and begin to notice details that you did not realize were in the images the last time you were there.

If you have chosen to go to a different past life, one that you have not visited before, proceed with your regression by focusing in on the first images that come into your unconscious mind. If they are unpleasant, you can change your screen either backward or forward and turn down your sensitivity of the experience. Remember that you can always open your eyes and come back to your conscious mind relaxed and refreshed anytime you want or need to. Proceed through your regression with the plan that you have developed and gather your information to record in your journal when you return.

Filling in the Blanks

If you are revisiting a lifetime, you will already be familiar with some of the details there. Now you can begin to focus in on the details you may have missed before. Give yourself the suggestion that you can count from five to zero any time you want during your regression and while you are doing so, the images you are experiencing will become clearer and clearer. It is like adjusting the lens on a camera so that you can bring it more into focus.

You may experience the same situation a little differently this time, or you may replay it exactly the same. Either way can be productive. You may be able to clear up some of the details with this visit. Every new piece of information can help you fill in the blanks. Don't worry if it is different. All you need to do is record the results in your journal afterward where you can compare your regression with information you gathered earlier.

On the other hand, if you experience the same images over and over, especially if you can approach them from different viewpoints, it is a good indication that you have a clear concept of what happened in your past life. This may give you confidence and perhaps validation that your past life experiences were real and not imagined. If you are seriously trying to prove something about your past lives to yourself, the more consistent your story becomes, the easier it is to believe.

The blanks in your past life story will begin to fill in a little more with each visit. You should be able to develop a good *time line* where you can trace your main character from birth to death. You can go right to different points in the story and start to collect your information. You can study not only your character but also others to learn how their lives intertwined with yours.

You can study the geography of where you traveled in your past life and experience what it was like to live during that time. You can try out the food and smell the aromas that were there. You can feel the emotions and watch karmic situations develop and resolve. You can study many aspects about your life in the past.

Words to Remember

A **time line** is a system for recording events in the order that they took place. It could be similar to a flow chart mentioned in the previous chapter that uses symbols.

If you are journeying to a new past life, you can look for relationships that spilled over into other regressions. Look for similarities of themes and characters. Is there any karma that could begin and be continued between lifetimes? Are there any characters that appear together in more than one life? If so, how did their roles differ or stay the same?

Every time you experience a past life regression, you fill in more of the blanks in the journey of your soul. On your way back to your conscious mind, suggest to yourself that the information will continue to surface from your soul's memory even after you have come out of trance. Suggest that every time you study your journal, more insights about your past will be revealed. Remind yourself that the images of your past will come to you at a rate that is positive and comfortable, and you will only get the ones that are right for you at the time. Also suggest that every time you use self-hypnosis to travel back in the past, you will be able to do so at an easier and faster rate. You will begin your journey the moment you start your countdown.

When you are ready, come back to the surface of your mind feeling relaxed, refreshed, and comfortable. Take a little time to readjust and make notes in your journal about your latest regression experience. Fill in any missing details.

Research the Story

Now that you have experienced more than one past life regression, you may find that you have a unique story emerging from the memories of your soul. You may want to take your research further and write it down, not only for yourself but for others like your family, friends, or other people who might find it interesting reading. In fact, a lot of great writers wrote best-sellers while in a trance state. They reached back into their soul's memory to provide the research material for their books. One such writer is Taylor Caldwell, who wrote *Dear and Glorious Physician* (Doubleday, 1959) and *Great Lion of God* (Doubleday, 1970) while in a trance state.

Soul Stories

Jenny Cockell was haunted by an early childhood memory that she had lived before as Mary Sutton, a young Irish mother who died while she was raising eight children. Jenny was able to use hypnosis to help her research the information in her soul's memory. She eventually found her children again, now much older than she. Her book *Across Time and Death* (Simon & Schuster, 1994) tells the story of her search.

I'll tell you more about putting talents from your past lives to use in Chapter 22. Even if you aren't interested in writing your past life story, you may want to research as many facts as you can find when you journey back in time. There are many types of information that can help you prove your case that you lived before. The best way to begin is to get as many researchable details from your regression as possible:

♦ **Names of people.** Note in your journal as many names as you can. Try to get the whole name. Then find as many names as you can that are related to the person. Parents, children, other relatives, and people in the same geographic location are very important. Note any name that you can find in your regression sessions. There are several ways to get names. You can ask the character to write them down through you. You can hear someone call a person by name. You can look for something that their name has been written on, such as an envelope. Remember that some of the characters in your past may not be literate.

♦ **Names of locations.** Note the names of countries, towns, states, and streets. Record the names of streets, buildings, boats, trains, etc., as well as any written information you locate in your past. You may have names that you don't even know where they go. That's okay. Just make a note of them in your journal.

♦ **Dates.** You will want to know the dates of your past life. When were you born and when did you die? What are the dates of other characters in your story? What were the dates when significant events took place during your regression? You can get dates from the past by looking for someplace where they are written down, such as a calendar. You might hear someone mention a date. You can also get a general idea of a date by observing clothing styles, hairstyles, modes of transportation, household furnishings, and even physical locations. Or you may know the date, and dowse to help determine the time period of your past life regression.

♦ **Good descriptions.** Record the best descriptions you can of the characters. Look at their dress from head to foot. Describe the scenery, the buildings, the temperatures, the feelings, the music, the smells, and what the food is like. Make sketches of what you see, if possible. Make sure you note anything that will help you research your past life story.

♦ **Get other facts.** Note what activities are taking place either up close or in the background. These could include war, social situations, childhood games, and even the lifestyle that the characters live. Don't leave any stone unturned when you research your past. It can be both fun and educational. The more you research, the more complete the story of your soul's journey will become. You may have a book in your hands when you finish.

The Least You Need to Know

◆ What you have learned during a past life regression will help you set your goals for your next return.

◆ When you regress more than once you have the opportunity to refine your method for more productive trance states.

◆ Going back again will help you learn more about your past.

◆ The more you go back to the same life, the more blanks of your soul's story you will be able to fill in.

◆ Your past life makes an excellent research project!

Chapter 20

Was That Really My Past Life?

In This Chapter

- How the story of Bridey Murphy captivated the world
- Were you really *you?*
- Could you have more than one life at the same time?
- Tapping into the collective unconsciousness
- Channeling and communicating with spirits

Just when you have begun to think that this past life stuff is not too complicated, this chapter might change your mind. You will look at several different examples of other things that might be taking place during the time you are experiencing a journey into your past. You will first consider one of the most publicized past life experiences in the last hundred years, the Bridey Murphy story.

As you read about the theories in this chapter, remember that you should make up your own mind as to what you believe. You have a good guidance system already in place inside yourself and looking over you. Always rely on your belief and your intuitive mind to help you bring clarity and balance to your life.

The Bridey Murphy Story

If you have not read the book *The Search for Bridey Murphy* (see Appendix B), you may find it fascinating. It chronicles the research by Colorado businessman Morey Bernstein, done through hypnosis, on a past life of 29-year-old Virginia Tighe. In the book Tighe is known as Ruth Simmons. Like many of you, Bernstein became intrigued with the mysteries of the mind. In his case, a series of events in his life exposed him to hypnosis and sparked a compelling desire to research and learn all he could about the subject. That hunt brought him to Virginia Beach and the home of Hugh Lynn Cayce, the son of Edgar, who provided a list of people who had known and worked with the great psychic.

Bernstein interviewed doctors who verified the results of his work, business people who had been healed by Cayce's cures, and people who had had life readings based on the events of their past lives. Although skeptical at first, he was convinced that Edgar Cayce was not a fraud, and he became intrigued with the concept that people had lived before.

Bernstein further discovered that research was being done through hypnosis taking subjects back before birth and into other lifetimes. Even though he was classified as an amateur, he had developed the skills to become an effective hypnotist by this time. His next logical step was to find a good subject and take them back into a past life.

The subject turned out to be Virginia Tighe. Bernstein discovered that she was an excellent candidate when she slipped easily into trance while he was doing a relaxation exercise for a group of friends one evening. Later he had an occasion to hypnotize her again, and she regressed back to age one. When he decided to try a past life regression, he knew that she would be an excellent subject for his first attempt.

On November 29, 1952, Bridey Murphy emerged from the unconscious mind of Virginia Tighe and started an adventure into the past that would captivate many Americans over the next few years. The Irish woman who came through Mrs. Tighe, Bridget (Bridey) Murphy, was born in County Cork, Ireland, in 1798 and lived until 1864 when she died from a fall down a set of stairs. Over several hypnotic sessions conducted in late 1952 and early 1953 until Mr. Tighe put a stop to the regressions, Bernstein was able to follow the life of this woman and bring out a good many details that seemed inconceivable to be consciously known to Virginia Tighe.

As Bernstein shared the tape recordings of his research, interest grew, and it was suggested to him that he write the story for publication. The result was a book followed by a movie on the search for Bridey Murphy. Interest in reincarnation soared throughout the country until a rival newspaper of the one that had covered the story decided to debunk it.

It seems that Virginia Tighe had an elderly Irish neighbor with the nickname of "Bridey." Worse yet, this woman had a son who was an editor for the paper that had helped publicize the story. Almost overnight, despite the denials of Virginia Tighe of prior knowledge of the details of her past life, the public lost interest in her story. You may want to read the book for yourself and make up your own mind as to whether you think she had lived before or was just bringing out unconscious memories that she wove into a fantasy about her life as Bridey Murphy.

Many of the facts in her story that were discovered through hypnosis were later proved, and they would have been very difficult for her to know during her lifetime. Was Bridey Murphy real or imagined? Regardless of what you believe, the story of the quest is well worth looking into for all of you who are serious about researching one or more of your past lives.

> **CAUTION**
>
> **Karmic Cautions**
>
> In countries and religions that believe in reincarnation, the Bridey Murphy story would have been accepted without question. Not so in this country. Until there is a time when absolute scientific proof can verify that people really do have past lives, there will always be skeptics.

How Do I Know That Was Me?

The Bridey Murphy story brings up that nagging question again, "Was my past life regression real or just imagined?" Of course, the answer is the same. You are the one who really knows in your mind, regardless of what others claim. If you believe that you have made a connection with your soul's memory, it can be very beneficial to you in helping you to answer and perhaps resolve a voice deep down in your unconscious mind. Remember, you may not find many others who will believe you if you do tell them about your past life regressions.

One of the best ways to decide for yourself whether you are the character you met in your past life regression is to ask yourself as many questions about your relationship with each of your selves as possible. You might imagine what it would be like to live in that time period. You also could imagine what it would be like for the character in your past life to live as you do now. Of course, you may not have been able to relate to anyone when you regressed into the past.

Did you feel one of the characters you visited from the past was you in a different life? If so, how do you make the connection? What are your intuitive feelings? Can you explain the bond that you may feel bridges the gap between lifetimes?

What similarities did you have? Do you have the same emotions? Do you have the same interests? These could include music, food, locations, and professions. Make a note in your journal of anything that you can think of that links the memories of your soul with yourself in this life.

Do you share the same fears or phobias? Do you exhibit the same wounds from your past life? Do you have the same interests in relationship types? Do you share any of the same skills, athletic abilities, or artistic talents? Do you dream about the character you were in a past life? Do you have déjà vu experiences that you think may relate to your past life experiences?

Would you rather live now or in the era of your previous life? Do you resent some of the modern conveniences of today and try whenever possible to live a much simpler lifestyle? Since you have met the character of your past, do you often think of how they would feel or act as you go about your daily life?

Were you your own relative? Did you go back and experience the life of someone you are related to? Are there still people alive who would have known this relative? If so, can you compare notes on this character and obtain pictures of them? Do their pictures look anything like you do now or did at a different age in your life?

What is different about you now and you before? Were there things that your character did in a past life that you cannot stand to do in this lifetime? Are you trying to make up for something you failed at or were deprived of in a past life? Perhaps you have a fear of being poor from a time when you were poor. You may hoard items of food because you did not have enough before.

What other things can you compare about your different lifetimes? What can you research from the past that you can prove was a part of your other lifetime? When you have collected all the evidence both for and against the case of you being you before, let yourself be the judge and mediator. Let the answer be one that both you and your soul can live with.

Two or More Lives at the Same Time

It may be possible to actually experience more than one life during the same time period. Now that can really confuse the picture! How do you explain that you could be more than one person during the same reincarnation? The answer is, you weren't. One of the characters could have been you, but the other had leftover energy from their soul memories that you were able to absorb.

Have you ever been able to know exactly what another person was thinking? You may be able to synchronize your mind so that each of your thoughts are almost exactly alike. You may be able to feel the emotions of someone else and imagine what it would be like to be them.

Soul Stories

When Julie was researching her past life through many hypnotic regressions, she discovered that she was able to experience many different characters during one lifetime. With each one she would speak in a different tone and take on the personality of that individual. She would be an old man one time and a young girl the next. She was not only able to understand how she felt about other characters, but she could feel how other characters felt about her.

Not every one of you will be able to experience other characters besides your own. It is your own mental DNA that will determine how you will be able to access the characters in your past life. The things that you can do in this life you can take back with you when you experience your past lives. The more you trust in your image ability as you journey back in time, the more you will be able to relate to the many different characters you meet along the way.

In the case of Bridey Murphy, researcher Morey Bernstein was able to have Virginia Tighe demonstrate Irish dances in a hypnotic trance that she knew from her past life. Was this actually the memory of her soul, or something that she may have observed in her current lifetime? Again, the question will probably remain unanswered, at least for the skeptics that need scientific proof. However, there is another question: How did her muscles "know" how to do a dance she had apparently never physically attempted before, at least in this lifetime?

One word of caution: If you decide you would like to involve yourself in physical acts that you were able to do in another life, it's advisable that you work with a professional past life specialist. You want to make sure that you don't do anything that could result in injury. Someone trained in hypnosis and regression can carefully monitor and control physical demonstrations, while someone who is inexperienced and unprepared may forget what to do and leave you at risk.

With this said, you might try out other past life abilities with a partner and some by yourself. These activities include artistic abilities of several types including music, painting, or writing. You can even bring forward a psychic or healing gift from before. There will be much more on this subject in Chapter 22.

You can also work with your unconscious mind to help you get to the truth about who you were in your past life. The pendulum is a good way to do that (see Chapter 14). After you have determined yes and no and have requested permission from your soul, you can ask whether or not a character from your past life was you. You may find your answer this way.

Words to Remember

Soul fragmentation is the belief that your soul can divide when it reincarnates. This means that there could be two or more parts of yourself wandering around the world seeking to reunite. Imagine how that would compound over different lifetimes. Under this theory you could be communicating with several parts of yourself through the various characters in your past.

There are many more theories on what you are communicating with during a hypnotic past life regression. An interesting one is *soul fragmentation*. Under this theory you could be communicating with several parts of yourself through the various characters in your past.

Make sure you keep records of whom you can communicate with and whom you cannot. You will not be able to step into the soul memories of some characters. Some of the soul energies have been pulled back to the other side and are not able to communicate with you, at least not at the present time.

The Collective Unconscious: Meeting All Kinds of People

Swiss psychologist Carl Gustav Jung (1875–1961) advanced the theory of the collective unconsciousness. He believed that beyond one's own unconscious mind, which contained personal repressed memories, was a greater consciousness that contained the memory of the mental energy of the universe. The universal mind is often considered to be the same as the collective unconsciousness. In other words, all knowledge is accessible to almost anyone who desires to open him- or herself to it.

Under this theory, when you regress to a past life, you are absorbing the knowledge of what was there when the actual experience happened. All the actions and thoughts represented in the energy of each character in your past life may be accessible to you when you open yourself to them. This may create confusion when you try to determine which person you were.

When Edgar Cayce visited the Akashic Records, he was able to peer into the history of any soul that he wanted. He could see the pitfalls and hindrances that potentially lay ahead because of the knowledge of the soul's past. You may have that same ability.

If you can go to the Akashic Records through a hypnotic trance, you may want to look up the record of your soul and compare it to the different characters you have met in your past life.

> **Soul Stories**
>
> You may have heard the story of the hundredth monkey. It goes something like this: There was an island where a colony of monkeys lived. One of the monkeys decided that it would wash its food in the water before he ate it. The other monkeys on the island all decided that they would do the same. Before long all the monkeys on the island were washing their food before they ate. Soon, on another island halfway across the world, a monkey began to wash *its* food in the water before it ate. Was this an act of coincidence or universal communication?

Regardless of whose past lives they were, the energy of the collective unconsciousness could be a great benefit to you. Just imagine what it would be like to consult the masters of knowledge who have gone on to the other side. Perhaps you would like to understand the secrets of the universe or the painting technique of a famous artist. The collective unconsciousness has the record of all knowledge, thoughts, and actions. All you have to do is connect to it.

There are many other benefits of contacting others during a past life regression. One is that you have a greater chance for gaining better insights into your own past life by observing through the eyes of others. You can study relationships and perhaps gain a better perspective of those that have been carried over into your current lifetime. The more you learn about the story of your past, the better you will be prepared to be in tune with your soul's journey into the future.

The next time you experience a regression, you may wish to try visiting the collective unconsciousness. After you have counted yourself down and traveled back to the lifetime that you want to visit, see how many different characters in your story you can communicate with. Can you directly have a conversation with them? Can you hear what they are telling you? Can you move them around in their lifetime? Can you feel their emotions and image through their eyes? See how well you do communicating with the collective unconsciousness.

> **Ageless Insights**
>
> You don't necessarily need to go into a deep trance to experience the collective unconsciousness. You can tap into the energy through the feeling of déjà vu. You may sense the energy from a different time period from a location that is rich in history, such as a Civil War battleground or a disaster site. Places where many people congregated during a time in history can contain the energy of their souls.

Channeling and Spirit Communication

To compound your past life research even further, consider that you may have opened yourself up to be a channel for another entity. It may be a friendly voice that speaks through you with words of wisdom from the collective unconsciousness. You could become a medium for an entity that wants to get a message out through you.

Channeling is a different type of trance experience. The subject enters an altered state, and another personality comes through. During the time that the altered state is in effect, the subject is consciously unaware of what is being said through them. This can also happen through automatic writing and other artistic forms. Two of the most noted channels in the second half of the twentieth century were Jane Roberts, who brought through an entity known as Seth, and Arthur Ford, through whom an entity named Fletcher spoke. Roberts chronicled her experiences in a book called *Seth Speaks* (see Appendix B).

It's possible to confuse a channeling experience with a past life experience. This can easily happen when the entity identifies the time when they lived, especially if it is coincidentally in the time you experienced a past life. The difference between a channeling and a past life experience can in part be determined by the language the subject used. The past life focus is on another time period while a channel often focuses on the present and future.

Words to Remember

Spirit communication is the ability to speak to the soul of someone who has died, usually in thought form. People who have this ability will each do it a little differently using imagery from their five senses.

You may also run into ghosts and other spirits when you attempt a past life regression. Hypnosis can be an excellent method for *spirit communication*. This can be accomplished by giving yourself the suggestion that you will be open to the energies that may be connected to the location where you are when you are experiencing a trance state. At the same time you may be open to these energies without realizing it. Remember to ask your belief for protection from unwanted spirit visitors when you are in hypnosis.

A good hypnotic subject can actually visualize a ghost and then communicate with it. The purpose is usually to help a spirit who is trapped within the earth plane move on to the other side. A good way to accomplish that is to ask the ghost to ask someone close to them who has died to help guide them over to the other side.

Do you think you can talk with space aliens while you are in a hypnotic trance? It's possible that you might channel an entity that claims they are from another planet.

Their message might be for the entire world as either encouragement or as a warning about the future. This book does not make a judgment on what may be speaking through you. The important thing to remember is that all communication should be positive and nonthreatening. If you have continuous negative voices in your head you should stop experiencing regressions and seek professional counseling immediately.

There are a lot of religions that consider communication with spirits and regressing into your past lives the work of the devil. If the church becomes aware that a member of their congregation practices hypnotic trances, they may be asked to leave the group. If you are connected to a conservative membership of any kind, you may want to consider seriously whom you tell about your interest of going into your past.

As I stressed in Chapter 13, it's very important for you to be grounded in your belief. If you ask that your inner and outer guidance systems help guide and protect you as you experience your past life regressions, you will have a much better chance of having a positive regression experience. The more you are comfortable with your past life plan, the better you will be able to understand something that might pop up unexpectedly. You know that anytime you want to, you can always take a deep breath, exhale, and open your eyes feeling relaxed and positive.

Delving into the history of your soul can be a very positive, educational, and life-changing experience. Once you are prepared to go beyond a possible negative experience, you will be able to go about your past life research with confidence. Always keep track of the different types of past life regression experiences you have. You may want to come back and work with something that you uncover which may not be your own character from before.

The Least You Need to Know

- ◆ *The Search for Bridey Murphy* is a story worth reading.
- ◆ The character whom you identify with in a past life can be insightful to you in this life regardless of whether it was you or not.
- ◆ You can experience more than one life during a past life regression.
- ◆ The collective unconsciousness is also there for you to communicate with.
- ◆ Hypnosis is an excellent way to channel spirit communication.

Chapter 21

Resolving the Old Karma

In This Chapter

- What goes around comes around
- How your free will may be prolonging your karma
- Change is good—or is it?
- Understanding and resolving your karma

You now know that you run into your old karma many times each day. It could be in a thought or a communication with someone else. You may be held captive by an issue that started many lifetimes ago. Up until now you have not found a way to move beyond its old emotions.

As you may remember, in Chapter 12 you learned how past karma can catch up with you. In this chapter you will discover ways to make a fresh start in your life. You can actually get yourself back in tune with your soul's purpose. There's only one thing that stands in your way. It's your free will. It is the voice inside you that represents your ego.

Now it is time to put your detective skills to work so that you can discover and crack the case of your past life karma. Once you understand it, you can move forward in your life. You may never view an old karma in the same way again.

Old Karma Dies Hard

What goes around comes around. That old saying can certainly apply to the actions that you took in your past lives. Did you discover anything when you visited your past that could be connected to your current lifetime? You may have been looking for something specific. You may not have had karma on your conscious mind when you went into your past. Either way, it exists around you most of the time. Some of it is so strong that it is impossible not to notice while some is so subtle that you are only momentarily affected by it. What happened during your past life?

Did you identify any karma when you regressed back in time? If so, do you have a section in your journal on your discoveries? If not, it might be a good idea to make one. You will want to note anything that seemed to conflict with the positive universal energy flow throughout your body. In other words, did you run into anything that indicated issues that have not yet been worked out in your actions, your relationships, or your internal communication with yourself? Have you found yourself in conflict with others or yourself? If you have, you may have karma to resolve.

What lifetime was the karma in? Were you able to follow it back through your past lifetimes until you found the beginning? When you do this, you are actually using the affect-bridge regression technique to trace a feeling or emotion back through your past life rather than your current one. The goal is to get to its beginning and examine it as you are now so that you can get a different view of an old situation.

If you haven't yet uncovered your karma, here is a way that you can try identifying it through a past life regression. This technique will deal with looking for previously undiscovered karma in a past life.

After you have completed your basic self-hypnotic induction, suggest to yourself that when you regress in time you will let your unconscious mind reveal to you any karma that either began or was continued over into the life you are visiting. When you go back, allow yourself to experience what the suggestion brings out of your soul's memory. Then begin to collect the information that is brought forward from your unconscious mind. Focus on the first images you get and deepen them through all your different senses. Don't forget to zoom in and out so that you can get more than one view if that works for you.

You may have several options for discovering your karma, depending on what you have learned about it. If it went back before this life, you can ask your unconscious mind to take you back to the life before that contains the same karma. Then focus on the first images that come to you. Use all your senses to help deepen your hypnotic trance. Once you have established a strong image, move the karma back through that life until you come to the beginning of it when the character was born.

Now go forward until you reach the end of the life and examine the last thoughts and the after-death feeling that they may have carried over into the next lifetime. Again, examine the relationships of the characters in that lifetime to learn how they are connected with other lifetimes and you in your current lifetime. Also look for a theme of that life and what may have been carried over into another one.

Did your karma remain the same, or did it follow a theme through several past life plays? Did you have repeat characters sharing your past lives? If so, what was the same and what was different from life to life? Did you have an emotional karma that only involved yourself and not others? What other karma did you uncover in your journey into the memory of your soul?

> **Karmic Cautions**
>
> You might need to examine several lifetimes before you have identified your karmic relationship with the past. It may take more than one regression session to follow the karma back to its beginnings. After all, it may have existed for a very long time. After each regression, make notes in your journal about the karma you encountered and then develop a plan for your return visit.

Free Will: You Don't Have to Change

Okay, now that you have gathered some information about your karma, what do you want to do about it? You don't have to do anything if you don't want to. You can keep on going along the same path that you are on, but you can alter your life plan if you so choose. Of course, if you choose unwisely, you may have to revisit the lessons you are currently working on at a later date.

As you already know, the choice to follow your life plan or not is free will. Your life plan is dictated by how you followed your plan during your previous life. If you chose to stick with your lesson there, you moved forward in your soul's journey. If you didn't, you are now dealing with the leftover karma from your past. You may have a lot to work on or you may have already made improvements.

It seems that the more developed your soul is, the more resistance you may encounter for staying in tune with your life purpose. As your soul evolved over many lifetimes, it has slowly worked its way through the lessons of the universe. Of course, when all the lessons are learned, the "old soul" will return to the place where its journey began. There it will exist as a part of the collective unconscious and the knowledge of all its experiences.

A younger soul may create a lot of karma, but does so out of desire to satisfy its ego. It is more prone to act without consciously thinking about the results of its actions. It is only later that it realizes it has followed its will for personal satisfaction rather than staying in tune with its purpose. At this point in its development, it may not be paying attention to its potential.

An old soul, on the other hand, knows that it needs to stay true to its purpose. It may resent that it is not free to make its own decisions like a young soul. It is bound by its conscience or awareness that there is a purpose in life beyond material comfort and ego satisfaction. If you are an old soul, you know what it means to be out of sync with most everyone, and you probably resent that fact.

The old soul will often have many more arguments with him- or herself than a younger soul. These arguments are often over the right to do what one pleases rather than to listen to the inner voice that says to do the right thing. An old soul will observe younger souls that seem to enjoy life without an awareness of the consequences of following their own free will. The old soul knows the consequences, but may choose to ignore them.

Now that you have identified some of your karma and traced it back into other life-times, do you want to do anything about it or do you want to keep it as it is? You may have found that in one life your karma gave you a lot of pleasure, and in another it gave you a lot of pain. The pleasure comes when you are taking self-gratifying actions that do nothing to help you learn the lessons of the universe. That brief respite of self-indulgence can result in a much longer period of karmic payback.

"What goes around, comes around" means that your quest for self-gain may allow you to serve many of those you mistreated during the time you were in control. If you are now in a vocation that seems menial and you have to serve many people, you may be able to regress back to a lifetime when you were in power and find that those you serve now, served you then. If you can locate such a lifetime, how did you treat others when you were in a position of power? If you are in a position of power or wealth now, you may want to consider how you are currently treating those who cross your life journey. Remember that every action you take now may result in karma in the future.

Soul Stories

Jane feels that her current life is karmic payback for her actions in the past. She wanted to regress back to the times when she strayed from the lessons of her soul's journey. She located a life where she was extremely beautiful and used her gift to gain power and wealth. In this life she has the wealth, but does not see herself as beautiful. She had been using money to buy her friends rather than trusting her "inner" beauty, which is the lesson of this lifetime. Once she accepted that, she went on to resolve a lot of her old karma.

The choice is yours. You have the opportunity to create and resolve karma with every thought and action. You can go with your heart and soul, or you can listen to the voice inside that seeks to satisfy your ego. You may want to develop a karmic balance sheet in your journal and consider the actions that you have taken and those that you are contemplating. (Do you need a bigger journal yet?)

Would It Be Good to Change?

Yes, you do have a choice, but do you consider the potential long-term results of actions you take that are meant to satisfy your ego? Do you consider the results of what you do in relationship to what the total effect will be on others, not only in the next moment, but in the future as well? There are many people who dwell on a past action in their minds long after the others involved are finished with it. Do you know anyone like that? They are still experiencing actions of the past, and are unable to allow themselves to move forward into the future.

It may be that someone took away your self-confidence when they made you feel you had little value or were not intelligent. Because of a single moment in time, you continue to be held back by their words or actions. Now every time you think that you are making headway, something happens that reminds you of your past, and you are thrust back into your memories. Your old karma continues to play out inside your mind.

You may not even be aware of your old karma consciously because you are stuck in a narrow view. If you can change your focus to take in the big picture, you can examine the past in a different manner. You may ask yourself if you caused the past situation, or were you only a part of what someone else caused? Chances are that the bigger view will show you that you were not the cause but just a victim of the actions of others. Do you want to continue to be the victim, or do you want to resolve the past for yourself, regardless of the other characters? You do have that choice. You can go beyond the karma that someone else created and advance in your soul's purpose.

Once you begin to learn about karma, you may never look at the way you take an action in your life the same way again. You may also become aware of the little karma that goes on in your life all the time. You can now see the second view. That view is the one that allows you to pull back and examine your future, present, and past actions without getting caught up in the emotional part of them. Once you begin to consciously examine the possibility that you have karma, you will have begun to develop a second view of a situation that can help you resolve and move beyond it.

Can you think of situations where you may have met someone for the first time and immediately stepped into a karmic situation? It may have been an issue from a past lifetime that has brought the two of you together again. You may or may not have resolved it. That might have been the only chance you will get in your current life. In that case you will meet them again in some future time.

Are you aware when you are involving yourself in a past life karma? If you think you are, would it be good for you to resolve it so that you can move forward in your life? As you review the history of your karma, imagine how it would help you to be able to make a fresh start as you get back in tune with your soul's purpose.

Ageless Insights

You can do your part to resolve karma, but what if another person or persons involved choose not to cooperate? Does that mean that you all have to work on it again? Not necessarily. If you do your part as honestly as you can and believe that your action is the best for your soul's development, you have done what you can. Now the other characters in the play own the action and they will need to deal with it in the future.

Do you know someone who is so self-centered that they can only focus on themselves? They may not be able to pull back from their narrow focus and take in the whole picture. As long as they stay in that view, they will continue to experience the karma that accompanies it.

You have the choice of prolonging your karma or taking steps to resolve it. Imagine for a moment how it would be to go about your daily life free of some of the current karmic distractions that you have. If you think you might want to change some of your patterns, let's see how you can develop a plan to resolve some of your karma.

Try It Out in Your Mind

Have you identified some karma that you would like to resolve? If you haven't, now is the time to identify it. Have you traced it back to where you think it began? Can you identify the type of karma it is? Have you determined the relationship or relationships that you have with the different characters in your karma over one or more lifetimes? Have you found the theme that connects your karma from lifetime to lifetime?

If you have done all this and are ready, let's use some self-hypnosis to help you resolve the old views your karma has given you. Find a place where you will not be interrupted and get comfortable. Begin to breathe in and out slowly and let yourself focus on your third eye. When you are ready, begin your countdown from five to zero. Go at a speed that is right for you as you let yourself enter a deep hypnotic trance. You will always be aware of many things, and you know that at any time you want or need you may always take a deep breath, exhale, open your eyes, and come back to the surface of your conscious mind.

As you count yourself down, remind yourself to relax and feel positive as you breathe in the peaceful energy of the universe. There are many muscles in your body, and every time you allow one to relax that is stiff, you will go deeper and deeper into hypnosis.

Once you get to zero, allow yourself some time to enjoy the peaceful and loving energy of the universe that surrounds and flows through your body. When you are ready, ask your unconscious mind if it is willing to work with you to help you resolve old karma from your past. You may request that if the answer is yes, one of your fingers or thumbs will lift itself into the air to signal the affirmative answer. Now continue to breathe slowly in and out as you wait to receive the answer from your unconscious mind.

> **Soul Stories**
>
> Lisa had a fear of needles. She could not bear the thought of having one stuck into her arm. When she needed to have blood work done, she sought the help of a hypnotist. Lisa was regressed to a life where she had received a lethal injection from a needle. After she learned the origins of her fear, she was able to overcome it and complete her tests.

When you receive the okay, suggest to yourself that you will review your karma to help you understand how it began and has carried forward to where your soul's map is at the moment. Ask your belief that as you visit your past you may understand your old behavior and learn how you may change it in the future to help you get back in tune with your soul's purpose.

You may use any method of regressing that works best for you. Start by reviewing your current life and go back through all the karma relating to it over as many lifetimes as it takes until you get back to the beginning. You may have already done much of this in earlier regressions, but there might be something on the way back that you did not notice before. You may be able to do this quickly or it may take some time to complete. Just go at a pace that is comfortable for you and don't forget to use all of your senses to help produce the best images possible.

Get as clear a definition of each karmic situation as possible. Make note of how you emotionally felt about each situation and compare them to help you identify the ongoing theme of your feelings. Once you have gotten back to the beginning, go back a little farther and then move forward until you get to where the karma started.

Once you have gotten as much information as possible, bring yourself back to your present life as you are now, but continue to remain in your comfortable and peaceful hypnotic trance. Take a moment or so to readjust. Now allow your unconscious mind to provide you with positive images as to how you can go forward into the future and resolve your old karma.

Ask your belief to help you know the right way to respond and take actions that are different from the ones you used to take. You may ask that the right words be given to you to say that will be the best for all concerned, not just to satisfy your ego. Allow the peaceful and loving energy of the universe to wash over your old karma and feel it begin to heal. You may request that you do the best you can for the good of the whole in relationships in your life and give yourself permission to let your mind move beyond old situations that happened in the past. Ask for the right way to avoid conflict and to overcome old fears.

Now try these new concepts out in your mind. Imagine now how you can use the information gained from regressing into your past lives to help you resolve the old karma and put yourself back in tune with your soul's purpose. Try out some potential future situations and see how you will react to them differently than the way you used to.

How were you able to view your future? Could you experience yourself overcoming and resolving situations that in the past would have led to the continuation of your karma?

Karmic Cautions

Remember that if there are others beside yourself involved in your karma, they may not choose to resolve your differences. If that is the case, imagine how your actions in the future could put you in tune with your belief and your soul purpose, letting others use their own free will to do the same. They now own your good intentions. What they do with them is their choice. They can work to resolve them or not. Your personal goal is to be free of your karma.

Now ask your unconscious mind if you have completed the process of resolving the karma and if you are prepared to take the proper actions in the future if similar situations arise again. Ask that one finger rise if the answer is yes and two fingers rise if you still need to review your old karma more. If the answer is no, ask that the right images be given you from your unconscious mind to help you find the right information to be able to move forward in your life.

Go through the process of review if needed and project this into the future. When you have finished, ask again if you have completed your resolution. When you have gotten an affirmative answer, slowly count yourself up from zero to five to the surface of your mind. Take a deep breath, exhale, and open your eyes feeling the positive and peaceful energy of the universe flowing through your body.

The Least You Need to Know

- ◆ You may currently be affected by the actions you took in your past lives.

- ◆ You have the right to choose if you want to resolve your karma or not.

- ◆ Resolving your karma can help get you back on track with your soul's purpose and move forward in your life.

- ◆ Once you are aware of karma, you always have the opportunity to change and resolve it.

Part 5

Updating Your Past

Now that you are an experienced mind detective of your own past lives, it's time to update your old abilities and put them to use again. Were you a writer, a poet, an artist, or someone with great psychic skills in a past life? You may want to look into what your potential will be in a future life. Then there is another intriguing place to go. What happens in between lifetimes? If you'd like to explore group regression, you could host a past life regression party for your family and friends.

Finally, it's time to take a look at your past life regression abilities and decide how they might be useful to you. You now have the tools to learn from your past and can use them to build on your future. Your past will always be a part of your present and your future. That past includes your many past lives.

22

Putting Past Talents to Use Again

In This Chapter

- ◆ Learning about your past life skills
- ◆ Revisiting artistic talents from a past life
- ◆ Rediscovering the writer in your past
- ◆ Using your psychic gifts from another lifetime
- ◆ How past fame can help you in this life

Have you discovered any past life talents yet on your journeys back in time? If so, what are they? Perhaps you were an artist, a writer, a great athlete, highly intuitive, or a famous person. If you were any of these, wouldn't it be nice to pick up where you left off during your other lives?

You may be able to do just that. This chapter will help you to identify and update the talents you had during a past life. You might think about reconnecting with your past life talents, as a Kellogg's cereal commercial suggests. To get you to retry the product, the commercial invites you to "discover it again for the first time."

You may already be drawn to and even excel in a past life ability. You just may not be aware that you were born already knowing how to use it. At the same time, you may have a special gift that is so natural that you dismiss it and do not use it in this life. Finally, it's possible that you do not want to have anything to do with a past life talent in this lifetime because of the unfinished karma attached to it. This chapter will help you to identify and understand how you can use your abilities from the past if you so desire.

Rediscovering Your Skills

Have you identified any abilities in a past life that you would like to put to use again? Perhaps you discovered that you did something that you haven't remembered yet in your current life. If you excelled at a profession, you might want to try it again during this lifetime. You may have already made note in your journal of the occupations you had before. How do you suppose a prospective employer would react to your resume if it listed your past life occupations as well as those in your current life? Do you think they would be ready for such a claim? Of course, it might be a little difficult to get any references for your past life abilities.

Knowing that you did something well in a past life might give you encouragement and confidence to redevelop what you were able to do before. The goal is for you to reacquaint yourself with your past life skills. To accomplish this, you will want to go back and experience again what you could do before.

> **Soul Stories**
>
> Donald had the potential for being a gifted athlete. His physical shape and natural coordination were the envy of many of his high school friends, and yet he refused to even try out for team sports. He was much happier going on runs and walks by himself. It wasn't until a few years later that he learned through a past life regression how he had used his great strength in a past life to cause pain for others. He wanted nothing to do with the combative nature of sports in this lifetime.

Remember that each of you will image your past life differently. If you can project yourself into your character, you will be able to feel what it was like when you first developed your abilities. The goal is for you to bring these old feelings of success back with you so that you can update them for your current life.

If you know the life that you want to regress to, prepare to return to it. Once you have entered your self-hypnotic trance and counted down to zero, suggest to yourself that when you go back you will feel what it was like to have and use your skill from before. Now go back to that lifetime.

When you have arrived, let yourself experience the past life skill again. Project yourself into the mind of the character. How and what did they think like? Feel the movements of the character in your past. Suggest to yourself that your muscles will remember these movements after you come back to your conscious mind. The experience may be like Bridey Murphy's when she danced again in the body of Virginia Tighe (see Chapter 20). It might be possible for you to remember the muscle movements that you experienced before.

Once you have finished experiencing your past life, slowly bring yourself back to consciousness. Did you videotape yourself? Now while you are still in a relaxed state, recall to the best of your ability what you learned from your past life experience. Will your muscles respond to your past life experience? Be patient; the more you focus on your past muscle movements, the more your present body will respond to the memories. If for any reason you feel uncomfortable experiencing the muscle movements from your past life, take a deep breath, exhale, and bring yourself back to consciousness feeling relaxed and positive.

You may have to revisit the same past life a few times for your muscles to respond to their soul memories. You may have different physical traits now than you did before. The more you imagine your muscles responding, the better the chance for them to start producing your old skills again.

Is there anything you know in your mind you can do very well but you have a resistance to even giving it a try? If you do, you may want to understand where you learned it in the first place, and where you learned not to want to do it. Maybe you have karma that has prevented you from using a past life skill or natural ability in this lifetime. Maybe it is being blocked by a *suppressed memory* because of a traumatic situation connected to it.

You can bridge yourself back through this life into the past life or lives that relate to your gift and your karma attached to it. Note where you first developed it and where and how you learned to either mistrust or hate it. When you have finished, reunite your past life skills with yourself in this life and give yourself permission to use your ability in a positive way for yourself and others.

> **Words to Remember**
>
> A **suppressed memory** is one that is buried in your unconscious mind and is only remembered when a situation jogs it. Then it may come flooding back to the surface and cause you to replay the original experience in your mind. Once you resolve the negative part of the memory, you can reconnect with the ability you had before, as you would use it now.

Were You an Artist?

Artistic abilities surface in many different ways. You may have been such a natural as a child that you eventually lost interest because it was not challenging enough for you. You may still use your creative talent but wish you could develop it further. You may not think that you have ability, but others tell you that you do.

Do you have a natural creative talent? It may be arranging flowers, redecorating your house or apartment, designing and building your own furniture, or putting colors together in ways that bring many compliments. It may be so easy for you that you think everyone else has the same ability. If you get a lot of positive feedback about something creative that you do, it is a talent that others probably do not have. If that's the case, perhaps you would like to develop it even further.

> **Ageless Insights** _____
>
> Did you ever wonder why some people excel at art while others can't draw a straight line? Maybe they have developed their talent over several lifetimes. Remember that everyone has a creative gift. Your gift is directly linked to your mental DNA. You will use your strongest senses to produce your best work. If you have no pictures in your mind, you will paint differently than someone who has strong visual imagery.

The goal of this chapter is to help you identify where you first learned your "natural" talent and to help you update your abilities from previous lifetimes to the present. To accomplish this, you may first identify what artistic interest you would like to investigate from your past. It may be something you already do or did do at one time in your life. It may be something that you have always had a great interest in and want to learn where it came from. It may be a time period when great artists lived that you would like to visit to see if you have some sort of a connection with it. Put your travel plan together.

If you have a specific artistic medium that you would like to try or perfect, you will want to have some material ready to practice with. It could be paper and pencils, or paint, brushes, canvas, clay, or some other material. You may already have the right equipment, or you may want to purchase or borrow some. If you are able to put yourself in the mind and body of the character in your past life, you can try to let yourself be taught by who you were then.

You may want to work with a partner at first to assist you when you try out your artistic talent in a trance state. They can help hand you your supplies and guide you through your project. This will help you focus on the artistic experience that you had in a past life. It may take a few attempts before you are able to put yourself in the artistic trance zone. Once you are used to the procedure, you should be able to accomplish your creative trance without the help of someone else.

When you are ready, get comfortable and count yourself down from five to zero using the induction that works best for you. Once you have entered a comfortable and relaxing self-hypnotic trance, suggest to yourself that when you regress back to the lifetime where you were an accomplished artist, you will allow yourself to experience the skills of the person you were in the past. Also suggest that you will feel your muscles moving the same way and that you will understand how you thought in the past. Suggest that you will remember this when you come back to your conscious mind and will be able to continue developing your artistic gifts from your past.

Karmic Cautions

If there was karma attached to your artistic talent, suggest to yourself that you only need to feel just enough of the emotion so that you will be able to experience your old gift. If the feelings are too intense, you can always take a deep breath, exhale, open your eyes, and come back to your conscious mind.

Now regress to the life where you first developed your artistic skills. Before your experience, go through the lifetime and learn as much about the artist as possible. First be the observer, and when you're ready, step into the experience. Now work with the material and let the artist of old create again. Once you have completed your experience, suggest that you will continue to open your unconscious mind to your soul's artistic gifts after you have returned to your conscious state. Count yourself back up to five.

Were you able to bring your artistic talent from a past life forward to where you are now? The more you practice what you already know, the more you will hone your soul's skills again. Be patient with yourself now and with who you were in the past. If you work together, you will again find yourself in tune with your abilities of old.

Were You a Writer?

A lot of great books have been written from the past. The writer may have developed the skills to produce beautiful and powerful written words some time ago. They may have captured the memories of their soul and are now able to write them for others to benefit. Taylor Caldwell's books are a great example of how her memories from past lives surfaced when she wrote novels about specific time periods. She was able to write descriptions imaged through her unconscious mind that actually proved to be historically accurate. You may be able to have the same past life recall that provides stories of your own soul's memories.

Do you have an interest in writing? Do you write now or do you have a deep feeling that you want to be a writer? You may be hearing the whispers of a memory locked deep in your unconscious mind. Did you tell stories from different times when you were a child? Do you have an imagination that is rich in memories from the past? If you do, perhaps you were a writer in another life. Do you use this talent in your present lifetime? If not, perhaps you would like to give it a try.

Do you keep a journal? If you do, you may already have the seeds that will help your ideas grow into a novel. You may have had stories come to you in your dreams or just pop out of your unconscious mind with such clarity that they seem to be already written. Perhaps they were, and by you. Now you may be able to reconnect with the writer within.

There are two ways to work with the writer in your past. One is to go back through hypnotic regression and connect with your soul's experience. Just as with other art forms, you can feel what it was like to be the writer of old. You can study that lifetime and understand how the ability to write was first developed. You can also resolve any old karma that may be hindering your ability to write in this lifetime.

To go back, follow a normal regression procedure, counting down and then suggesting to yourself to regress to the time when you were a writer before. Make sure you have something to write with and plenty of paper for your adventure. If you have a partner for the first few times, it may help you focus on your regression. Review the life first, and then if you are able, let yourself experience how the writer thought and what it felt like to write during that time. Try holding a pen or pencil over a piece of paper and see what happens. Suggest to yourself that you will bring forward your writer soul memory to your conscious mind and update your old skills into your current lifetime.

You may also access your past life memories through automatic writing. Automatic writing happens while you are in a hypnotic trance. You can focus your conscious mind on many different things while you write down your unconscious thoughts and images. You don't even need to know what your hand is writing.

Soul Stories _____

When Jackie was in her 20s, she had unlimited access to her unconscious mind. Anything she wanted to know, all she had to do was open herself to it. She became obsessed with writing down everything she knew. Of course, that was impossible. She wrote all day long, forgetting to eat or sleep. Her obsession finally led to a complete mental breakdown. Remember that you only need to know what is right for you to know at the moment. If you have such a compulsion, please seek the help of a professional counselor.

To try automatic writing, choose the way you want to set the words of your soul down on paper. It may be with pencil, pen, typewriter, or computer. You can sit at a desk or in a chair, whatever is best for you. Start out with a basic relaxation exercise, and enter a light self-hypnotic trance. Suggest to yourself that when you are ready, your unconscious mind will connect you with your soul memories and you will let the writer in your past come through your fingers. You may or may not be consciously aware of what you are writing. It may take a little practice to find the best technique for you, but you could have a great story of the past waiting to be told again.

Did You Have a Psychic Gift?

Are you psychic? Actually, everyone is psychic to some degree. Many times a psychic gift is more like a curse. You may know things that you don't want to know. If you have this ability, you probably live in constant dread that you will suddenly get images of something that will have a negative outcome in the future. It may be a premonition of a death of a family member or friend, or a world disaster.

This type of psychic experience often starts during your teen years at a time when you are very open to the images of your unconscious mind. You actually enter a light trance such as a daydream, and all of a sudden you focus on what your unconscious mind is projecting up to you. The images may be of things that you do not understand. You may even become aware that you are leaving your body and are floating up into the universe. That experience can be very scary to anyone when they experience it for the first time, especially to a teenager who is totally unprepared. After the first time people live in constant fear of it happening again.

The word *psychic* means "from the human soul." It is the belief that your intuitive abilities in this life are a direct result of past life experiences. This could be true for you. You may be directly influenced by your soul's memories of past life psychic talents. The more you developed your gifts in the past, the stronger their images may be in your unconscious mind today.

Do you have a psychic ability that you would like to understand? Perhaps it is something that you would like to use more or just understand more about. It is experienced through the senses that are strongest for you. If you are visual, you may get pictures of events that have not yet happened. If you have a strong sense of hearing, you may have a voice in your head give you information about the future or the past. The same goes for feelings, smell, and taste. These senses have all been developed in a past life to the point that they now work for you. Understanding how you developed them can help you put them to use again in your current lifetime.

Psychic ability and karma can go hand in hand. As I've said, many intuitive people do not enjoy having their gift at all. The experiences you have had before may have been related to survival or overcoming extreme circumstances that gave you great strength. When those abilities are triggered now, the situations are probably a lot different. An old adversary from your past may have a much different role to play in this lifetime, but your unconscious mind may not know about the change. It is still involved with the conflict from before. Your old survival skills surface without warning. If this is the case for you, you may want to go back and resolve the karma related to your psychic talent from the past.

To go back and investigate a past life when you developed and used psychic abilities, let yourself go into a hypnotic trance and count yourself down from five to zero. Suggest to yourself that you will go back to a lifetime where you learned and developed your psychic talents. Now let yourself travel back to that time. Review the entire life and look for any resulting karma that might have begun because of your abilities. Look for any characters that may also be a part of your life now and note the relationship. Let yourself resolve any karma that may have resulted from your psychic power from the past. Suggest that when you come back to consciousness, you will again be able to reunite your psychic gifts of the past with where you are at the moment.

Now let yourself experience what it was like to be psychic in that lifetime. Bring forward how the different senses imaged so that you will be able to use them again. Feel yourself reuniting with your psychic gifts of the past as they update to your current life. Suggest that you will remember how to use this ability when you come back to the surface of your conscious mind. When you are ready, count yourself back from zero up to five and open your eyes feeling relaxed, positive, and filled with the peaceful and loving energy of the universe.

Were You Famous?

Perhaps you really were a person of great stature and fame in the past. Do you think you might have been? If this is the case, you may be able to bring your leadership qualities or other qualities forward to help you and others in this lifetime. Of course, just because you were famous doesn't mean you were on the right side of the law. You might have been a powerful scoundrel or controlling ruler.

You may have brought some of these issues with you into your current lifetime. The difference here is, your role in the play is not the same as it was before. This life may be one of service or humility. You may be dealing with the karma you created back then.

Karmic Cautions _____

Edgar Cayce cautioned about the dangers of finding out you were a famous person in a past life. The problem that can arise from knowing is that the individual wants to be treated and have all the wealth and power that they may have had before. Of course, the scene of the play has changed, and their role is different now. Trying to live in the past can keep you from addressing the lessons of this lifetime.

Knowing your past can be helpful to you as you journey through your current life. It can help you avoid the pitfalls that are always waiting to pull you offtrack. The key is to work toward updating the power you held from before in a way that keeps you in tune with your soul's journey. The famous person you were before can lend expertise to help you work to find the balance for the character you are now.

To go back and visit the famous person that you once were, let yourself go into a self-hypnotic trance and count yourself down from five to zero. When you get to zero, suggest that you will go back to a lifetime when you were famous. You may already have an idea of when that might be, or you may not have a clue at all. Use the regression technique that you are the most comfortable with. Let yourself travel back in time.

As in other regressions, let yourself focus on the first images you receive. Experience them in all your five senses. Move forward and backward through the lifetime and review the theme, look for the characters that relate to your life now, and resolve any karma that might be connected to your life as a famous person. Now let yourself experience how you felt then, and suggest that you will remember in your conscious mind when you return. When you are ready, count yourself back up to five, and open your eyes feeling positive and relaxed.

When you are awake again, make notes in your journal and compare how you see your role in your current life, to how it was back then. You may get some insights as to how you have been focusing on the role you are playing at the moment. You may find that your famous self can be a positive influence in helping you stay in tune with your soul's journey.

The Least You Need to Know

- ◆ You can bring your talents from another life with you.

- ◆ You can draw upon your past artistic ability in this lifetime.

- ◆ You may have some stories from the past to write.

- ◆ Psychic abilities do not have to be a burden if you learn from your past how to use them again.

- ◆ If you were famous before, it may be a help in your current life.

Chapter 23

Visiting Future and In-Between Lives

In This Chapter

- Finding out about future lifetimes
- How to create a progression travel plan
- What's it like to go forward in time?
- Between-lifetime experiences

Many of you may invest a lot of money visiting psychics who can predict your future. You want to know about your relationships, your prosperity, and your health. You may spend a lot of time and energy worrying about a day that has not yet come.

Just imagine what it would be like to know the future in this lifetime as well as the next lifetime. What would you do with the knowledge? Would it be a help or a hindrance to you in your current situation?

You might also want to know what happens to your soul when it is between lifetimes. Where does it go? What does it do? Besides questions about your past, these questions may also be addressed with the help of a self-hypnotic trance.

Progression: A Peek into the Future

By now you have plenty of experience regressing to your past lives. What do you think about progression? You might ask what that is. Progression is the use of a self-hypnotic trance to project yourself forward into a future lifetime. The concept is similar to regression except that you are going ahead in time instead. Do you think this is a good idea or even possible?

Karmic Cautions

You should not attempt to do a future life progression alone. Always work with a qualified regression specialist or a psychic who has a recognized ability to see into your future lives.

Words to Remember

Quantum mechanics is the theory that every particle or cell contains energy and exists independently of each other. On the metaphysical level, every cell contains the universal life energy that holds the keys to the knowledge of the universal mind.

Have you ever imagined what the future will be like? If this is of interest to you, you will get your chance to find out before this chapter is over. Perhaps you are already in the habit of visiting psychics who can help you anticipate and plan your future in this lifetime. A progression may take you one step further down the path of your soul's journey.

Is a future lifetime experience real or imagined? You'll have to decide that for yourself just as you did about past life regression. It may be just your imagination, or you may be able to tap into the universal knowledge that knows all facets of time—the past, the present, and the future. The theory of *quantum mechanics* states that everything in the universe is related. Psychiatrist Carl Jung believed that all time is accessible on the unconscious level. Therefore, the collective unconsciousness contains not only the knowledge of the past but of the future as well. If you believe this theory, you may be able to go to the Akashic Book of Records and look up your future lives.

To take the quantum mechanics theory a little further, there are those who believe that all time exists at once. In other words, the past, present, and future all are happening together. There are even organizations that attempt to go back in time and heal some of the events that happened in the past, such as wars and other oppression. There are also those who put great faith in the predictions of Edgar Cayce, Nostradamus, and the Bible. They live their lives preparing for events that have not yet happened.

There are both pros and cons about going forward in time. Just as Edgar Cayce warned about letting the knowledge of a past life interrupt your current lessons, so could the knowledge of a future lifetime. If you develop a clear objective in your travel plan, it can help clarify your goals when you journey into your future. Your reason for your progression may influence the type of information you receive when you get there.

What about free will? What will you do with the information you receive about your future lives? Will you use it for self-gain, or will you use it to help find a better balance in your life now? You may not know how you will react until you have experienced a progression. It is your free will to do as you want or should. Your belief system plays an important role in the outcome of your travels into the future.

Soul Stories

Nancy had experienced several past life regressions that were very beneficial to her in her current life, so she wanted to do a progression. The result was not what she expected. She was shown a string of paper dolls, all connected together. She knew that one of the lives was very short, and she was told that she was not to know any of the details about her future lives because it would interfere with her lessons in her current one.

In your journeys, did you ever wind up between lifetimes? Some of you may have already experienced what it is like between lives. You may have felt the pull into the tunnel of light or gently floating out of your body as your soul left your physical body. You may have been confused by what you experienced. The last section of this chapter will explain some of what happens when you are in between lifetimes.

Establish a Travel Plan

Why do you want to see into the future? It's important to establish clear objectives as a part of your travel plan. As you consider some of the reasons for traveling into the future, make notes in your journal to help you define your goals. Part of your plan should be the flexibility to just go with the experience.

Your reasons for progression could come from a combination of your experiences in past lives and your present lifetime. You may wish to find out how a karmic relationship may get resolved. Or you may have an affliction that has no cure at the moment. Perhaps you could find an answer in the future that you could bring back with you, just as memories and talents from the past have been brought forward into the present.

You may just be curious to find out what it will be like in a future time. You may want to write about the future and would like to research it with a progression. You may want to find out if your struggle in this lifetime will be rewarded the next time around. You might be looking for motivation and encouragement to continue on in the direction you are headed. There are many different reasons why you would want to know what your future lifetimes could be like.

For example, one young man who was suffering from a serious debilitating disease wanted to know what his next life would be like if he chose to end the pain and suffering he was currently experiencing. What do you think? Would he have karma? Is his situation caused by past karma? Even if his body is deteriorating, he could use his mind in a positive way to inspire others. If he did this, would he advance his soul's journey? If he doesn't address his lessons now, will they come back again next time?

When you create your future life progression script, you may find it helpful to work with a partner the first few times to help guide you. Much of the preparation will be the same as you did when you experienced a past life regression. You can write it out and record it, or have your partner read it to you, or you could memorize it and repeat it to yourself as you experience your progression. You will want to have materials available for making notes about your journey, and it would be helpful to record or videotape the session.

You should be in a comfortable place where you will not be interrupted during your progression. Have a warm blanket ready in case you get a chill on your journey. If you are a veteran of past life regression, this is all something that you are familiar with. However, it doesn't hurt to review the process from time to time. You can choose the technique that you feel will work the best for you. Those were addressed in Chapter 16.

Remember to use the who, what, when, where, and why observation methods for a progression (see Chapter 15). If you are not familiar with your mental DNA, you will also want to review Chapter 8 so that you will be prepared to use all five of your sensory image abilities. The better the flight checklist you develop and use before each travel into time, either backward or forward, the greater the chance is that you will have an informative and productive experience.

- ◆ WHO do you want to visit in a future lifetime? Would you like to know what kind of a relationship you would have in the next life with someone you are connected to in this life? It could be a relative, a friend, or even someone you have a conflict with. You may have more than one person that you want to do future research on.

- ◆ WHAT do you want to learn when you go forward in time? The better the definition, the clearer your information may be. There are many different questions that you could ask in a future life. Try to focus on just one or a few at a time so that you will not receive more information than you can remember.

- ◆ WHEN is the time period that you want to progress to? Do you want to go just to your next life or to several future lives? You may have a certain time period that you want to investigate, such as the twenty-fifth century. You may want to go forward in time and check out what it's like a hundred years from now. If you know when you want to visit, write it into your travel plan.

◆ WHERE would you like to go when you progress into the future? Do you have a particular location in mind? You may want to know what the area where you live will look like, or you may have an interest in a certain country or geographical location. Of course, your soul may be assigned there in lives to come.

◆ WHY do you want to progress? The better you can define your reasons, the greater the possibility that you will not be disappointed when you get there. This goal will also address why you want to have this information and how you will use it once you have returned from your progression into a future lifetime.

Soul Stories

Willie wanted to progress to a future life to see if he would still have the ability to play the drums. It has been a passion in this lifetime, and he hopes that as he journeys into the unknown his gift will remain with him. He went to a lifetime a couple of hundred years from now and saw himself on another planet playing a very fancy set of space age drums!

Create a Future Self-Hypnotic Trance

If you're ready to travel into the future, find a place where you will not be interrupted, and get comfortable. To begin your relaxation exercise, take a deep breath of air, exhale slowly, and continue to do so. Let yourself focus on your third eye and begin to feel the peaceful and loving energy of the universe start to flow into your body. Feel the golden protective light of the universe surrounding your body as you continue to breathe slowly in and out. You may allow the muscles in your body to begin to relax as you prepare to count downward from five to zero. Let yourself feel in tune with your belief and your inner and outer guidance systems that are always with you to watch over you.

You may suggest to yourself that if you want or need to end your self-hypnotic progression into a future lifetime, you can always take a deep relaxing breath, exhale, open your eyes, and come back to your conscious mind. You will always feel relaxed and positive after a trip into the future. You will always feel the peaceful and loving energy of the Universe protecting you.

When you are ready, begin to enter your hypnotic trance by counting slowly backward from five to zero. With each count you may feel yourself going deeper and deeper into hypnosis. With each count you will feel more and more relaxed as you prepare to progress into a future lifetime.

Ageless Insights

You may repeat positive words to yourself during your progression, such as *relax, peaceful, loving, deeper,* and you will feel their meaning every time you say them. With each count you will go deeper and deeper into your trance.

When you get to zero, you may enjoy the peaceful and loving energy of the universe as it flows from your unconscious mind. You may ask permission of your soul to go forward in time by asking a finger to rise when your unconscious mind is ready. If for some reason this is not the right time for you to visit your future, ask that one of your thumbs rise to indicate it would be better to wait until another time. Once you have gotten permission and you are ready, you may follow your travel plan ahead in time to the life that you want to visit.

If you want to go to the Akashic Records, you may feel yourself gently floating upward until you come to the place where they are stored. Once there, you may begin to look up your future lifetimes in the book of your soul. You may find a computer waiting for you, or even a video center. In whatever form the Akashic Records appear, just let yourself go with the experience. Look for the potential advances in your soul's journey and karmic hazards that may be ahead of you. Once you have gathered your information, you may come back to your body and count yourself back up from zero to five, open your eyes and come back to consciousness feeling relaxed, positive, and full of peaceful loving energy.

If you are using a movie or library technique, you may enter your progressive trance just as you did your regressive ones and follow your travel plans. Focus on the first images you receive with the strongest of your senses. First review the life and look for the theme and the relationships to any of the characters there and compare it to your current life.

Once you have done this, put yourself into the image and experience what it's like to live in a future time. Make as many notes as you can, and when you are ready, count yourself back up from zero to five and return to your conscious mind. Take some time and review your experience. Make notes in your journal so that you can sift through the data whenever you want to.

Can Future Knowledge Help You Right Now?

What will you do with the information you got from a visit into the future? Will you use it for self-gain to avoid your soul's lessons, or will you use it in a way that helps you stay in tune with your current purpose? You have the free will to do with it as you choose. The question is, "Will you create or resolve your karma?"

> **Karmic Cautions** _____
>
> Is the future cast in stone? Will it come true as you imaged it? It may be similar to getting a psychic reading. When you are told about something that will happen in the future, what if you take action now to change the outcome? Imagine that you were told that if you drove on a certain road at a certain time, you would have an accident. Would you drive on that road at that time? Probably you would not. So what about the prediction? Why didn't it come true?

The question brings you back to the concept of quantum mechanics. At the time of the prediction, the outcome is just a probability that will result if the current life pattern continues to be followed. The future is constantly changing, depending on the actions taken in every moment. You can take a chance that your next lifetime will be what you want it to be, or you can work with your current one to prepare for the next one in the best way you can.

What if a future lifetime doesn't look very promising? Remember Mr. Scrooge? The character in Charles Dickens' story *The Christmas Carol* dreamed of what the future held in store for him. He didn't like it, and he changed the outcome, not only for himself, but also for other characters in the story. You may want to make some positive changes in your current life that will be good for you as well as for others as you prepare for the future.

What do you do now if you think you will have a fabulous life next time? The answer is the same. Concentrate on your current lifetime, regardless of what you see in the future. If you stay in tune with your soul's purpose in this lifetime, you may advance beyond the lessons that your soul needed to learn. That decision is yours; it is also part of your free will and can have a positive effect on your future lives.

Can future knowledge help you right now? The answer is yes if you use it in a way that helps you stay in tune with your soul's purpose. The answer may not have been exactly what you wanted to know, but it may be what is currently right for you. It is up to you to decide.

Regressing to a Place Between Lifetimes

In any of your past life regressions up until now, have you experienced what it was like to be between lifetimes? It could have been a floating sensation as your soul began to leave your physical body. It is the same experience that many have had when they encountered a near death situation. Near death experiences usually happen when a person's heart stops beating for a period of time. At that point they are clinically dead. When they come back to life again, many describe the feeling as being "slammed" back into their body.

Soul Stories

Jan had an unusual experience while she was regressing to a past lifetime. She was describing a house that she had lived in before when she began to see two different images of it. One was a small building and the other had been enlarged. As the regression continued, it was discovered that after she had died in that lifetime, her soul continued to exist on the earth plane for a period of time. As a ghost she lived in the house while it was expanded to its later size. This was the explanation for her two different views of the same location.

Just the sensation of leaving your body can be very unsettling. It's the feeling that is often experienced when someone has his or her first astral projection. Perhaps you have knowingly or unknowingly encountered an astral projection or a near death experience. If you have, you may be familiar with what it's like to regress to between two lifetimes.

Astral projection occurs when the mental and/or spiritual parts of yourself separate from your physical body. It is usually felt as a floating sensation, and it usually happens when you are in a state of trance. If you are not prepared for it, it can be very unsettling. Many times, a first experience can linger in your mind for a long time. Astral projection is similar to a near death experience, except that you are not necessarily drawn to the light. It is believed that astral projection is a soul's memory of an early life where there was no physical body that accompanied the soul.

Sometimes the soul continues the emotions that are first encountered after physical death. The trauma of the event may continue and develop into a karma that carries over into the next lifetime. Past life regression therapist Thelma Freedman has studied the lives of several people who suffered from agoraphobia, the fear of leaving their homes, and discovered that many of them had a common denominator as to the beginnings of their phobias. She found the roots of the agoraphobia with the soul in between lifetimes. The confusion resulting from a sudden and/or traumatic death when they were suddenly separated from and unable to reenter their body, transferred to the fear of leaving the body of their house.

There are many beliefs about what happens after a person dies. Most Christians believe that there is no such thing as reincarnation, and you either go to heaven or hell, depending on your behavior while on Earth. There are those who feel that you create your own heaven or hell depending on what you believe when you die. If you believe or fear that you are going to hell, then that is what you will experience after you die. The same goes for heaven.

There has been a lot of evidence collected that souls may linger around the earth plane for a period of time after death and even communicate with loved ones or continue to exist on a spiritual plane in the same physical location. The need to stay may be caused by something that was left unfinished while they were still alive.

There has also been research using hypnosis to follow the migration of the soul after it leaves the physical body. Some go to a place where the lessons of the past lifetime are reviewed and plans are made while the soul rests for the next incarnation. Some near-death survivors tell about being shown back through their life map and examining their lessons just before they came back to life.

You may be interested in exploring in-between lifetimes. You could find yourself there by chance when you are regressing or progressing. The important thing to remember is to let yourself go with the experience. If you collect the information while you are there, wherever that is, you will have the opportunity to clarify it later after you have returned to your conscious mind. As long as you know that you can always end your self-hypnotic trance any time you want to and feel safe and protected by your belief, you are free to explore.

To try an in-between lifetime hypnotic trance, follow your normal induction. When you reach zero, suggest to yourself that you will go back in time to the end of a life where you can follow your soul as it ascends into the universe. Also suggest that you will be surrounded and protected by the peaceful and loving energy of the universe as you follow your soul to its home on the astral plane. Ask that what you will be shown will be useful to you currently as you continue your journey on your soul's path. Go with the experience.

The Least You Need to Know

- ◆ It's important to establish clear progression goals.
- ◆ Use the knowledge of future lives to help you stay in tune with your soul's lessons in your current life.
- ◆ You can encounter in-between lifetimes when you progress or regress.
- ◆ You may be able to follow your soul to its home between lifetimes.

24

Let's Have a Past Life Party!

In This Chapter

- Can more than one person regress at the same time?
- Deciding who will participate in your past life regression party
- Facilitating a group regression
- Reading a past life group regression script
- Taking time to share the experiences

Have you been sharing this book or discussing your past life adventures with anyone else? If you have, how do they react? Chances are that if you have been sharing your stories, the people you have shared with have been drawn into the mysteries of the journeys of the soul. Most people have either a fascination or a fear of the unknown whether they will admit it or not.

Have you and a partner been working together? Perhaps you have already let some of your friends or family watch your regression sessions in person or on tape. One of the reasons that the story of Bridey Murphy (see Chapter 20) was made into a book was because others listened to the audiotapes that led to the interest in publishing the story.

Party Time: Group Past Life Regression

More than one person can participate in a past life regression at the same time. They may or may not share a common experience. In other words, you and others could go back to the same destination, or you could each go to a different place and time along your soul's own paths.

Edgar Cayce spoke of souls that traveled together through time. This is the premise that all of you are in a universal play together with each scene producing a change of roles. Of course, there are karmic themes that carry over from one life to the next. With this in mind, it is possible for several of your friends and family to have lived together before. A group regression to examine specific lifetimes, karmic patterns, or changing relationships could be very beneficial to all of you.

You could all work on regressing back to a common time period separately or together. Each method can have its benefits and drawbacks. If you work by yourself, you can independently document your experiences. You can keep a journal and then get together with others involved in the project and compare results. They may be similar, or they may not match at all. One major drawback with this way is to get everyone motivated to complete his or her part of the group goals.

The advantage of a group regression is that you will have everyone together at the same time, and the results will be compared right after the regression. If you do not establish clear goals for information sharing, you may find that some of the participants won't reveal everything they imaged. They might hold back sharing some of their past life encounters, and that would distort the group findings. It is also possible for some to be influenced by the experiences others had, and their views could change from what they actually encountered.

Another way to have a group past life regression party is to bring together a few people who do not have a common goal. They are all interested in traveling back into a past life and can have the experience while in a group, each researching their own goals rather than making a single group focus. After the regressions are completed, everyone will share their experiences. The evening can be a very enjoyable time and could begin with a meal, perhaps a potluck supper.

Everyone will have a different regression. Some might find themselves between lifetimes, and some might not have much of an experience at all. Still others may have a communication with a spirit or even their guides. It's a lot of fun to compare each different experience at a past life regression party.

Who Should Participate?

How many guests should you invite? How many do you have room for? You want enough so that you have a good blend and balance of experiences, but you do not want so many that you are pressed for time to get everyone's reactions after the regression. A good number might be between six and a dozen. You may have a guest who just wants to watch the process who could help record the session. You don't want too many watching, but one or two may add to the gathering.

Karmic Cautions _____

Obviously you want to invite friends, neighbors, and family who will have a good time. But if you have someone in attendance who is a vocal skeptic or doesn't mix well with others, it will put a damper on your gathering. Also, please don't bring young children because they don't have a long enough attention span to complete a regression and can break the focus of your other guests. The same might be said of some pets. Teenagers are good subjects, but you will want to have their parents' written permission if they are less than 18 years old, unless their parents come with them.

If you would like a theme for your past life regression party, you will want to host a group of people that have a similar goal. You may want to all go back to the same time, place, or karmic themes. You may all believe that you have been together before and would like to examine that lifetime. Or you could all visit a historic event or time period together and then compare notes afterward.

You might want to request that every participant be familiar with this book. If each person has a copy and understands the concept of past life regression and has practiced relaxation and self-hypnotic exercises, it will help save pre-induction time. It also helps when the participants know how their individual DNA produces strong images in their minds. Each person will experience their regression differently even though they are participating together. When everyone that participates is at least partly prepared for his or her journey into the past, it will help the evening go smoothly and may produce better results.

Soul Stories _____

Diane is highly psychic, but she is not a professional. She can visualize in mental pictures what other people are seeing in their minds. She was invited to a past life party and was able to describe details that the other guests did not remember about their own pasts when they gave their post-regression reports. She was the hit of the party.

Do you know any psychics? They don't have to be professional psychics, just have the ability to synchronize their minds with others'. You may know someone who is just beginning to realize that he or she has intuitive abilities. Once this person learns how to understand her mental DNA, she may discover that she has a psychic gift that will enable her to visualize what someone else describes regarding a past life regression experience—making her a valuable participant in the party.

If for some reason you do not plan to have an individual review of each experience after the regression, you can have a larger group. You can even rent a hall if you have a lot of participants. There are professional past life regression specialists who do group regressions. They can work with large numbers, but they also have the training to handle groups of that size. If you are responsible for the party, you will want to keep an eye on everyone so that you can watch to see if anyone is feeling uncomfortable with their experience.

The Role of the Facilitator

The facilitator is the most important element of a past life regression party. He or she needs to be knowledgeable about past life regressions and able to explain the process simply to those who have little or no experience in going back into the memories of their soul. (It would be most helpful for the participants to be familiar with this book before the gathering to ensure that everyone has at least a general knowledge of what to expect and how to experience relaxation and self-hypnosis.) The facilitator needs to be able to induce a hypnotic trance in those attending and be able to watch everyone to make sure that their trip is going smoothly.

You may want to hire a professional to facilitate the regression. There may be a certified hypnotist in your area who can do past life group regressions. You could find out their fee and divide it up among the number of guests at the party. Some regression specialists may have a set fee for each participant. They may collect the money themselves or bring someone with them to take care of the business portion. Some regression specialists recruit hosts for a regression party. The host usually gets to experience it free as a thank you for taking care of the arrangements.

Here are some tips for finding a qualified past life regression specialist:

◆ Check the local telephone directory for listings of hypnotherapists and past life regression specialists in your area.

◆ See Appendix B of this book for websites of hypnosis and past life regression organizations. Ask the organization for a referral to someone in your area.

◆ When you find someone, ask for references of past life work, the type of credentials the person has, and where he or she earned them.

◆ Ask if the specialist has an upcoming event you can attend and perhaps participate in.

You may want to try to facilitate a past life regression party yourself. If you do, you will want to be thoroughly familiar with the material in this book. There are also places that you can train and become certified in hypnosis and past life regression. Check the websites listed in Appendix B if you would like to study this subject in greater depth.

> **CAUTION**
>
> **Karmic Cautions** _____
>
> At first you will want to practice on friends and family who are forgiving of any mistakes you make in conducting the regression. Just like learning any other skill, it takes time to develop and hone your past life regression techniques. You can record the induction if you wish. This way if you slip up in your dialogue or are nervous about doing it live, you can make any corrections needed ahead of time. I include a general script for you to follow later in the chapter.

The most important part of a past life regression party is to make sure the guests feel safe and secure and are having a good experience. You may want to have one or more people assisting the facilitator. They can keep watch on the participants, and if anyone experiences something unpleasant, they can help them feel calm and come back to consciousness. Those assisting the facilitator should be experienced in the knowledge of past life regression. They may even be someone who is training to be a hypnotist or a past life regression specialist.

Establishing Regression Goals

Talk over your idea for a past life regression party with a few others and get their feedback. It is possible that you are the only one familiar with a regression experience, so you can try out your ideas on your friends and family.

Decide what type of regression party you want to host. Will you ask people who want to work toward a common goal? Will you decide to have a gathering that will offer each participant a chance to regress to unrelated lives? You may want to start by just giving others the experience before you focus in on future regression goals. It is very possible that a regression party could inspire follow-up past life research.

Ageless Insights

When you invite your guests, give them enough advance notice so that they can fit it into their schedule. A couple weeks to a month may be a good lead time. That will also give them time to review a copy of this book in order to prepare for the gathering.

Select a good location where interruptions and noise will be at a minimum. If it's a home, unplug any phones and put pets in another room. It should be a place where everyone can feel comfortable, and roomy enough to spread out. Some people may be more comfortable lying down, so if you do not have enough seating space, a soft carpeted floor will do, particularly if you suggest that your guests bring a blanket and pillow. (Sometimes a person will feel chilly after a regression.)

You may want to start the evening with dinner to give your guests time to become comfortable with each other and have the opportunity to discuss their ideas or questions about a past life regression. You will want to have someone who is not going to do a regression to oversee the serving and cleanup of the food. You could hold off on dessert and coffee until the windup period.

Have everything ready:

◆ Writing materials for making notes and sketches

◆ Soft instrumental background music

◆ Dim lighting

◆ Video equipment or tape recorder and someone to run it

◆ Extra blankets and pillows

The pre-induction talk given by the facilitator should include an explanation of the format the party will follow. Give an overview of reincarnation and the lessons each soul encounters as it journeys through each lifetime. Explain what relaxation and self-hypnosis is like. Some of your guests may already practice them. Include a discussion and examples of how to identify each guest's mental DNA and how each one may expect to image.

Also discuss the importance of belief and staying grounded, safe, and protected. Include the possibility that each person has an external and internal guidance system. Explain the relationship between the conscious and unconscious minds. Make sure they are secure in knowing that they can open their eyes and come back to consciousness any time they want or need to.

Finally, tell them how the regression experience will be conducted and encourage them to stay with the experience whether it makes sense or not. Let each one decide which of the regression techniques shown in Chapter 16 they would like to use. If everyone is familiar with this, the evening should go smoothly. You should plan on up to 30 minutes for this portion of the party.

The regression itself should last no more than 30 minutes from the beginning induction to counting back to consciousness. With a group of people, each individual will have their own length of focus time. You don't want some of your guests who may come back earlier to get restless and bored waiting for the others to return.

Soul Stories

When Jenny took part in a past life regression party, she wasn't able go back like the rest of the group. Unbeknownst to her, there was a resident ghost in the old house where the regression took place. Jenny was very psychic and she found herself communicating with the ghost instead of finding a past life.

Assign 15 minutes for the participants to make notes and to collect their thoughts after the regression ends. It is also a good time to take a break. Some will not have had enough time to write, while others won't have much to write about.

The windup and sharing portion of your evening can take up to 45 minutes, depending on the number of guests that you have. The more you have, the less the time each will have to give a summary. Be sure to stay on schedule so that everyone has an equal chance to share their story. Some of your guests may be shy about talking about their experiences. The more the others encourage them, the more they will feel comfortable and open to telling about their encounters.

Past Life Group Script

What follows is a sample of a script that a facilitator would read to the participants in a past life regression session:

If you are ready to begin your past life regression, make yourself comfortable and prepare to start your journey into your unconscious mind and the memories of your soul. Begin by taking a deep breath and slowly exhaling. Continue to do this as you let your mind focus on your third eye, which is in the center of your forehead. You may even feel a sensation there, such as a warm or vibrating feeling. That is normal when you are beginning to connect to the universal energy of peace and love.

When you are ready, close your eyes as you focus on the sound of my voice and the soft music playing in the background. You will be aware of different sounds from time to time. That is perfectly normal as you experience a self-hypnotic trance. As you continue to slowly breathe in and out, you may be aware that you have many muscles throughout your body. Some are relaxed and some are stiff. Every time you relax a stiff muscle, you will relax more and more.

For a moment imagine that you are going to go to a very special place where you feel very comfortable. This place may be real or imaginary. It may be just deep in your unconscious mind. In a few moments I am going to start counting down from five to zero. When you reach zero, you may imagine that you are in your special place, and you may experience it in as many of your five senses as work well for you. If you want to, you may go faster or slower than my counting.

When you begin your countdown into your unconscious mind, you may begin to feel the peace and love of the universe flow through and around your body. You will feel safe and secure and know that anytime you want or need to, you may always take a deep breath, exhale, open your eyes, and come back to consciousness. You will now begin to count down from five to zero. With each count you will feel yourself going deeper and deeper into self-hypnosis as you relax more and more.

- ◆ FIVE. You may begin to feel yourself relaxing more and more as you start to enter into your self-hypnotic trance. With each breath you may relax more and more. You may imagine your favorite relaxing smell or calming music. You may let your mind go wherever it would like to go. You may focus on one image or many different ones. You can hear the music playing softly in the background as you continue to go deeper and deeper.

- ◆ FOUR. With each count you may feel yourself gently sinking deeper and deeper into your self-hypnotic trance. You may feel very relaxed and comfortable. You may continue to breathe slowly in and out as you go deeper and deeper.

- ◆ THREE. You are now halfway to zero and a deep comfortable trance where you will be open to the images of your unconscious mind. With each breath you may go deeper and deeper and relax more and more.

- ◆ TWO. You are getting closer and closer to the images of your unconscious mind. You are relaxing more and more. You are going even deeper into self-hypnosis. You feel calm and positive.

- ◆ ONE. You are almost in a deep hypnotic trance where you will be open to the images of your unconscious mind. With each breath you may feel more and more relaxed. In a moment I will count from five to zero and you may enter a deep and relaxing positive trance as you prepare to travel back in time to a place where the memories of your soul will be open to you. When you get to zero, you will ask permission from your unconscious mind to go back to the time that is right for you at this moment.

◆ FIVE. FOUR. THREE. TWO. ONE. ZERO. You are now in a deep self-hypnotic trance and open to the images that will come through your unconscious mind. Take a moment and enjoy the peaceful and loving energy of the universe as it flows through and around you. Ask your unconscious mind for permission to go back to the images of your soul that are right for you. To receive permission, ask one of your fingers to slowly rise into the air. If it is better for you to wait a little longer to regress into a past life at this time, you may feel one of your thumbs rise up. If this is the case, you may take this time to communicate positively with the messages there for you from your unconscious mind.

Now you may begin to let yourself drift back in time to another lifetime that is right for you at the moment. Take your time and focus on the first images you receive. It may be a picture, a sound, a feeling, a smell, or a taste. Collect as much information as you can. Can you feel your hair, your clothes, or see the location where you are? Remember to look for the who, what, when, where, and why information that is in your regression. Look for the characters that are in your regression. Take a few minutes to focus on these images.

(Allow for several minutes of silence while the group regresses.)

When you are ready, move to the next important scene in this lifetime. Image the scene from different positions. You may go backward or forward. Take your time. Continue to move through that lifetime and make note of as much information as possible. As you move about, look for the theme of that lifetime.

(More silence)

When you are ready, move to the end of that life. You may know the last feelings that your character had when they were alive and how they felt about their life. After you have done this, go back over the entire lifetime and look for the theme, any karma and relationships that may relate to your life now. Imagine how you can use this knowledge in a positive way as you move forward into the future. In a few minutes I will count you back up to the conscious level of your mind.

(More silence)

Now I am going to count you slowly back up from one to five and the conscious level of your mind.

◆ ONE. You are beginning your journey back to consciousness.

◆ TWO. You are feeling relaxed and positive.

◆ THREE. You are coming back to the surface.

◆ FOUR. You are almost there. Take a deep breath, exhale, and open your eyes.

◆ FIVE. You are back to the surface of your conscious mind feeling relaxed and full of the peaceful and loving energy of the universe.

The Windup: Sharing the Experiences

Take up to 15 minutes for everyone to process the information, make notes, and take a break. Next, divide up the remaining time for each participant to share their past life regression experiences. Some of the participants will be very comfortable sharing while others may not want to tell about what they encountered. If someone is reluctant, that's okay. The important thing is to give everyone who wants an equal chance to tell his or her stories.

Finally ask for feedback from your guests. Did they have a good time? What would they suggest for another time? You could give them a form on which to answer the questions you are asking, or you can allow a few minutes for them to voice their views. If everyone had a good time, you may want to make plans for another past life regression party.

The Least You Need to Know

◆ A past life regression party can be a lot of fun and yield valuable insights.

◆ Choose your guest list wisely.

◆ The facilitator is very important to the success of the regressions.

◆ Careful planning will help the party go smoothly.

◆ Allow time for everyone to share their past life experiences.

Balancing Your Past, Present, and Future

In This Chapter

- ◆ Putting your positive and negative experiences from the past to use
- ◆ Getting in touch with your soul's purpose
- ◆ Using self-hypnosis to redevelop your past life abilities
- ◆ Continuing to use past life regressions in the future
- ◆ How knowledge of your past can help you create goals for the future

The evidence has been gathered and examined. Now it's time to present it to the judge and jury—you! What is your verdict on the case for past life regression? Did you find enough evidence to support it? Do you need further research? Is it really necessary to believe?

If you have found that doing the exercises in this book has helped you, regardless of whether or not you believe in past lives, now is the time to make your plans for the future. You can use your newfound knowledge from the past to help you as you move forward. Now is the time to put your rediscovered abilities to use.

Using Past Positive and Negative Experiences in the Present

Have you ever had a perfect experience in your life? It could have been something that you made or a place you lived or visited. It may have been a relationship or an event such as a holiday. It was a time when everything came together and you were in absolute bliss. Have you ever had an experience that was that perfect?

Words to Remember

Perfection is the highest degree of excellence or experience or proficiency at something that one can achieve. Do you try to match a standard that you were able to reach only once before? If you do, where did you learn to recognize that standard in the first place? Did you acquire it during this life, or were you born with it?

You are the product of your past. Once you have had a perfect experience, can you ever call anything less a success? A perfectionist couldn't. Their experiences are often painful because their standards required to achieve *perfection* are very high. A tiny flaw can be amplified so that it covers up everything else that may be right.

The search for perfection can expand beyond one lifetime. You may have been searching for something that you experienced a long time ago in one or more past lives. Up until now your soul memories have been the responsibility of your unconscious mind. Now you know how to retrieve them.

Perhaps you look at the world through "rose-colored glasses" and never see anything wrong. You only see the good in someone who would take advantage of you if they were given the slightest opportunity. Your detached view of the world could have been created during a lifetime when the good you saw was good. There was no bad to experience. You may not be able to see the warning signs until it is too late because you have never learned how. This could be karma that started in a past life that you have not yet learned to resolve.

All of the experiences from your past lives, both negative and positive, are a wealth of knowledge that you can learn from. You know this now, but look around you at the many people who are unaware of how they may be influenced by their past. They may be stuck in karmic patterns that you have learned to resolve. At the same time, you may have some more to discover and resolve.

You have probably been told that you learn from your mistakes. You may have made some in your past lives that are still haunting you in this life. Now you have a choice of continuing the same cycle or finally resolving these mistakes. In fact, you have more of an opportunity to do this from negative past life experiences than positive ones. The positive ones are those that often drive you to match them again, and that is nearly impossible. The negative ones give you the chance to change rather than repeat them. When you find something that went wrong in a past life regression, you now can change its pattern.

> ## Soul Stories
>
> Sonya has always felt out of place in her life. She spent years searching for something that seemed to be missing. The problem was that she didn't know what. Finally she had a past life regression and discovered that she had had an idyllic lifetime in her last reincarnation. She had not been emotionally ready for the differences she found in this lifetime. Once she understood, she surrounded herself with her feelings from the time period before, and made the adjustment in her current life.

You may have heard the saying, "If life hands you a bunch of lemons, make lemonade." Your past life mistakes as well as your accomplishments can help you get in tune with your soul's purpose. It just takes the willingness to look for and practice your lessons that are waiting for you in this lifetime.

Remember, you can resolve the negative karma from your past lives. You can also use the positive experiences even during current situations that may cause you to wish you lived in the past. In other words, a perfect life before can be used as a model to reach toward again. Remember that you need to update the past and readjust it for your present life. If you are open to the memories of your soul, you will constantly learn from all of your past.

Get in Tune with Your Soul's Purpose

You know how to experience a past life regression, and you have a journal filled with notes on your encounters. You have identified your old karma and have taken action to resolve it. Now you have begun to take the steps that will help you get in tune with your soul's purpose.

So how do you know what that purpose is? It isn't something that is presented to you when you began this reincarnation, such as a master plan or a blueprint of what you should be learning and accomplishing during your time on earth, or is it? There is nothing that could be called tangible evidence, so what really is locked away in your unconscious mind? Does it contain instructions for your soul?

How can you get to the truth regarding your soul's purpose? Where do you look for the answers? Is it through religion? Can you find it in the many books and workshops that advise you on the way to live your life? Do you listen to your conscience and make decisions as to how you feel inside? Do you live for today and let tomorrow take care of itself? Do you live in fear of tomorrow? Where can you find the answer? Have you consciously been searching for the truth?

Whether you are aware of it or not, your unconscious mind is always searching for the truth. That search, unfortunately, can take many detours along the winding journey of your soul. You may have been trying to live your life in a past life pattern that is not the same now as it was before. There may be positive and negative components to that pattern. You may not have to get rid of the whole, just the part that is holding you back from your life purpose. You can change old behavior patterns; it just takes the willingness to examine them and to communicate with the voice inside you that represents your free will.

An old fault from a past life may actually be a gift or talent in this lifetime if you are willing to resolve the karma attached to it. Where you used your abilities for self-satisfaction and gain in another life, you can use for good in your current life. Of course you can still use your power for self-gain. The choice is yours.

Soul Stories

Matthew was very strong-willed, and for much of his early life he used his ability to take advantage of many people for his own personal gain. Then he had a near death experience, and his awareness of the universe changed. He began to devote his life to helping others instead of himself. During a past life regression he discovered how he had misused his power, so his passion for helping others now is actually a way of resolving the karma he had compiled from before.

You may already be unknowingly working toward getting your soul's purpose back on course. It happens to many people who do not believe in past lives or the nature of karma. They may endure a traumatic experience mentally, physically, or spiritually, and suddenly change. They find it impossible to go back to their old lifestyle because the unconscious knowing of their soul's purpose is now influencing them. They cannot explain it, and they still have the free will to fight it, but they are changed. They have been given the opportunity to get in tune with their life map.

It takes patience and practice to develop your ability to communicate with your soul. Just like learning to tune and play a stringed musical instrument, there is a learning period. Many beginners never get beyond that stage because they expect instant success. Success is an ongoing process. To a beginner, an intermediate can sound like a well-trained master. The master, however, is always seeking to improve. They are well aware of what is left to accomplish.

The same is true as you learn to play the music of your soul. The more you practice, the more in tune you will become. There is always more that you can learn. You have at your fingertips the masters of the universe and the memories of your soul; all you need to do is to be open to their wisdoms to help you fine-tune your soul's purpose.

Use Self-Hypnosis to Redevelop Past Life Abilities

As you have learned, hypnosis is totally integrated into your life. You are constantly going in and out of trance. It is your natural way of communicating with your unconscious mind, whether you are aware of it or not. Why not learn to use it to help you stay on track with your soul's purpose?

You have special talents that are unique. They have been honed over many lifetimes. Have you updated them yet for this lifetime? If not, you can always use your self-hypnosis ability to do just that.

You can develop an anchor that will help you contact your soul's memories in the blink of an eye. It can be as simple as focusing on your third eye. The more you practice self-hypnosis, the easier it is to step through the window and into the essence of your soul. Knowing becomes a way of life. It is there for you to access.

> **Ageless Insights**
>
> The memories of your soul are always available to you. All you need to do is stay in touch with your unconscious mind. You can do this easily through the use of self-hypnosis. You have learned to peek through the veil and open the window to your past.

This type of soul communication is not new. The ancients could, the Gnostics knew, and so did Edgar Cayce when he looked into the Akashic Records. You are on your way to doing the same if your free will so chooses. Like any other talent, it will dry up if it is not used.

> **Soul Stories**
>
> Amy has a very active conscious mind that would often over-think her life situations. Her tendency to dwell on her worries kept her off-balance much of the time. She would spend hours analyzing situations that had occurred and worrying about those that had not happened yet. After she learned to use her past lives as insights, she started to spend some quiet time every day examining her thoughts from a different perspective. This resulted in her being able to resolve a lot of stress in her life.

When you reach into your unconscious mind you have opened yourself to your soul. You do not have to regress into a past life to access memories and special abilities. Just by spending some quiet time while in trance, you will begin to be aware of the whispers of your soul.

You might try counting yourself down from five to zero into a relaxing and comfortable deep, self-hypnotic trance. When you get to zero, suggest to yourself that you will be open to the images of your soul. You may be seeking an answer to a question about the direction of your life or looking for the courage to make a decision. You may need an affirmation that you are going in the direction that puts you in tune with your life map. Remember to include your belief and your inner and outer guidance systems. Ask that the peace and love of the universe surround and flow through you.

Ask your belief that you may know how to use your abilities from your past to help you become in tune with your soul's purpose. Let all of your five senses be open to the wisdom. As you spend time with the incredible knowing of the universe, feel the peace, strength, and love that surround you. Feel the awesome power of the universe and open to its knowledge.

Take a moment and turn over any concerns or worries you may have to the guardians of your soul to help guide you safely through your life map. Ask that you may have the knowledge you seek at the time that is right for you to know it. Ask that your guides and angels help watch over your journey. Above all, feel the peace and love that surrounds and comforts you. Ask that your past life abilities automatically come to the surface of your conscious mind when it is time to use them to help you get in tune with your soul's purpose.

Suggest to yourself that you can use a key word or focus on your third eye and come back to this special state any time that you want or need to. When you are ready, count yourself up from zero to five and the conscious level of your mind. Take a deep breath, exhale, and open your eyes feeling relaxed, comfortable, and full of universal peace and love.

Now try triggering your word or physical anchors, and go back into your trance state. If it is your third eye, focus on it and then relax. Try it several times to help you get comfortable with the experience of going into instant hypnosis.

Continue to Use Your Ability to Experience Past Life Regressions

Now that you have developed the ability to experience past life regressions, what do you want to do with it after you finish this book? It's not unusual for someone to get very excited about something new that they have learned and make great plans to continue their study after they have finished their initial experience. Unfortunately, as time separates them, their enthusiasm diminishes, and it is not long until their new-found skills become rusty and unused. Perhaps you can think of similar occurrences in your life.

Once you have learned to experience and interpret a past life regression, you do not have to make much of an effort to keep your new skills honed and ready to use. You may have spent a great deal of time during the course of reading this book and doing the exercises. Your investment can really pay off if you continue to use your ability to consult with your past.

> **Ageless Insights**
>
> Just being conscious of the fact that every thought and daily encounter can be connected to the past can help you be more aware of life itself. When you consider every action you take in terms of your soul's journey, you are also focusing your mind on your present. You may never look at life the same way again!

You now have the opportunity to examine two different views, the old and the new. The new perspective is actually gained from examining your past. That past, of course, spans many lifetimes. Your knowledge and ability to regress into your soul's memories provides you with the opportunity to consider your life differently.

There will be times ahead when the pressures of your current life temporarily block your memory of the lessons in this book, and then, all of a sudden, a flash of insight will pop into your conscious mind. It will be a message from your unconsciousness that still remembers your links with your past. When that happens, you have the opportunity of listening to the message or not. Before, you would have missed it altogether. Now you have the skills to be aware of the messages from your soul.

When that flash arrives, you can consider what you received on the spot, or you can delve into it deeper at a more appropriate time. Having a set time every day when you can communicate with your soul can provide many insights for you in the future. It doesn't have to be long. Only a few minutes can do the trick. What the process does is open you to the messages from your unconscious mind. It will make the link back to the memories of your soul and send up the appropriate information for you when you need it.

Your belief can be an important source of support and awareness. When you practice self-hypnosis, ask for the guidance necessary to help you understand the daily situations in your life. You may also request that your inner and outer guidance systems work with your belief to remind you of the lessons of your past that relate to where your soul's journey has progressed.

The more you are open to that concept, the more you will be aware of your past lives. That flash of insight you receive from your unconscious mind may come in any of the five senses. You may have a picture come into your mind, a voice, a feeling, a smell, or a taste in your mouth. You may just *know*. The insights may come while you are awake or asleep. They may appear as déjà vu. These are all forms of instant past life regressions. They may have been with you before you experienced this book, but now you know how to recognize the memories of your soul.

> **Soul Stories**
>
> Jake didn't believe in the concept of past lives until a chance encounter with someone involved in Edgar Cayce's work presented a view that he could not shake from his mind. Jake was given a book on the life of Cayce, and when he read of the struggles that this common man had endured as he began to use his psychic gifts, it gave him new insights into his own life situation. Jake began to compare his life to karmic patterns and discovered by relating his problems to other lifetimes he had a new and different view. He was also able to make some positive changes in his life because of his new concept of past lives. He feels he is advancing on the journey of his soul.

Chances are you have been regressing into your past lives since you were born. Everyone does, but most people do not know or want to understand the importance of connecting themselves to the past. It can make a great difference in your view of life situations if you continue using your ability to experience past life regressions.

What You Were and What You May Be

You are a work in progress. You can trace your journey from the beginnings of your soul. You can look into the potential of future lives, but the real focus is on your present lifetime. What you do now can greatly influence what you will have to do in the future. What you may be depends on what you are doing with what you have done. You may have some karma to resolve. You may have an ability that needs to be developed and used for the good. Now is your chance to let yourself become in tune with your life map and your soul's current purpose. You even have the opportunity to go beyond your lessons in this life if your free will lets you.

Remember the suggestion that when you encounter images you don't understand during a past life regression, you should just go with the experience. You have the opportunity to go with and work with your current life experiences. If you believe that your soul has a great potential, you may find hope where there is little to find.

The more you focus on the love and peace that is waiting to be experienced when you tap into the universe through your unconscious mind, the more you will be open to the wisdoms from your soul to help guide you into the future. You are never alone. Just by changing your focus you have the wisdom and strength of the Universe with you. It will help temper the past and provide hope for the future.

Do you know what patina on a gold ring is? When you buy a ring that is brand new and freshly polished, it has no patina. The ring needs to be worn before it acquires it. You see the patina in all the scratches that are created from its wear. Every little scratch causes the gold to reflect the light much more brilliantly than the new ring. You need to use the ring for its true beauty to be revealed. In the same way, you have acquired a lot of patina from your past life experiences.

Serving the greater whole is a lofty ambition, and yet many strive for it unknowingly. An unfinished mission started in a past lifetime may drive you to see it through now. You may not even know what that mission was, but you have the overwhelming emotion that you need to get going. Yet at the same time you may be frustrated that you can't find a way to get started. You may feel like you're spinning your wheels, and time is running out.

So get started. Spend some time with your past and get to know who you have been. Spend some time with your belief and guidance systems so that you may begin to move into the future. Your goal is one step at a time. You may think that you take two steps forward and then one back. If you could sit on a high mountain and follow your soul's progress since the beginning, what would the journey look like? Would it be a straight line or a meandering road as it spans the lifetimes of your past?

How do you think the path of your soul will look in the future? Will it still wander back and forth, or will it show a new direction as you work on the lessons of the universe? You can learn from your past and create a new and positive direction to your future.

You are the master of your soul.

The Least You Need to Know

- ◆ You can use all the experiences from your past lives to help you in the future.

- ◆ You are ready to stay in tune with your soul's purpose.

- ◆ There are always new past life insights to discover.

- ◆ You can now recognize when you are instantly regressing into the past.

- ◆ You can use your knowledge of the past to help you in the moment and on into the future.

Appendix A

Glossary

affect-bridge regression   A hypnosis technique that takes a subject back through their life to events that relate to a specific emotion. As they regress, they may transfer the emotion to a similar emotion that they experienced earlier.

Akashic Book of Records   Also known as the "Book of Life." It contains a record of every soul that has ever existed. It is believed to hold every deed, word, feeling, thought, and intent of every soul in the Universe.

altered state of consciousness   A trance.

anchor   A special word or physical action such as a touch that can help you recreate a state of heightened focus.

astral projection   When the mental and/or spiritual parts of yourself separate from your physical body. It is usually felt as a floating sensation, and it usually happens when you are in a state of trance.

automatic writing   Writing from images received in a self-hypnotic trance.

channeling   When another entity comes through one's unconscious mind for the purpose of communicating.

collective unconsciousness   The place in the universe where it is believed all thoughts and experiences from the past are recorded.

conscious mind   The part of the mind, approximately ten percent, that thinks, processes information, and makes decisions.

conscious reality   Your awareness of the present and what is taking place in close proximity to you.

convergent thinking   A thought process that eliminates options rather than examining them. Eventually there will be no options left and the process will be stuck.

déjà vu   A French word that means "seen before."

detachment   The ability to observe, or even experience, a potentially upsetting image with little or no emotional feeling.

divergent thinking   A thinking process that examines options, especially when you can't go forward. By trying out options you can find another route and succeed in reaching your goal.

DNA   Deoxyribonucleic acid, a chemical found at the center of the cells of living things that controls the structure and purpose of each cell. It carries genetic information.

dowsing   Finding information by using a device such as a pendulum controlled by the unconscious and universal minds of the individual holding it.

external guidance system   Angels, spirits, guides, and other unseen elements that are a part of your daily life and usually are there to help watch over and assist you.

false memory   The recall of events in a way that never happened, due to external influences such as the power of suggestion.

fantasy prone personality   Someone that imagines a great deal in his or her mind and easily enters a hypnotic trance.

flow chart   A simple map to help follow the sequence of events of one or more past lives that might use symbols to depict persons, places, occupations, etc.

free will   The term given to your ability to do as you want rather than follow your soul's life plan. If you choose not to follow your purpose, you will have the opportunity to do it over in a future lifetime.

genealogy   The record or study of your family: the record of your ancestors and descendents. You can develop a past life family tree through the use of regression.

hypnosis   An altered state of consciousness where the unconscious mind is receptive to suggestions.

hypnosis script   The dialogue used by a hypnotist to induce a trance in a subject. It can also be the words that individuals practicing self-hypnosis say to themselves to help them go into a trance and may contain suggestions for obtaining their desired goals.

imagination   The power of the mind to reproduce images or concepts stored in the memory.

internal belief system   The set of values that you were born with.

karma   The unfinished lessons created by a person's actions in one or more of their lifetimes. These actions influence some of the situations they currently face now and in their future lives.

labyrinth   Like a maze except there are no dead ends. Once you enter, you continue inward until you reach the center. If you view the layout of a labyrinth from above, it looks much like the design of a human brain. There is a right sphere and a left sphere. As you progress through it, you can actually balance your own energy flow.

library   A real place with books or one that you imagine in your unconscious mind where you may find one book of your soul's memories or a series of books, each featuring one of your past lives.

life cycle   A theme or situation that keeps coming up or happening over and over again. It is usually connected to an unresolved karma.

life map   The lesson plan (blueprint) a soul follows during one incarnation.

lucid dreaming   The process of continuing a dream in your waking state.

manifest reality   What can be seen, touched, heard, tasted, and smelled by whoever is in the same vicinity.

mental DNA   The way your mind works in the five senses which may be shaped by past life experiences.

mesmerize   To induce someone into a hypnotic trance. Named for Anton Mesmer (1734–1815).

old souls   People who are further along their soul's lessons and often don't seem to fit in with others. They know more than they can tell anyone. If they try, they may be looked at as odd or a misfit.

operator   The person who is guiding a subject into a hypnotic trance and usually asks questions that will help produce desired information from a regression session.

past life regression   When a person goes back in his or her mind in a trance state to experience a past life.

past life regression specialist   Someone who has been trained to conduct and interpret a past life regression experience. The training may be recognized by acceptance to an organization such as IBRT, the International Board for Regression Therapy.

pendulum   A weight such as a crystal, a pendant, or anything that can dangle from a chain or string so that it will swing freely.

perfection   The highest degree of excellence or experience or proficiency at something that one can achieve.

phobia   A fear that becomes so powerful the one who experiences it temporarily loses touch with their surroundings and enters a second reality that is connected to a traumatic moment in their past (that past may not be in this lifetime!). When the phobia starts, they relive that memory again without realizing it.

progression   The use of a self-hypnotic trance to project yourself forward into a future lifetime. The concept is similar to regression except that you are going ahead in time instead of back.

psychic   A person whose soul knowledge is accessible to them through their unconscious mind. This knowledge may come through at unexpected times until the individual learns to access it.

quantum mechanics   The theory that every particle or cell contains energy and exists independently of each other. On the metaphysical level, every cell contains the universal life energy that holds the keys to the knowledge of the universal mind.

reincarnation   The belief that the soul returns to live in different physical bodies over a series of lifetimes. These lifetimes are a continuation of the lessons that the soul encounters working its way back to being a part of the universal mind.

self-hypnosis   When a person induces him- or herself into a hypnotic trance.

soul   The element of life, feeling, thought, and action in humans. Considered to be a separate part of the mental, physical, and spiritual self. It is believed to survive beyond death.

soul fragmentation   The belief that a soul can divide into more than one part when it reincarnates. This belief makes it possible for your soul to be also a part of another person.

soul mate   Someone that you have been together with before in at least one or more lifetimes. The connections in the past were often very close.

spirit communication   The ability to speak to the soul, usually in thought form, of someone who has died.

spontaneous memory recall   A memory that is stored in your unconscious mind and suddenly becomes part of your conscious thinking without any effort to remember. This is different than one that you may have been trying to remember.

subject   The individual experiencing a trance state.

suggestibility test   An exercise to determine how well a subject for hypnosis follows suggestions.

suppressed memory   A memory that is buried in your unconscious mind and is only recalled when a situation jogs it. Then it may come flooding back to the surface and cause you to replay the original experience in your mind.

theosophist belief   A belief system that dates back to the third century C.E. and became popular again after Madame Helena Petrovna Blavatsky founded the Theosophical Society in 1875. Its followers strove to learn the secrets of the universe in order to achieve the same perfection as their supreme deity.

third eye   The energy center where your "psychic sight" comes into your body from the "Source." Located in the center of your forehead at a point that is above and centered between your two seeing eyes.

time line   A system for recording events in the order that they took place. Similar to a flow chart, which uses symbols.

trance   An altered state of consciousness in which the unconscious mind is open to suggestion and loses its ability to make critical decisions.

transmigration   Means essentially the same as reincarnation. It is a term that was incorporated into one of the Christian beliefs until it was finally purged from the church that would become today's Christian religion.

tunnel vision   A focus that is so narrow that it is like looking through a tunnel. All you can see out the other side is the area in front of the opening. The further away you are, the smaller your actual view is.

unconscious mind   The storage area for all your memories up to this point in time. It makes up ninety percent of your total mind.

universal mind   Your connection to the source or the knowledge of the universe that also contains your soul's memories.

unmanifest reality   Something that is real to one person but not to another. It is a reality that most others have no awareness of as it cannot be touched or experienced by most others.

vortex   A place where earth energies converge and create a swirling cylindrical stream that rises upward into the universe. It is a place where souls can be transported to the other side and where the universe can send through reincarnated souls.

zone   A state of hyper-focus where a person is able to mentally change time, distance, and energy.

Appendix B

Resources

General

Advanced Book Exchange
#4-410 Garbally Road
Victoria BC
Canada V8T2K1
www.abebooks.com
Online marketplace for used books: 40,000,000 books, 10,000 booksellers

Akashic Record Consultants International
PO Box 14994
Odessa, TX 79768
915-368-5059
www.arc-akashicrecords.org
Consultants, classes, and teachers for people who want to learn more
about the Akashic Records

American Society of Dowsers
PO Box 24
Danville, VT 05828
1-800-711-9530
www.dowsers.org
A nonprofit educational and scientific society dedicated to preserving an
open forum of ideas regarding dowsing

Association of Research and Enlightenment
215 67th Street
Virginia Beach, VA 23451
1-800-333-4499
www.edgarcayce.org
Information about Edgar Cayce, holistic health, personal spirituality, intuition, and education

Association for the Study of Dreams
PO Box 1166
Orinda, CA 94563
925-258-1822
Information on everything to do with dreams

Cambridge Dictionaries Online
Cambridge University Press
Edinburgh Boulevard, Shaftesbury Road
Cambridge, England CB2 2RU
www.dictionary.cambridge.org
A search engine for English vocabulary using the many dictionaries published by Cambridge University Press

International Association for Regression Research and Therapies
PO Box 20151
Riverside, CA 92516
909-784-8440
www.iarrt.org
Nonprofit organization dedicated to increasing the acceptance and use of professional and responsible regression therapy through education, association, and research

International Board for Regression Therapy
9091 Beach Road
Canastota, NY 13032
315-762-4453
www.ibrt.org
Examining and certifying board for past life therapists, researchers, and training programs

National Guild of Hypnotists
PO Box 308
Merrimack, NH 03054
603-429-9438
www.ngh.net
Information on hypnosis and hypnosis training

National Nightmare Hotline
866-DRMS911
www.asdreams.org
A project for the Association for the Study of Dreams created in response to the
September 11 tragedy

Parapsychology Foundation, Inc.
228 East 71st Street
New York, NY 10021
212-628-1550
www.parapsychology.org
A nonprofit educational organization to encourage and support impartial scientific
inquiry into such psychical aspects of human nature as telepathy, clairvoyance, pre-
cognition, and psychokinesis

White Mountain Hypnosis Center
PO Box 276
Madison, NH 03849
603-367-8851
www.whitemountainhypnosiscenter.com
The director is Michael R. Hathaway, author of this book, hypnotherapist, and
hypnosis trainer

Books

Ackerman, Diane. *The Natural History of the Senses*. New York: Random House, 1990.

Bennett, Dean B. *The Forgotten Nature of New England*. Camden, Maine: Down East
    Books, 1996.

Bernstein, Morey. *The Search for Bridey Murphy*. New York: Doubleday & Co., 1956.

Bolduc, Henry Leo. *The Journey Within. Past-Life Regression and Channeling*. Virginia
    Beach, VA: Inner Vision Publishing Co., 1988.

Caldwell, Taylor. *Dear and Glorious Physician*. New York: Doubleday, 1959.

———. *Great Lion of God*. New York: Doubleday, 1970.

Freedman, Thelma. *Soul Echoes: The Healing Power of Past Life Therapy*. New York:
    Citadel Press, 2002.

Grant, Robert J. *The Place We Call Home. Exploring the Soul's Existence After Death*.
    Virginia Beach, VA: A.R.E. Press, 2000.

Guiley, Rosemary Ellen. *Harper's Encyclopedia of Mystical & Paranormal Experience.* San Francisco, CA: HarperSanFrancisco, 1991.

Kirkpatrick, Sidney D. *Edgar Cayce. An American Prophet.* New York: Riverhead Books, 2000.

LaBerge, Stephen, and Howard Rheingold. *Exploring the World of Lucid Dreaming.* New York: Ballantine, 1990.

Lethbridge, T. C. *The Power of the Pendulum.* Penguin Books, England, 1976.

Pliskin, Marci, and Shari L. Just. *The Complete Idiot's Guide to Interpreting Your Dreams.* Indianapolis: Alpha Books, 1999.

Roberts, Jane. *Seth Speaks: The Eternal Validity of the Soul.* Englewood Cliffs, New Jersey: Prentice Hall, 1972.

Stearn, Jess. *The Search for a Soul. Taylor Caldwell's Past Lives.* New York: Berkley Books, 1994.

Stevenson, Ian. *Where Reincarnation and Biology Intersect.* Praeger Publishers, 1997.

Sugrue, Thomas. *There Is a River.* New York: Henry Holt, 1942. Reprinted by Holt, Dell, A.R.E. Press.

Washington, Peter. *Madame Blavatsky's Baboon. A History of the Mystics, Mediums, and Misfits Who Brought Spiritualism to America.* New York: Schocken Books, 1995.

Weiss, Brian L. *Many Lives, Many Masters.* New York: Simon & Schuster, 1988.

———. *Through Time into Healing.* New York: Simon & Schuster, 1992.

Woolger, Roger J. *Other Lives, Other Selves. A Jungian Psychotherapist Discovers Past Lives.* New York: Bantam Books, 1988.

Index

U-V

W–X–Y–Z